THE

MANDARIN CHINESE
PHRASEBOOK

Compiled by
LEXUS

www.roughguides.com

Credits

Mandarin Chinese Phrasebook

Compiled by Lexus with Julian Ward
and Xu Yinong
Lexus series editor: Sally Davies
Layout: Jessica Subramanian
Picture Research: Scott Stickland

Rough Guides Reference

Director: Andrew Lockett
Editors: Kate Berens,
Ian Blenkinsop, Tom Cabot,
Tracy Hopkins, Matthew Milton,
Joe Staines

Publishing information

First edition published in 1997
This updated edition published October 2011 by
Rough Guides Ltd, 80 Strand, London, WC2R 0RL
Email: mail@roughguides.com

Distributed by the Penguin Group:
Penguin Books Ltd, 80 Strand, London, WC2R 0RL
Penguin Group (USA), 375 Hudson Street, NY 10014, USA
Penguin Group (Australia), 250 Camberwell Road, Camberwell,
Victoria 3124, Australia
Penguin Group (New Zealand), Cnr Rosedale and Airborne Roads,
Albany, Auckland, New Zealand

Rough Guides is represented in Canada by Tourmaline Editions Inc.,
662 King Street West, Suite 304, Toronto, Ontario, M5V 1M7

Printed in Singapore by Toppan Security Printing Pte. Ltd.

256 pages

A catalogue record for this book is available from the British Library.

978-1-84836-733-3

1 3 5 7 9 8 6 4 2

CONTENTS

How to use this book

The Rough Guide Mandarin Chinese Phrasebook is a highly practical introduction to the contemporary language. It gets straight to the point in every situation you might encounter: in bars and shops, on trains and buses, in hotels and banks, on holiday or on business. Laid out in clear A–Z style with easy-to-find, colour-coded sections, it uses key words to take you directly to the phrase you need – so if you want some help booking a room, just look up "room" in the dictionary section.

The phrasebook starts off with **Basics**, where we list some essential phrases, including words for numbers, dates and telling the time, and give guidance on pronunciation, along with a short section on the different regional accents you might come across. Then, to get you started in two-way communication, the **Scenarios** section offers dialogues in key situations such as renting a car, asking directions or booking a taxi, and includes words and phrases for when something goes wrong, from getting a flat tyre or asking to move apartments to more serious emergencies. You can listen to these and download them for free from www.

roughguides.com/phrasebooks for use on your computer, MP3 player or smartphone.

Forming the main part of the guide is a double dictionary, starting with **English–Chinese**, which gives you the essential words you'll need, plus easy-to-use phonetic transliterations. Then, in the **Chinese–English** dictionary, we've given the phrases you'll be likely to hear (starting with a selection of slang and colloquialisms), followed by the **Signs** section, which explains many of the signs, labels, instructions and other basic words you'll come across in print or in public places. Scattered throughout the sections are travel tips direct from the authors of the Rough Guides guidebook series.

Finally, there's an extensive **Menu reader**. Consisting of separate food and drink sections, each starting with a list of essential terms, it's indispensable whether you're eating out, stopping for a quick drink or looking around a local food market.

Note: one abbreviation is used in this book: *adj* for adjective.

一路顺风
Yílù shùnfēng!
Have a good trip!

BASICS

Basic phrases

yes shìde shur-dur 我同

no bù boo 不

OK hǎo how 好

hello ní hǎo nee how 你好

good morning nǐ zǎo nee dzow
你早

good evening nǐ hǎo ni how
你好

good night wǎnān wahn-ahn
晚安

goodbye/see you! zàijiàn
dzai-jyen 再见

see you later huítóujiàn
hway-toh-jyen 回头见

please qǐng ching 请

yes, please hǎo, xièxie
how hsyeh-hsyeh 好谢谢

could you please-...?
qǐng nín-..., hǎo ma? ching
nin ..., how mah 请您 ..., 好
吗？

thank you xièxie
hsyeh-hsyeh 谢谢

thank you very much duōxiè
dwor-hsyeh 多谢

no, thank you xièxie, wǒ bú
yào hsyeh-hsyeh wor boo yow
谢谢我不要

don't mention it bú kèqi
boo kur-chee 不客气

how do you do? nǐ hǎo
ni how 你好？

how are you? nǐ hǎo ma?
mah 你好吗？

fine, thanks hén hǎo, xièxie
hun how hsyeh-hsyeh 好谢谢

nice to meet you jiàndào nǐ
hěn gāoxìng jyen-dow nee hun
gow-hsing 见到你很高兴

excuse me (to get past) láojià
low-jyah 劳驾

(to get attention) láojià, qǐng
wèn-... ching wun 劳驾请问

excuse me/sorry duìbuqǐ
dway-boo-chee 对不起

sorry?/pardon me? nǐ shuō
shénme? shwor shun-mur
你说什么？

I see/I understand wǒ míngbai
le wor ming-bai lur 我明白了

I don't understand wǒ bù dǒng
我不懂

do you speak English?
nín huì jiǎng Yīngyǔ ma?
hway jyang ying-yew mah
您会讲英语吗？

I don't speak-Chinese
wǒ búhuì jiǎng Hànyǔ
wor boo-hway hahn-yew
我不会讲汉语

could you speak more slowly? qǐng shuō màn yìdiǎnr ching shwor mahn yee-dyenr 请说慢一点儿

could you repeat that? qǐng nǐ zài shuō yíbiàn, hǎo ma? ching nee dzai shwor yee-byen how mah 请你再说一遍好吗？

Dates

Dates in Chinese are written in the following order:

year + month + number

To write the year, place the relevant numbers in front of nián (**year**); this is followed by the month and then the number of the day plus hào:

the first of September
jiǔyuè yīhào jyoh-yew-eh yee-how 九月一号

the second of December
shíèryuè èrhào shur-er-yew-eh er-how 十二月二号

the thirtieth of May
wǔyuè sānshíhào woo-yew-eh sahn-shur-how 五月三十号

the thirty-first of May, 2006
èrlínglíngliù nián wǔyuè sānshíyīhào ur-ling-ling-lyoh nyen woo-yew-ehsahn-shur-yee-how 二零零六年五月 三十一号

1942 yījiǔ sìèr nián yee-jyoh sur-er nyen 一九四二年

Days

Sunday xīngqītiān hsing-chee-tyen 星期天

Monday xīngqīyī hsing-chee-yee 星期一

Tuesday xīngqīèr hsing-chee-er 星期二

Wednesday xīngqīsān hsing-chee-sahn 星期三

Thursday xīngqīsì hsing-chee-sur 星期四

Friday xīngqīwǔ hsing-chee-woo 星期五

Saturday xīngqīliù hsing-chee-lyoh 星期六

Months

January yīyuè yee-yew-eh 一月

February èryuè er-yew-eh 二月

March sānyuè sahn-yew-eh 三月

April sìyuè sur-yew-eh 四月

May wǔyuè woo-yew-eh 五月

June liùyuè lyoh-yew-eh 六月

July qīyuè chee-yew-eh 七月

August bāyuè bah-yew-eh 八月

September jiǔyuè jyoh-yew-eh 九月

October shíyuè shur-yew-eh 十月

November shíyīyuè
shur-yee-yew-eh 十一月

December shí'èryuè
shur-er-yew-eh 十二月

Time

When telling the time, the word diǎn is added to the number to indicate the hours. Zhōng (**clock**) is optional and is placed at the end of most time expressions. The word fēn (**minutes**) is added to the number of minutes.

what time is it? jǐdiǎn le?
jee-dyen lur 几点了？

o'clock diǎn zhōng dyen joong
点钟

one o'clock yīdiǎn (zhōng)
yee-dyen 一点（钟）

two o'clock liǎngdiǎn (zhōng)
lyang-dyen 两点（钟）

at one o'clock yìdiǎn (zhōng)
yee-dyen 一点（钟）

it's one o'clock yìdiǎn (zhōng)
一点（钟）

it's two o'clock liǎngdiǎn
(zhōng) lyang-dyen
两点（钟）

it's ten o'clock shídiǎn (zhōng)
shur-dyen 十点（钟）

five past one yìdiǎn wǔfēn
yee-dyen woo-fun 一点五分

ten past two liǎngdiǎn shífēn
lyang-dyen shur-fun 两点十分

quarter past one yìdiǎn yíkè
yee-dyen yee-kur 一点一刻

quarter past two liǎngdiǎn yíkè
lyang-dyen yee-kur 两点一刻

half past two liǎngdiǎn bàn
bahn 两点半

half past ten shídiǎn bàn
shur-dyen 十点半

twenty to one yìdiǎn chà
èrshí yee-dyen chah er-shur
一点差二十

twenty to ten shídiǎn chà èrshí
shur-dyen 十点差二十

quarter to one yìdiǎn chà
yíkè yee-dyen chah yee-kur
一点差一刻

quarter to two liǎngdiǎn chà
yíkè lyang-dyen 两点差一刻

a.m. (early morning up to about 9)
zǎoshang dzow-shahng 早上
(from about 9 till noon)
shàngwǔ 上午

p.m. (afternoon) xiàwǔ
hsyah-woo 下午
(evening) wǎnshang
wahn-shahng 晚上
(night) yèli yur-lee 夜里

2 a.m. língchén liǎngdiǎn ling-
chun lyang-dyen 凌晨两点

2 p.m. (14.00) xiàwǔ liǎngdiǎn
hsyah-woo 下午两点

6 a.m. zǎoshang liùdiǎn dzow-shahng lyoh-dyen 早上六点

6 p.m. (18.00) wǎnshang liùdiǎn wahn-shahng 晚上六点

10 a.m. shàngwǔ shídiǎn shahng-woo shur-dyen 上午十点

10 p.m. (22.00) wǎnshang shídiǎn wahn-shahng 晚上十点

noon zhōngwǔ joong-woo 中午

midnight bànyè bahn-yur 半夜

hour xiǎoshí hsyow-shur 小时

minute fēn fun 分

two minutes liǎng fēnzhōng lyang fun-joong 两分钟

second miǎo myow 秒

quarter of an hour yí kèzhōng kur-joong 一刻钟

half an hour bàn xiǎoshí bahn hsyow-shur 半小时

three quarters of an hour sān kèzhōng sahn kur-joong 三刻钟

nearly three o'clock kuài sān diǎn le kwai sahn dyen lur 快三点了

Numbers

See Measure words, p.13.

0 líng 零

1 yī yee 一

2 èr, liǎng lyang 二

3 sān sahn 三

4 sì sur 四

5 wǔ 五

6 liù lyoh 六

7 qī chee 七

8 bā bah 八

9 jiǔ jyoh 九

10 shí shur 十

11 shíyī shur-yee 十一

12 shíèr shur-er 十二

13 shísān shur-sahn 十三

14 shísì shur-sur 十四

15 shíwǔ shur-woo 十五

16 shíliù shur-lyoh 十六

17 shíqī shur-chee 十七

18 shíbā shur-bah 十八

19 shíjiǔ shur-jyoh 十九

20 èrshí er-shur 二十

21 èrshíyī er-shur-yee 二十一

22 èrshíèr er-shur-er 二十二

30 sānshí sahn-shur 三十

31 sānshíyī sahn-shur-yee 三十一

32 sānshíèr sahn-shur-er 三十二

40 sìshí sur-shur 四十

50 wǔshí woo-shur 五十

60 liùshí lyoh-shur 六十

70 qīshí chee-shur 七十

80 bāshí bah-shur 八十

90 jiǔshí jyoh-shur 九十

100 yìbǎi 一百

101 yìbǎi líng yī 一百零一

102 yìbǎi líng èr 一百零二

110 yìbǎi yìshí yee-shur
一百一十

111 yìbǎi yīshíyī shur-yee
一百一十一

200 èrbǎi 二百

201 èrbǎi líng yī 二百零一

202 èrbǎi líng èr 二百零二

210 èrbǎi yīshí yee-shur
二百一十

300 sānbǎi sahn-bai 三百

1,000 yìqiān yee-chyen 一千

2,000 liǎngqiān lyang-chyen 两千

3,000 sānqiān sahn-chyen 三千

4,000 sìqiān sur-chyen 四千

5,000 wǔqiān woo-chyen 五千

10,000 yíwàn yee-wahn 一万

50,000 wǔwàn 五万

100,000 shíwàn shur-wahn 十万

1,000,000 bǎiwàn 百万

10,000,000 qiānwàn
chyen-wahn 千万

100,000,000 yí yì 一亿

Counting

When counting 'one, two, three' and so on, yī (**one**) is written and said with the first tone (see

Tones, p.17). In other situations, the fourth tone is used:

one, two, three yī, èr, sān
yee er sahn

a fish yìtiáo yú yee-tyow yoo

a tree yìkē shū yee-kur shoo

The exception to the above is if yì is followed by a fourth tone, in which case it changes to second tone:

an object yíjiàn dōngxi
yee-jyen doong-hshee

In number sequences yāo is used for '**one**' instead of yī, as in the two examples below:

32518 (phone number)
sān-èr-wǔ-yāo-bā
sahn-er-woo-yow-bah

number one hundred and nineteen (room number)
yāoyāojiǔ yow-yow-jyoh

There are two words for **two** in Chinese: èr and liǎng. Èr is used in counting or for phone, room or bus numbers:

one, two three… yī, èr, sān…
yee er sahn

number two (room, house etc)
èr hào er how

number two bus èr lù chē
er loo chur

Èr also occurs in compound numbers:

thirty-two sānshí'èr
sahn-shur-er

Liǎng is similar to 'a couple' in English and is used with measure words (see below):

two friends liǎngwèi péngyou
lyang-way pung-yoh

two buildings liǎngsuǒ fángzi
lyang-swor fahng-dzur

Líng (**zero**) is used when there are zeros in the middle of a number sequence:

one hundred and three
yìbǎi líng sān yee-bai ling sahn

one thousand and three
yìqiān líng sān yee-chyen ling sahn

Note that Chinese has a unit for **10,000** (wàn) and for **100,000,000** (yì)

Ordinals

1st dì yī 第一
2nd dì èr 第二
3rd dì sān sahn 第三
4th dì sì sur 第四
5th dì wǔ 第五
6th dì liù lyoh 第六
7th dì qī chee 第七

8th dì bā 第八
9th dì jiǔ jyoh 第九
10th dì shí shur 第十

Measure words

Chinese uses measure words between a numeral and a noun or between a word like '**this**' or '**that**' and a noun. In English, a word like '**pat**' in '**two pats of butter**' could be seen as a measure word.

There are different measure words for different types or categories of noun. Some common measure words are:

bǎ bah **for chairs, knives, teapots, things with handles, bunches of flowers**

bēi bay **for cups, glasses**

běn bun **for books, magazines**

kuài kwai **for lumps, pieces**

liàng lyang **for vehicles**

tiáo tyow **for fish and long narrow things**

zhāng jahng **for tables, beds, tickets**

There is also a general measure word ge. This can also be used if the correct measure word is not known.

Here are some examples of measure words in use:

zhèiběn shū	jay-bun shoo	**this book**
zhèiliàng zìxíngchē	jay-lyang dzur-hsing-chur	**this bicycle**
sānzhāng piào	sahn-jahng pyow	**three tickets**
sìshíge rén	sur-shur-gur run	**forty people**

Pronunciation

Throughout this book Chinese words have been written in the standard romanized system known as pinyin (see below). Pinyin, which was introduced in China in the 1950s, can for the most part be used as a guide to pronunciation. However, some syllables are not pronounced in an immediately obvious way, so a simplified transliteration is also provided in almost all instances. This transliteration should be read as though it were English, bearing in mind the notes on pronunciation below:

Vowels

ah	long 'a' as in art	eh	'e' as in bed
ai	'i' as in I, eye	oh	'o' as in go, oh
ay	as in hay	ow	as in cow

Consonants

ch	as in Chinese	ts	as in tsar
dz	like the 'ds' in heads	y	as in yes
g	hard 'g' as in get		

Pinyin

Chinese words are made up of one or more syllables, each of which is represented in the written language by a character. These syllables can be divided into initials (consonants) and finals (vowels or vowels followed by either n or ng) In spoken Chinese, the consonant finals are often not fully sounded. A full list of initials and finals, along with the closest equivalent sound in English appears below. There are, however, some sounds that are unlike anything in English. In this pronunciation guide, words containing these sounds are given in Chinese characters as well; ask a Chinese person to pronounce them for you.

Initials

Pinyin – Initial	Pronunciation
f, l, m, n, s, w, y	are all similar to English
b, d, g	similar to English, but a shorter sound
p, t, k	a more emphatic pronunciation as in pop, tap and cap (more strongly pronounced than b, d and g above)
h	slightly harsher than an **h** in English, closer to the **ch** sound in lo**ch** or Ba**ch**
j, q, x	pronounced with the lips positioned as if you were smiling:
j	'j' as in **j**eer
q	'ch' as in **ch**eer
x	'sh' as in **sh**eer, but say it with your lips in a smile and the tip of your tongue pointing up. This sound is shown in the book with **hs**
c	'ts' as in **ts**ar 菜
z	'ds' as in head**s** 自
ch, sh, zh, r	the last group of initials is the most difficult for a non-Chinese to perfect; they are all pro nounced with the tip of the tongue curled back till it touches the palate:
ch	as ch in bir**ch** 茶
sh	as sh in **sh**ower 少
zh	as ge in bud**ge** 中
r	as r in **r**ung 人

Finals

Pinyin – Final	Pronunciation
a	as in art
ai	as in aisle
an	as in ran, but with a longer 'a' as in art
ang	as in hang, but with a longer 'a' as in art
ao	'ow' as in cow
e	like the 'e' in the or the 'u' in fur
ei	as in weight
en	as in shaken
eng	like 'en' followed by a softly spoken 'g'
er	similar to err, pronounced with the tongue curled back so that it touches the palate
i	usually pronounced as in margarine; however, after the initials c, ch, r, s, sh, z and zh it is pronounced like the 'i' in shirt or first
ia	'ya' as in yarn
ian	similar to yen
iang	yang ('i' plus 'ang', but with shorter 'a' sound)
iao	'yow' as in yowl
ie	'ye' as in yeti
in	as in din
ing	as in bring
iong	yoong ('i' plus 'ong')
iu	'yo' as in yo-yo
o	as in lore
ou	like oh
ong	oong ('ung' as in lung, with the vowel given a longer, more rounded sound)

u	as in rule; or like French une or German über
ua	wah ('wa' plus 'a' as in art)
uai	similar to why
uan	wahn in most cases ('w' plus 'an'); after 'y', the second pronunciation of 'u' plus 'an'
uang	wahng ('w' plus 'ang')
ue	the second pronunciation of 'u' plus 'e' as in bet
ui	'wai' as in wait
un	as in fungi
uo	similar to war
ü	like French une or German über
üe	'ü' followed by 'e' as in bet

Northern Chinese

In Northern Chinese, the suffix r is often placed at the end of a syllable, producing a sound reminiscent of the burr of southwest England. This is represented in pinyin by the addition of an r to the syllable so that men (**door**), for example, becomes menr, with the n barely pronounced. Such pronunciation is most apparent in Beijing.

Tones

The Chinese language only uses about four hundred different sounds. The number of sounds available is increased by the use of tones: the particular pitch at which a word is pronounced determines its meaning. The same combination of letters pronounced with a different tone will produce different words. There are four tones: first tone (‾), second tone (′), third tone (˘) and fourth tone (`).

Not all syllables are pronounced with tones; where there is no tone, the syllable is written without a tone mark. Often when you have a word consisting of two syllables, the second syllable, for example, xuésheng (**student**), is written without a tone.

In Chinese, the tone is as important a part of the word as the consonant and vowel sounds. Context usually makes the meaning clear, but it is still important whenever possible to use the correct tone in order to reduce the chance of misunderstanding. The character ma mah has five meanings, differentiated by the tones:

mā	妈	mother
má	麻	hemp
mǎ	马	horse
mà	骂	abuse, scold
ma	吗	(added to the end of a sentence to turn it into a question)

To help you get a clearer idea of how the tones sound, Chinese character equivalents are given for the words in this section. Ask a Chinese speaker to read the words for you so that you can hear the tonal differences.

First tone (‾). High, level tone, with unchanging volume, held briefly:

gū	goo	孤	solitary
guān	gwahn	观	look at
kāi		开	open
yān	yahn	烟	cigarette

Second tone (´). Starting about mid-range, rising quickly and becoming louder; a shorter sound than the first tone, similar to a question showing surprise such as 'eh?':

héng	hung	衡	balance
rén	run	人	person
shí	shur	十	ten
yán	yahn	言	speech

Third tone (ˇ). Starts low and falls before rising again to slightly above the starting point; starts quietly then increases in volume; slightly longer than first tone:

běn	bun	本	book
fǎ	fah	法	law

| qǐ | chee | 起 | **rise** |
| yǎn | yahn | 掩 | **cover** |

Fourth tone (ˋ). Starts high, falling abruptly in pitch and volume; shorter than the second tone:

bèn	bun	笨	**stupid**
dà	dah	大	**big**
pà	pah	怕	**fear**
yàn	yahn	雁	**wild goose**

The tones can be illustrated in diagram form like this:

In speech, a third tone which precedes another third tone becomes a second tone.

Regional accents

Mandarin, or modern standard Chinese, derives from the language spoken by the Han ethnic group and is the official language of modern China. It takes the Beijing pronunciation of Chinese as standard. In its spoken form it is also known as Putonghua.

Many regions of China either have their own language (for example, Mongolian, Tibetan) or speak dialects (for example, Gan, Wu, Xiang, Min, Yue or Cantonese, Kejia or Hakka). Someone speaking in one of these dialects will not usually be understood by a speaker of another dialect, although these days most Chinese people also speak Mandarin. The Chinese government has made great efforts to establish Mandarin as a *lingua franca* and it is the working language of the media and government and in schools and businesses all over the country. It is becoming more influential in Hong Kong and Macau, although here the language used in schools and the media is still mainly local Cantonese. These days most people, and especially younger people, will be able to communicate in Mandarin Chinese so you will usually be understood throughout China if you use the Mandarin pronunciation system given in this book.

① Beijing and around
② Hebei and Tianjin
③ Dongbei
④ The Yellow River
⑤ Shanghai and around
⑥ Jiangsu and Zhejiang
⑦ The Yangzi basin
⑧ Fujian, Guangdong and Hainan Island
⑨ Hong Kong and Macau
⑩ Guangxi and Guizhou
⑪ Yunnan
⑫ Sichuan and Chongqing
⑬ The Northwest
⑭ Tibet

But there are some accent differences. Here are some examples of distinctive characteristics that can be heard in the regional pronunciation of Mandarin by speakers influenced by the local dialect. Note that, in some cases, there are tone changes as well.

	Standard Chinese	Northeast	South	Northwest
ch becomes c	chū	cū	cū	chu
fei becomes hui	fēi	fēi	hūi	fei
hu can become fu	hú	hú	fú	hú
n becomes l	niúnǎi	niùnǎi	liúlǎi	niúnài
ng becomes n	chuáng	cuáng	cuán	chuáng
r becomes y or l	ròu	yòu	lòu	rōu
sh becomes h or s	shá	há	sá	shá
sh becomes zh or s	shuāi	zhuāi	suāi	shuai
y can become n	yīn	yīn	yīn	nīn
z becomes zh or j	gōngzī	gōngzhī	gōngjī	gongzi
zh becomes z or j	zhāng	zāng	jiāng	zhang
ai is preceded by n or ng	ài	nài	ài	ngai
an is preceded by n or ng	ān	nān	ān	ngān
ue becomes e	yuē	yuē	yē	nüe

SCENARIOS

Download these scenarios as MP3s from
www.roughguides.com/phrasebooks

1. Accommodation

▶ Is there an inexpensive hotel you can recommend?
Nǐ kěyǐ gěi wǒ tuījiàn yīge búguì de fàndiàn ma?
nee kur-yee gay wor tway-jyen yee-gur boo-gway dur fahn-dyen mah

    ▶▶ I'm sorry, they all seem to be fully booked.
    Duìbuqǐ, hǎoxiàng shì dōu mǎnle.
    dway-boo-chee, how-hsiang shur doh mahn-lur

▶ Can you give me the name of a good middle-range hotel?
Nǐ kěyǐ gěi wǒ tuījiàn yīge zhōngjí fàndiàn ma?
nee kur-yee gay wor tway-jyen yee-gur joong-jee fahn-dyen mah

    ▶▶ Let me have a look, do you want to be in the centre?
    wǒ lái kànkan, nǐ xiǎng zài shìzhōngxīn ma?
    wor lai kahn-kahn, nee hsyang dzai shur-joong-hsin mah

▶ If possible.
Rúguǒ kěyǐ de huà.
roo-gwor kur-yee dur hwah

    ▶▶ Do you mind being a little way out of town?
    Rúguǒ lí shìzhōngxīn shāo yuǎn yīdiǎnr, kěyǐ ma?
    roo-gwor lee shur-joong-hsin show-yew-ahn-yee-dyenr, kur-yee mah

▶ Not too far out.
Wǒ bù xiǎng tài yuǎn.
wor boo hsyang tai yew-ahn

▶ Where is it on the map?
Nǐ kěyǐ zài dìtúshang gěi wǒ zhǐyīxià ma?
nee kur-yee dzai dee-too shahng gay wor` jur-yee-hsyah mah

▶ Can you write the name and address down?
Nǐ kěyǐ gěi wǒ bǎ míngzi hé dìzhǐ xiěxiàlái ma?
nee kur-yee gay wor bah dee-jur hsyeh-hsyah-lai mah

▶ I'm looking for a room in a private house.
Wǒ xiǎng zhù sīrén fáng.
wor hsyang joo sur-run fahng

2. Banks

bank account	yínháng zhànghù	yin-hahng jahng-hoo
to change money	huàn qián	hwahn-chyen
cheque	zhīpiào	jur-pyow
to deposit	cúnqián	tsun-chyen
pin number	gèrén mìmǎ	gur-run mee-mah
pound	yīngbàng	ying-bahng
renminbi	rénmínbì	run-min-bee
to withdraw	qǔqián	chew-chyen

▶ Can you change this into renminbi?
Qǐng nín gěi wǒ huànchéng rénmínbì, kěyǐ ma?
ching nin gay wor hwahn-chung run-min-bee, kur-yee mah

▶▶ How would you like the money?
Nín yào shénme yàng de chāopiào?
nin yoh shun-mur yang dur chow-pyow

▶ Small notes.   ▶ Big notes.
Xiǎo chāopiào.   **Dà chāopiào.**
hsyow chow-pyow   da chow-pyow

▶ Do you have information in English about opening an account?
Nǐmen yǒu guānyú kāizhàng de yīngyǔ yìnshuāpǐn ma?
nee-mun yoh gwahn-yew kai-jahng dur ying-yew yin-shwah-pin mah

▶▶ Yes what sort of account do you want?
Yǒu, nín xiǎng kāi nǎzhǒng zhànghù?
yoh, nee hsyang kai nah-chung jahng-hoo

▶ I'd like a current account.
Huóqī cúnkuǎn.
hwor-chee tsun-kwahn

▶▶ Your passport, please.
Qǐng gěi wǒ kàn yīxià nínde hùzhào.
ching gay wor kahn yee-hsyah neen-dur hoo-jow

▶ Can I use this card to draw some cash?
Kěyǐ yòng zhège kǎ qǔ xiànjīn ma?
kur-yee yoong jur-gur kah chew hsyan-jin mah

▶▶ You have to go to the cashier's desk.
Nǐ děi dào chūnàyuán nàr qù.
nee day dow choo-nah-yew-ahn nar chew

▶ I want to transfer this to my account at the Bank of China.
Wǒ xiǎng bǎ qián zhuǎndào wǒ zài Zhōngguó yínháng de zhànghù shang qù.
wor hsyang bah chyen jwahn-dow wor dzai chung-gwor yin-hahng dur jahng-hoo-shahng chew

▶▶ OK, but we'll have to charge you for the phonecall.
Hǎo, nínde diànhuà děi shōufèi.
how, nin-dur dyen-hwah day shoh-fay

3. Booking a room

shower	línyù	lin-yew
telephone in the room	fángjiānlǐ de diànhuà	fahng-jyen-lee dur dyen-hwah
payphone in the lobby	dàtīnglǐ de tóubì diànhuà	da-ting-lee dur toh-bee dyen-hwah

▶ Do you have any rooms?
Yǒu fángjiān ma?
yoh fahng-jyen mah

▶▶ For how many people?
Jǐge rén?
jee-gur run

▶ For one / for two.
Yīge rén / liǎngge rén.
yee-gur run / lyang-gur run

>> ▶▶ Yes, we have rooms free.
>> **Yǒu fángjiān.**
>> yoh fahng-jyen

>> ▶▶ For how many nights?
>> **Zhù jǐge wǎnshang?**
>> joo jee-gur wahn-shahng

▶ Just for one night.
Yīge wǎnshang.
yee-gur wahn-shahng

▶ How much is it?
Duōshǎo qián?
dwor-show chyen

>> ▶▶ 900 yuan with bathroom and 700 yuan without bathroom.
>> **Dài xǐzǎojiān de jiǔbǎi yuán rénmínbì, búdài xǐzǎojiān de qībǎi yuán.**
>> dai hshee-dzow-jyen dur jyoh-bai yew-ahn run-min-bee, boo dai hshee-dzow-jyen dur chee-bai yew-ahn

▶ Does that include breakfast?
Bāokuò zǎocān ma?
bow-kwor dzow-tsahn mah

▶ Can I see a room with bathroom?
Wǒ kěyǐ kàn yīxià dài xǐzǎojiān de fángjiān ma?
wor kur-yee kahn yee-hsyah dai hshee-dzow-jyen dur fahng-jyen mah

▶ OK, I'll take it.
Hǎo, wǒ yàole.
how wor yow-lur

▶ When do I have to check out?
Wǒ shénme shíhou jiézhàng líkāi?
wor shun-mur shur-hoh jyeh-jahng lee-kai

▶ Is there anywhere I can leave luggage?
Yǒu cún xíngli de dìfāng ma?
yow tsun hsing-lee dur dee-fahng mah

4. Car hire

automatic	zìdòng huàndǎng	dzur-doong hwahn-dahng
full tank	yóuxiāng mǎnde	yoh-hsyang mahn-dur
manual	shǒudòng huàndǎng	show-doong hwahn-dahng
rented car	zūde chē	dzoo-dur chur

▶ I'd like to rent a car.
Wǒ wiǎng zū chē.
wor hsyang dzoo chur

    ▶▶ For how long?
    Duō cháng shí jiān?
    dwor chahng shur-jyen

▶ Two days.
Liǎng tiān.
lyang-tyen

▶ I'll take the…
Wǒ yào…
wor yow

▶ Is that with unlimited mileage?
Kāi duō cháng lù yǒu xiànzhì ma?
kai dwor-chahng loo yoh hsyen-jur mah

    ▶▶ It is.
    Méiyou xiànzhì.
    may-yoh hsyen-jur

    ▶▶ Can I see your driving licence please?
    Wǒ kàn yīxià nǐde jiàshǐ zhí zhào, hǎo ma?
    wor kahn yee-hsyah nee-dur jyah-shur jur-jow, how mah

    ▶▶ And your passport.
    Hái yào nǐde hùzhào.
    hai yow nee-dur hoo-jow

▶ Is insurance included?
Bāokuò bǎoxiǎn ma?
bow-kwor bow-hsyen mah

    ▶▶ Yes, but you have to pay the first 1000 yuan.
    Bāokuò, búguò nín děi xiàn fù yīqiān yuán.
    bow-kwor, boo-gwor nin day hsyen foo yee-chyen yew-ahn

    ▶▶ Can you leave a deposit of 1000 yuan?
    Qǐng nín fù yīqiān yuán yājīn, hǎo ma?
    ching nin foo yee-chyen yew-ahn yah-jin, how mah

▶ And if this office is closed, where do I leave the keys?
Rúguǒ nǐmen zhèr guānménle, wǒ bǎ yàoshi fàng zài nǎr?
roo-gwor nee-mun jer gwahn-mun-lur, wor bah yow-shur fahng dzai nar

▶▶ You drop them in that box.
Fàng zài nàge hézi lǐ.
fahng dzai nah-gur hur-dzur lee

5. Car problems

brakes	shāchē	shah-chur
to break down	huàile	hwai-lur
clutch	líhéqì	lee-hur-chee
diesel	cháiyóu	chai-yoh
flat battery	diànchí méidiànle	dyen-chur may-dyen-lur
flat tyre	lúntāi biěle	lun-tai byeh-lur
petrol	qìyóu	chee-yoh

▶ Excuse me, where is the nearest petrol station?
Qǐngwèn, zuìjìnde jiāyóuzhàn zài nǎr?
ching-wun dzway-jin-dur jyah-yoh-jahn dzai nar

▶▶ In the next town, about 5km away.
Lízhèr wǔ gōnglǐ zuǒyòu, zài xiàyíge chéngshì.
lee-jer woo goong-lee dzwor-yoh, dzai hsyah-yee-gur chung-shur

▶ The car has broken down.
Chē huàile.
chur hwai-lur

▶▶ Can you tell me what happened?
Qǐng gàosu wǒ, fāshēngle shénme shì?
ching gow-soo wor, fah-shung-lur shun-mur shur

▶ I've got a flat tyre.
Lúntāi biěle.
lun-tai byeh-lur

▶ I think the battery is flat.
Diànchí sìhū méidiànle.
dyen-chur sur-hoo may-dyen-lur

▶▶ Can you tell me exactly where you are?
Qǐng gàosu wǒ nǐ xiànzài zài nǎr?
ching gow-soo wor nee hsyen-dzai dzai nar

► I'm about 2km outside of Suzhou on the ring road.
Zài Suzhou chéngwài dàyuē liǎng gōnglǐ zài huánchéng lùshang.
dzai soo-joh chung-wai dah-yew-eh lyang goong-lee dzai hwahn-chung loo-shahng

>> What type of car? What colour?
Nínde chē shì shénme xínghào de? Shénme yánsède?
nindur chur shur shun-mur hsing-how dur, shun-mur yahn-sur-dur

► Can you send a tow truck?
Nǐ néng pài yíliàng tuōchē lái ma?
nee nung pai yee-lyang twor-chur lai mah

6. Children

baby	xiǎo bǎobèi	hsyow bow-bay
boy	nán háir	nahn hair
child	háizi	hai-dzur
children	háizi	hai-dzur
cot	yīng'érchuáng	ying-er-chwahng
formula	pèifāng yīng'ér shípǐn	pay-fahng ying-er shur-pin
girl	nǐ háir	nyew hair
highchair	yīng'ér gāojiǎoyǐ	ying-er gow-jyow-yee
nappies (diapers)	niàobù	nyow-boo

► We need a babysitter for tomorrow evening.
Míngtiān wǎnshang wǒmen xūyào yīge yīng'ér bǎomǔ.
ming-tyen wahn-shahng wor-mun hsew-yow yee-gur ying-er bow-moo

>> For what time?
Jǐdiǎn?
jee-dyen

► From 7.30 to 11.00.
Cóng qīdiǎnbàn dào shíyī diǎn.
tsoong chee-dyen-bahn dow shur-yee dyen

>> How many children? How old are they?
Jǐge háizi? Tāmen dōu jǐ suì?
jee-gur hai-dzur, tah-mun doh jee sway

► Two children, aged four and eighteen months.
Liǎngge háizi, yíge sìsuì yíge shíbāge yuè.
lyang-gur hai-dzur, yee-gur sur-sway yee-gur shur-bah-gur yew-eh

▶ Where can I change the baby?
Wǒ kěyǐ zài nǎr gěi yīng'ér huàn niàobù?
wor kur-yee dzai nar gay ying-er hwahn nyow-boo

▶ Could you please warm this bottle for me?
Qǐng bǎ zhège píngzi rèyixià.
ching bah jur-gur ping-dzur rur-yee-hsyah

▶ Can you give us a child's portion?
Qǐng nǐ gěi wǒmen lái yìfèn értóng de.
ching nee gay wor-mun lai yee-fun er-tung dur

▶ We need two child seats.
Wǒmen xūyào liǎngge értóng zuòyǐ.
wor-mun hsew-yow lyang-gur er-toong dzwor-yee

▶ Is there a discount for children?
Yǒu értóng jiǎnjià ma?
yoh er-toong jyen-jyah mah

7. Communications: Internet

@	at	at
at sign	xiǎo lǎoshǔ	shyow low-shoo
computer	diànnǎo	dyen-now
email	diànzi yóujiàn	dyen-dzur yoh-jyen
Internet	hùliánwǎng	hoo-lyen-wahng
keyboard	jiànpán	jyen-pahn
mouse	shǔbiāo	shoo-byow

▶ Is there somewhere I can check my emails?
Wǒ néng chá diànzi yóujiàn ma?
wor nung chah dyen-dzur yoh-jyen mah

▶ Do you have Wi-Fi?
Yǒu wúxiàn wǎngluò ma?
yoh woo-syen wahng-lwor mah

▶ Is there an Internet café around here?
Zhèr fùjìn yǒu wǎngbā ma?
jer foo-jin yoh wahng-bah mah

▶▶ Yes, there's one in the shopping centre.
Yǒu, yǒu yíge zài gòuwù zhōngxīn.
yoh, yoh yee-gur dzai goh-woo joong-hsin

▶▶ Do you want fifteen minutes, thirty minutes or one hour?
Nǐ yào yòng shíwǔ fēnzhōng, sānshí fēnzhōng, háishi yíge xiǎoshí?
nee yow yoong shur-woo fun-joong, sahn-shur fun-joong, hai-shur yee-gur hsyow-shur

▶ Thirty minutes please. Can you help me log on?
Wǒ yòng sānshí fēnzhōng. Qǐng bāng wǒ shàngwǎng?
wor yoong sahn-shur fun-joong, ching bahng wor shahng-wahng

▶▶ OK, here's your password.
Hǎo, zhè shì nǐ mìmǎ.
how, jur shur nee mee-mah

▶ I'll take another quarter of an hour.
Wǒ hái yào shíwǔ fēnzhōng.
wor hai yow shur-woo fun-joong

▶ Is there a printer I can use?
Yǒu dǎyìnjī ma?
yoh da-yin-jee mah

8. Communications: phones

mobile phone (cell phone)	shǒujī	shoh-jee
payphone	jìfèi diànhuà	jee-fay dyen-hwah
phone call	diànhuà	dyen-hwah
phone card	diànhuàkǎ	dyen-hwah-kah
phone charger	shǒujī chōngdiànqì	shoh-jee choong-dyen-chee
SIM card	SIM kǎ	sim kah

▶ Can I call abroad from here?
Wǒ kěyǐ zài zhèr dǎ guójì chángtú ma?
wor kur-yee dzai jer dah gwor-jee chahng-too mah

▶ How do I get an outside line?
Wǒ zěnme wǎng wàibiān dǎ diànhuà?
wor dzun-mur wahng wai-byen dah dyen-hwah

▶ What's the code to call the UK/US from here?
Yīngguó/Měiguó de diànhuà qūhào shì shénme?
ying-gwor/may-gwor dur dyen-hwah chew-how shur shun-mur

▶ Hello, can I speak to Mrs Wang?
Wéi, qǐngwèn Wáng tàitài zài ma?
way, ching-wun wahng tai-tai dzai mah

zero	líng	ling
one	yī	yee
two	ér	ur
three	sān	san
four	sì	sur
five	wǔ	woo
six	liù	lyoh
seven	qī	chee
eight	bā	bah
nine	jiǔ	jyoh

▶▶ Yes, that's me speaking.
Wǒ jiù shì.
wor jyoh shur

▶ Do you have a charger for this?
Yǒu shǒujī chōngdiànqì ma?
yoh shoh-jee choong-dyen-chee mah

▶ Can I buy a SIM card for this phone?
Wǒ kěyǐ mǎi yìzhāng SIM kǎ ma?
wor kur-yee mai yee-jang sim kah mah

9. Directions

opposite	duìmiàn	dway-myen
turn (off)	guǎi	gwai
past the	guòle	gwor-luh
street	jiē	jyeh
near	jìn	jin
in front of	qiánmiàn	chyen-myen
back	wǎng huí	wahng hway
next	xià yíge	hsyah yee-gur
straight ahead	yìzhí wǎng qián zǒu	yee-jur wahng chyen dzoh
on the right	yòubiān	yoh-byen
further	yuǎn	yew-ahn
over there	zài nàr	dzai nar
just after	zài…zhīhòu	dzai…jur-hoh
on the left	zuǒbiān	dzwor-byen

▶ Hi, I'm looking for Nán Jiē.
Wǒ zhǎo Nán Jiē.
wor jow Nan Jyeh

▶▶ Sorry, never heard of it.
Duìbuqǐ, méi tīngshuōguo zhè tiáo jiē.
dway-boo-chee, may ting-shwor-gwor juh tyow jyeh

▶ Hi, can you tell me where Nán Jiē is?
Qǐng wèn, Nán Jiē zài nǎr?
ching wun, Nan Jyeh dzai nar

▶▶ I'm a stranger here too.
Wǒ duì zhège difang yě bù shúxi.
wor dway juh-gur dee-fahng yur boo shoo-hshee

▶ Hi, Nán Jiē, do you know where it is?
Qǐng wèn, nǐ zhīdao Nán Jiē zài nǎr ma?
ching wun, nee jur-dow Nan Jyeh dzai nar mah

▶ Where?
Zài nǎr?
dzai nar

▶ Which direction?
Nǎge fāngxiàng?
nah-gur fahng-hsyang

▶ Left at the second traffic lights.
Dàole dièrge hónglēdēng, wǎng zuǒ guǎi.
dow-luh dee-er-gur hoong-lyew-dung, wahng dzwor gwai

▶ Around the corner.
Guòle lùkǒu.
gwor-luh loo-koh

▶ Then it's the first street on the right.
Zhīhòu, zǒu yòubiān dìyì tiáo lù.
jur-hoh, dzoh yoh-byen dee-yee tyow loo

10. Emergencies

accident	shìgù	shur-goo
ambulance	jiùhùchē	jyoh-hoo-chur
consul	lǐngshì	ling-shur
embassy	dàshǐguǎn	da-shur-gwahn
fire brigade	xiāofángduì	hsyow-fahng-dway
police	jǐngchájú	jing-chah-joo

▶ Help!
Jiùmìng!
jyoh-ming

▶ Can you help me?
Bāngge máng, hǎo ma?
bahng-gur mahng, how mah

▶ Please come with me! It's really very urgent.
Qǐng gēn wǒ lái! Yǒu jǐnjí qíngkuàng.
ching gun wor lai! yoh jin-jee ching-kwahng

▶ I've lost my keys.
Wǒ diūle yàoshi.
wor dyoh-lur yow-shur

▶ My car is not working.
Wǒde chē bù gōngzuòle.
wor-dur chur boo goong-dzwor-lur

▶ My purse has been stolen.
Wǒde qiánbāo bèi tōule.
wor-dur chyen-bow bay tow-lur

▶ I've been mugged.
Wǒ bèi rén qiǎngle.
wor bay run chyang-lur

▶▶ What's your name?
Nínde míngzi?
nin-dur ming-dzur

▶▶ I need to see your passport.
Wǒ kànkan nínde hùzhào, hǎo ma?
wor kahn-kahn nin-dur hoo-jow, how mah

▶ I'm sorry, all my papers have been stolen.
Duìbuqǐ, wǒ suǒyǒu de wénjiàn bèi tōule.
dway-boo-chee, wor swor-yoh dur wun-jyen bay toh-lur

11. Friends

▶ Hi, how're you doing?
Nǐ hǎo ma?
nee how mah

▶▶ OK, and you?
Wǒ hěn hǎo, nǐ ne?
wor hun how, nee nuh

▶ Yeah, fine.
Hěn hǎo.
hun how

▶ Not bad.
Búcuò.
boo-tswor

▶ Do you know Mark?
Nǐ rènshi Mǎkè ma?
nee run-shur Mah-kuh mah

▶ And this is Hannah.
Zhè shì Hànnà.
juh shur Han-nah

    ▶▶ Yeah, we know each other.
    Wǒmen yǐjīng rènshile.
    wor-mun yee-jing run-shur-luh

▶ Where do you know each other from?
Nǐmen shì zěnme rènshide?
nee-mun shur dzen-mur run-shur-dur

    ▶▶ We met at Luke's place.
    Wǒmen shì zài Lúkè jiā rènshide.
    wor-mun shur dzai Loo-kur jyah run-shur-dur

▶ That was some party, eh?
Nàge yànhuì bàng jíle, dùi budùi.
nah-gur yen-hway bang jee-luh, dway boo-dway

    ▶▶ The best.
    Shì zuìhǎo de.
    shur dzway-how dur

▶ Are you guys coming for a beer?
Zánmen hējiǔ qù ba?
dzahn-mun huh-jyoh chew bah

> ▶▶ Cool, let's go.
> **Hǎo, zǒu ba.**
> how, dzoh bah

> ▶▶ No, I'm meeting Lola.
> **Wǒ búqù, wǒ yào qù jiàn Luólā.**
> wor boo-chew, wor yow chew jyen Lwor-lah

▶ OK, that's cool too.
Hǎo ba.
how bah

▶ See you at Luke's place tonight.
Wǎnshang zài Lúkè jiā jiànmiàn.
wahn-shahng dzai Loo-kur jyah jyen-myen

> ▶▶ See you.
> **Huítóu jiàn.**
> hway-toh jyen

12. Health

antibiotics	kàngjūnsù	kahng-joon-soo
antiseptic ointment	kàngjūn yóugāo	kahng-joon yoh-gow
cystitis	pángguāngyán	pahng-gwahng-yen
dentist	yáyī	yah-yee
diarrhoea	lādùzi	lah-doo-dzur
doctor	yīshēng	yee-shung
hospital	yīyuàn	yee-yew-ahn
ill	shēngbìngle	shung-bing-lur
medicine	yào	yow
painkillers	zhǐténgyào	jur-tung-yow
pharmacy	yàofáng	yow-fahng
to prescribe	kāi yàofāng	kai yow-fahng
thrush	ékǒuchuāng	ur-koh-chwahng

▶ I'm not feeling very well.
Wǒ juéde bù shūfu.
wor jew-eh-dur boo shoo-foo

▶ Can you get a doctor?
Qǐng gěi wǒ zhǎo ge yīshēng.
ching gay wor jow-gur yee-shung

▶▶ Where does it hurt?
Nǎr bù shūfu?
nar boo shoo-foo

▶ It hurts here.
Zhèr téng.
jur tung

▶▶ Is the pain constant?
Zǒngshì téng ma?
dzoong-shur tung mah

▶ It's not a constant pain.
Bù zǒngshì téng.
boo dzoong-shur tung

▶ Can I make an appointment?
Wǒ kěyǐ yùyuē yīshēng ma?
wor kur-yee yew-yew-eh yee-shung mah

▶ Can you give me something for…?
Gěi wǒ diǎnr … yào, hǎo ma?
gay wor dyanr … yow, how mah

▶ Yes, I have insurance.
Wǒ yǒu bǎoxiǎn.
wor yoh bow-hsyen

13. Hotels

maid	nǐ fúwùyuán	nyew foo-woo-yew-ahn
manager	jīnglǐ	jing-lee
room service	sòngfàn fúwù	soong-fahn foo-woo

▶ Hello, we've booked a double room in the name of Cameron.
Nǐ hǎo, wǒmen dìngle yíge shuāngrénfáng, míngzi shì Cameron.
nee how, wor-mun ding-lur yee-gur shwahng-run-fahng, ming-dzur shur cameron

▶▶ That was for four nights, wasn't it?
Nín dìngle sìtiān, shìbushì?
nin ding-lur sur-tyen, shur-boo-shur

▶ Yes, we're leaving on Saturday.
Shì, wǒmen xīngqīliù zǒu.
shur, wor-mun hsing-chee-lyoh dzoh

▶▶ Can I see your passport please?
Gěi wǒ kànyixià nínde hùzhào, hǎo ma?
gay wor kahn-yee-hsyah nin-dur hoo-jow, how mah

▶▶ There you are, room 323 on the third floor.
Nínde fángjiān zài sānlóu, fángjiān hào shì sānèrsān.
nin-dur fahng-jyen dzai sahn-loh, fahng-jyen how shur sahn-er-sahn

▶ I can't get this keycard to work.
Wǒ búhuì yòng fángkǎ.
wor boo-hway yoong fahng-kah

▶▶ Sorry, I need to reactivate it.
Duìbuqǐ, wǒ děi bǎtā jīhuó.
dway-boo-chee, wor day bah-tah jee-hwor

▶ What time is breakfast?
Zǎofàn jǐdiǎn?
dzow-fahn jee-dyen

▶ There aren't any towels in my room.
Wǒde fángjiān méiyou máojīn.
wor-dur fahng-jyen may-yoh mow-jin

▶ My flight isn't until this evening, can I keep the room a bit longer?
Wǒde fēijī jīntiān wǎnshang qǐfēi, wǒ néngbùnéng zài fángjiān dāi cháng yidiǎn?
wor-dur fay-jee jin-tyen wahn-shahng chee-fay, wor nung-boo-nung dzai fahng-jyen dai chahng yee-dyen

▶ Can I settle up? Is this card ok?
Wǒ jiézhàng, yòng xìnyòngkǎ, kěyǐ ma?
wor jyeh-jahng, yoong hsin-yoong-kah, kur-yee mah

14. Language difficulties

a few words	jǐge zì	jee-gur dzur
interpreter	kǒutóu fānyì	koh-tow fahn-yee
to translate	fānyì	fahn-yee

▶▶ Your credit card has been refused.
Nǐde xìnyòngkǎ bèi jùle.
nee-dur hsin-yoong-kah bay-jew-lur

▶ What, I don't understand. Do you speak English?
Shénme? Wǒ bù dǒng. Nǐ huì shuō yīngyǔ ma?
shun-mur wor boo doong, nee hway shwor ying-yew mah

> ▶▶ This isn't valid.
> **Xìnyòngkǎ wúxiàole.**
> hsin-yoong-kah woo-hsyow-lur

▶ Could you say that again?
Qǐng zài shuō yīxià, hǎo ma?
ching dzai shwor yee-hsyah, how mah

▶ Slowly.
Màn diǎnr.
mahn dyenr

▶ I understand very little Chinese.
Wǒ zhǐ huì yīdiǎnr zhōngwén.
wor jur hway yee-dyenr choong-wun

▶ I speak Chinese very badly.
Wǒ zhōngwén shuōde bù hǎo.
wor choong-wun shwor-dur boo how

> ▶▶ You can't use this card to pay.
> **Nǐ bù néng yòng zhège kǎ fùqián.**
> nee boo nung yoong jur-gur kah foo-chyen

> ▶▶ Do you understand?
> **Dǒngle ma?**
> doong-lur mah

▶ Sorry, no.
Duìbuqǐ, wǒ hái shì bù míngbai.
dway-boo-chee, wor hai shur boo ming-bai

▶ Is there someone who speaks English?
Zhèr yǒu rén huì yīngwén ma?
jur yoh run hway ying-wun mah

▶ Oh, now I understand.
Hǎo, wǒ míngbaile.
how wor ming-bai-lur

▶ Is that OK now?
Xíngle ma?
hsing-lur mah

15. Meeting people

▶ Hello.
Nǐ hǎo.
nee how

▶▶ Hello, my name's Wang Shen.
Nǐ hǎo, wǒ jiào Shèn, xìng Wáng.
nee how, wor jyow Shun, hsing Wahng

▶ Graham, from England, Thirsk.
Wǒ shì yīngguórén, wǒ jiào Graham, shì Thirsk rén.
wor shur ying-gwor-run, wor jyow Graham, shur Thirsk run

▶▶ Don't know that, where is it?
Thirsk wǒ bù zhīdao, zài nǎr?
Thirsk wor boo jur-dow, dzai nar

▶ Not far from York, in the North; and you?
Zài Yīnggélán běibù, lí York bù yuǎn; nǐ ne?
dzai Ying-guh-lan bay-boo, lee York boo yew-ahn; nee nur

▶▶ I'm from London; here by yourself?
Wǒ shì Lúndūn rén; nǐ shì yíge rén lái de ma?
wor shur Lun-dun run; nee shur yee-gur run lai duh mah

▶ No, I'm with my wife and two kids.
Búshì, wǒ gēn wǒ àiren hé liǎngge háizi yìqǐ láide.
boo-shur, wor gun wor ai-run huh lyang-gur hai-dzur yee-chee lai-dur

▶ What do you do?
Nǐ zuò shénme gōngzuò?
nee dzwor shun-mur goong-dzwor

▶▶ I'm in computers.
Wǒ shì gǎo diànnǎode.
wor shur gow dyen-nao-dur

▶ Me too.
Wǒ yě shì.
wor yeh shur

▶ Here's my wife now.
Zhè shì wǒ àiren.
jur shur wor ai-run

▶▶ Nice to meet you.
Hěn gāoxìng rènshi nín.
hun gow-hsing run-shur nin

16. Nightlife

heavy metal	zhòngjīnshǔ yīnyuè	joong-jin-shoo yin-yew-eh
folk	mínyuè	min-yew-eh
jazz	juéshì yuè	jew-eh-shur yew-eh
hip-hop	xīhā	hsee-hah
electro	diànzǐ yīnyuè	dyen-dzur yin-yew-eh
rock	yáogǔn yuè	yow-gun yew-eh

▶ I want to go to a club for...
Wǒ xiǎng qù yíge jùlèbù tīng...
wor hsyahng chew yee-gur jew-lur-boo ting

▶▶ There's going to be a great gig at Sanlitun tomorrow night.
Míngtiān wǎnshang zài Sānlǐtún yǒu yíge rènao de yǎnchū.
ming-tyen wahn-shahng dzai sahn-lee-tun yoh yee-gur rur-now dur yen-choo

▶ Where can I hear some local music?
Nǎr néng xīnshǎng dìfāng yīnyuè?
nar nung hsin-shahng dee-fahng yin-yew-eh

▶ Where's the best place for dancing?
Tiàowù zuìhǎo qù nǎli?
tyow-woo dzway-how chew nar-lee

▶ Can you write down the names of the best bars around here?
Qǐng nǐ bǎ fùjìn jiǔbā de míngzi xiěxialái, hǎo ma?
ching nee bah foo-jin jyoh-bah dur ming-dzur hsyeh-hsyah-lai, how mah

▶▶ That depends what you're looking for.
Zhè qǔjuéyú nǐ xiǎngyào shénme.
jur chew-jew-eh-yoo nee hsyahng-yow shun-mur

▶ The place where the locals go.
Dāngdìrén xǐhuan qù de dìfāng.
dahng-dee-run hshee-hwahn chew dur dee-fahng

▶ A place for a quiet drink.
Yíge ānjìng de jiǔbā.
yee-gur ahn-jing dur jyoh-bah

▶▶ The casino across the river is very good.
Hé duìmian de dǔchǎng hěn yǒu yìsi.
hur dway-myen dur doo-chahng hun yoh yee-sur

▶ I suppose they have a dress code.
Wǒ rènwéi tāmen yāoqiú chuān guīdìngde yīfu.
wor run-way tah-mun yow-chyoh chwahn gway-ding-dur yee-foo

▶▶ You can wear what you like.
Nǐ kěyǐ chuān nǐ yuànyi chuānde.
nee kur-yee chwahn nee yew-ahn-yee chwahn-dur

▶ What time does it close?
Jǐdiǎn guānmén?
jee-dyen gwahn-mun

17. Post offices

airmail	hángkōng	hahng-kung
post card	míngxìnpiàn	ming-hsin-pyen
post office	yóujú	yoh-jew
stamp	yóupiào	yoh-pyow

▶ What time does the post office close?
Yóujú jǐdiǎn guānmén?
yoh-jew jee-dyen gwahn-mun

▶▶ Five o'clock weekdays.
Gōngzuòrì wǔdiǎn.
gung-dzow-rur woo-dyen

▶ Is the post office open on Saturdays?
Yóujú xīngqīliù kāimén ma?
yoh-jew hsing-chee-lyow kai-mun mah

▶▶ Until midday.
Zhǐdào zhōngwǔ.
jur dow joong-woo

▶ I'd like to send this registered to England.
Wǒ yào wǎng yīngguó jì guàhàoxìn.
wor yow wahng ying-gwor jee gwah-how-hsin

▶▶ Certainly, that will cost 10 yuan.
Méi wèntí, guàhàoxìn shí yuán.
may wun-tee, gwah-how-hsin shur yew-ahn

▶ And also two stamps for England, please.
Hái yào liǎng zhāng dào yīngguó de yóupiào.
hai yow lyang-jahng dow ying-gwor dur yoh-pyow

▶ Do you have some airmail stickers?
Yóu hángkōng yóujiàn biāoqiān ma?
yoh hahng-kung yoh-jyen byow-chyen mah

▶ Do you have any mail for me?
Yǒu wǒde xìn ma?
yoh wor-dur hsin mah

国领	guójì	international
信	xìn	letters
国内	guónèi	domestic
包裹	bāoguǒ	parcels
待领邮件	dàilǐng yóujiàn	poste restante

18. Restaurants

bill	zhàngdān	jahng-dan
menu	càidān	tsai-dan
table	zhuōzi	jwor-dzur

▶ Can we have a non-smoking table?
Wǒmen yào bù chōuyānde zhuōzi, kěyǐ ma?
wor-mun yow boo choh-yen-dur jwor-dzur, kur-yee mah

▶ There are two of us.
Wǒmen liǎngge rén.
wor-mun lyang-gur run

▶ There are four of us.
Yīgòng sìgerén.
yee-gung sur-gur run

▶ What's this?
Zhè shì shénme?
jur shur shun-mur

> ▶▶ It's a type of fish.
> **Yī zhǒng yǔ.**
> yee joong yew

> ▶▶ It's a local speciality.
> **Shì běndì tèchǎn.**
> shur bun-dee tur-chahn

> ▶▶ Come inside and I'll show you.
> **Qǐng jìnlái kànkan.**
> ching jin-lai kahn-kahn

▶ We would like two of these, one of these, and one of those.
Zhège liǎngge, zhège yīge, nàge yīge.
jur-gur lyang-gur, jur-gur yee-gur, nah-gur yee-gur

> ▶▶ And to drink?
> **Hē diǎnr shénme?**
> hur dyenr shun-mur

▶ Red wine.   ▶ White wine.
Hóng pútaójiǔ.   **Bái pútaójiǔ.**
hung poo-tow-jyoh   bai poo-tow-jyoh

▶ A beer and two orange juices.
Yìbēi píjiǔ, liǎng bēi júzizhī.
yee-bay pee-jyoh, lyang bay jew-dzur-jur

▶ Some more bread please.
Qǐng zài lái xiē miànbāo.
ching dzai lai hsyeh myen-bow

>> ▶▶ How was your meal?
Chīde hǎo ma?
chur-dur how mah

▶ Excellent! Very nice!
Hěn hǎo! Búcuò!
hun how, boo-tswor

>> ▶▶ Anything else?
Hái yào shénme ma?
hai yow shun-mur mah

▶ Just the bill, thanks.
Wǒmen fù zhàngdān, hǎo ma?
wor-mun foo jahng-dan, how mah

19. Self-catering accommodation

air-conditioning	kōngtiáo	koong-tyow
apartment	dānyuán	dahn-yew-ahn
cooker	chuījù	chway-jew
fridge	bīngxiāng	bing-hsyang
heating	nuǎnqì	nwahn-chee
hot water	rèshuǐ	rur-shway
lightbulb	dēngpào	dung-pow
toilet	cèsuǒ	tsur-swor

▶ The toilet's broken, can you get someone to fix it?
Cèsuǒ huàile, qǐng pài rén lái xiūyíxià.
tsur-swor hwai-lur, ching pai run lai hsyoh-yee-hsyah

▶ There's no hot water.
Méiyou rèshuǐ.
may-yoh rur-shway

▶ Can you show me how the air-conditioning works?
Qǐng gàosu wǒ kōngtiáo zěnme yòng?
ching gow-soo wor koong-tyow dzun-mur yoong

>> ▶▶ OK, what apartment are you in?
Nín zhù zài nǎge dānyuán?
nin joo dzai nah-gur dahn-yew-ahn

▶ We're in number five.
Wǒmen zài wǔhào.
wor-mun dzai woo-how

▶ Can you move us to a quieter apartment?
Néngbunéng bāndào yíge bǐjiào ānjìng de dānyuán?
nung-boo-nung bahn-dow yee-gur bee-jyow ahn-jing dur dahn-yew-ahn

▶ Is there a supermarket nearby?
Fùjìn yǒu chāoshì ma?
foo-jin yoh chow-shur mah

▶▶ Have you enjoyed your stay?
Nǐmen wánrde hǎo ma?
nee-mun wahnr-dur how mah

▶ Brilliant holiday, thanks!
Wǒmen zài jiàqī wánrde hěnhǎo, xièxiè.
wor-mun dzai jyah-chee wahnr-dur hun-how, hsyeh-hsyeh

20. Shopping

付款台	fùkuǎntái	cash desk
关门	guānmén	closed
换	huàn	to exchange
开门	kāimén	open
大减价	dà jiǎnjià	sale

▶▶ Can I help you?
Mǎi diǎnr shénme?
mai dyenr shun-mur

▶ Can I just have a look around?
Wǒ kànkan, kěyǐ ma?
wor kahn-kahn, kur-yee mah

▶ Yes, I'm looking for...
Wǒ xiǎng mǎi...
wor hsyang mai

▶ How much is this?
Duōshǎo qián?
dwor-show chyen

▶▶ Thirty-two yuan.
Sānshí èr yuán.
san-shur ur yew-ahn

► OK, I think I'll have to leave it; it's a little too expensive for me.
Wǒ búyào, yǒu diǎnr tài guì.
wor boo-yow, yoh dyenr tai gway

>► ► How about this?
>**Zhège zěnme yàng?**
>jur-gur dzun-mur yang

► Can I pay by credit card?
Shōu xìnyòngkǎ ma?
shoh hsin-yoong-kah mah

► It's too big.   ► It's too small.
Tài dàle.   **Tài xiǎole.**
tai dah-lur   tai hsyow-lur

► It's for my son – he's about this high.
Gěi wǒ érzi mǎide – tā zhème gāo.
gay wor ur-dzur mai-dur, tah jur-mur gow

>► ► Will there be anything else?
>**Hái yào biéde ma?**
>hai yow byeh-dur mah

► That's all thanks.
Búyàole, xièxie.
boo-yow-lur, hsyeh-hsyeh

► Make it twenty yuan and I'll take it.
Wǒ zhǐ xiǎng fù èrshí yuán, kěyǐ ma?
wor jur hsyang foo ur-shur yew-ahn, kur-yee mah

▶ Fine, I'll take it.
Xíng.
hsing

21. Shopping for clothes

to alter	gǎiyíxià	gai-yee-hsyah
bigger	dà yìdiǎnr	dah yee-dyenr
just right	zhènghǎo	jung-how
smaller	xiǎo yìdiǎnr	hsyow yee-dyenr
to try on	shìshì	shur-shur

▶▶ Can I help you?
Nín mǎi shénme?
nin mai shun-mur

▶ No, thanks, I'm just looking.
Bùmǎi shénme, xièxiè. Jiùshì kànkan.
boo-mai shun-mur, hsyeh-hsyeh, jyoh-shur kahn-kahn

▶▶ Do you want to try that on?
Nín xiǎng shìshì ma?
nin hsyahng shur-shur mah

▶ Yes, and I'll try this one too.
Hǎo, wǒ hái xiǎng shìyíxià zhèjiàn.
how, wor hai hsyahng shur-yee-shyah jur-jyen

▶ Do you have it in a bigger size?
Yǒu dà yìdiǎnrde ma?
yoh dah yee-dyenr-dur mah

▶ Do you have it in a different colour?
Yǒu biéde yánsède ma?
yoh byeh-dur yahn-sur-dur mah

▶▶ That looks good on you.
Nín chuānzhe tǐng héshìde.
nin chwahn-jur ting hur-shur-dur

▶ Can you shorten this?
Nín néng bǎtā gǎiduǎn ma?
nin nung bah-tah gai-dwahn mah

▶▶ Sure, it'll be ready on Friday, after 12.00.
Xíng, xīngqīwǔ xiàwǔ shíèr diǎn yǐhòu nínlái qǔ.
hsing, hsing-chee-woo hsyow-woo shur-er dyen yee-hoh nin-lai chew

22. Sightseeing

art gallery	měishùguǎn	may-shoo-gwahn
bus tour	zuò dà bāshì lǚyóu	dzwor dah bah-shur lyew-yoh
city centre	shì zhōngxīn	shur joong-hsin
closed	guānmén	gwahn-mun
guide	dǎoyóu	dow-yoh
museum	bówùguǎn	bor-woo-gwahn
open	kāimén	kai-mun

▶ I'm interested in seeing the old town.
Wǒ duì cānguān lǎochéng yǒu xìngqù.
wor dway tsan-gwahn low-chung yoh hsing-chew

▶ Are there guided tours?
Yǒu dǎoyóu tuán ma?
yoh dow-yoh twahn mah

▶▶ I'm sorry, it's fully booked.
Duìbuqǐ, dōu dìngmǎnle.
dway-boo-chee, doh ding-mahn-lur

▶ How much would you charge to drive us around for four hours?
Wǒmen zuò nǐde chē sìge xiǎoshí, duōshǎo qián?
wor-mun, dzwor nee-dur chur sur-gur hsyow-shur dwor-show chyen

▶ Can we book tickets for the concert here?
Wǒmen kěyǐ zài zhèr dìng yīnyuèhuì de piào ma?
wor-mun kur-yee dzai jur ding yin-yew-eh-hway dur pyow mah

▶▶ Yes, in what name?
Kěyǐ, qǐngwèn, nínde míngzi?
kur-yee, ching-wun, nin-dur ming-dzur

▶▶ Which credit card?
Shénme xìnyòngkǎ?
shun-mur hsin-yoong-kah

▶ Where do we get the tickets?
Zài nǎr qǔ piào?
dzai nar chew pyow

▶▶ Just pick them up at the entrance.
Jiù zài rùkǒu (qǔ piào).
jyoh dzai roo-koh (chew pyow)

▶ Is it open on Sundays?
Xīngqītiān kāimén ma?
hsing-chee tyen kai-mun mah

▶ How much is it to get in?
Ménpiào duōshǎo qián?
mun-pyow dwor-show chyen

▶ Are there reductions for groups of six?
Liùgerén yīqǐ yǒu méiyou yōuhuì?
lyoh-gur-run yee-chee yoh may-yoh yoh-hway

▶ That was really impressive!
Zhēn shì hǎojíle!
jun shur how-jee-lur

23. Taxis

▶ Can you get us a taxi?
Qǐng bāng wǒmen jiào yíliàng chūzūchē?
ching bahng wor-mun jyow yee-lyahng choo-dzoo-chur

▶▶ For now? Where are you going?
Xiànzài? Dào nǎr qù?
hsyen-dzai, dow nar chew

▶ To the town centre.
Dào shì zhōngxīn.
dow shur joong-hsin

▶ I'd like to book a taxi to the airport for tomorrow.
Wǒ xiǎng dìng yíliàng míngtiān dào fēijīchǎng de chūzūchē.
wor hsyahng ding yee-lyahng ming-tyen dow fay-jee-chahng dur choo-dzoo-chur

▶▶ Sure, at what time? How many people?
Hǎo, jǐdiǎn? Jǐge rén?
how, jee-dyen, jee-gur run

▶ How much is it to the Temple of Heaven?
Dao Tiāntán duō shǎo qián?
dow tyen-tahn dwor show chyen

▶ Right here is fine, thanks.
Tíng zài zhèr jiù kěyǐ, xièxiè.
ting dzai jer jyoh kur-yee, hsyeh-hsyeh

▶ Can you wait here and take us back?
Nǐ zài zhèr děng wǒmen, zài sòng wǒmen huíqù, hǎo ma?
nee dzai jer dung wor-mun, dzai soong wor-mun hway-chew, how mah

▶▶ How long are you going to be?
Nǐmen zǒu duōcháng shíjiān?
nee-mun dzoh dwor-chahng shur-jyen

24. Trains

to change trains	huàn huǒchē	hwahn hwor-chur
platform	zhàntái	jahn-tai
return	wǎngfǎnpiào	wahng-fahn-pyow
single	dānchéngpiào	dahn-chung-pyow
station	huǒchēzhàn	hwor-chur-jahn
stop	tíngchē	ting-chur
ticket	huǒchēpiào	hwor-chur-pyow

▶ How much is…?
… duōshǎo qián?
dwor-show chyen

▶ A single, second class to…
Yīzhāng dānchéngpiào, érděng chēxiāng, dào…
yee-jahng dahn-chung-pyow, ur-dung chur-hsyang, dow

▶ Two returns, second class to...
Liǎngzhāng wǎngfǎnpiào, érděng chēxiāng, dào...
lyang-jahng, wahng-fahn-pyow, ur-dung chur-hsyang, dow

▶ For today.
Jīntiānde.
jin-tyen-dur

▶ For tomorrow.
Míngtiānde.
ming-tyen-dur

▶ For next Tuesday.
Xià xīngqīērde.
hsyah hsing-chee-ur-dur

▶▶ There's a supplement for the express.
Tèkuài jiāshōu.
tur-kway jyah-shoh

▶▶ Do you want to make a seat reservation?
Nǐ yào dìng zuòwèi ma?
nee yow ding dzwor-way mah

▶▶ You have to change at Shanghai.
Nǐ děi zài Shànghǎi huànchē.
nee day dzai Shahng-hai hwahn-chur

▶ Is this seat free?
Zhège zuò yǒurén zuò ma?
jur-gur dzwor yow-run dzwor mah

▶ Excuse me, which station are we at?
Qǐngwèn, zhèshì shénme zhàn?
ching-wun, jur shur shun-mur jahn

▶ Is this where I change for Suzhou?
Shì zài zhèr huàn dào Sūzhōu de huǒchē ma?
shur dzai jur hwahn dow Soo-joh dur hwor-chur mah

ENGLISH
→ CHINESE

A

a, an Chinese has no equivalent for the English 'a' or 'an'

about: about 20 èr shí zuǒyòu dzwor-yoh 二十左右

  it's about 5 o'clock wǔdiǎn (zhōng) zuǒyòu 五点钟左右

  a film about China guānyú Zhōngguó de diànyǐng gwahn-yew – dur dyen-ying 关于中国的电影

above (zài)-… shàng (dzai)-… shahng 在 … 上

abroad guówài gwor-wai 国外

absorbent cotton yàomián yow-myen 药棉

accept jiēshòu jyeh-shoh 接受

accident shìgù shur-goo 事故

  there's been an accident chūle ge shìgù choo-lur gur 出了个事故

accurate zhǔnquè jun-chew-eh 准确

ache téng tung 疼

  my back aches wǒ hòubèi téng wor hoh-bay 我后背疼

acrobatics záji dzah-jee 杂技

across: across the road zài mǎlù duìmiànr dzai mah-loo dway-myenr 在马路对面儿

acupuncture zhēnjiǔ jun-jyoh 针灸

adapter duōyòng chātóu dwor-yoong chah-toh 多用插头

address dìzhǐ dee-jur 地址

  what's your address? nín zhù nǎr? joo 您住哪儿？

address book tōngxùnlù toong-hsyewn-loo 通讯录

admission charge: how much is the admission charge? rùchǎng fèi shì duōshao qián? roo-chahng fay shur dwor-show chyen 入场费是多少钱？

adult dàrén dah-run 大人

advance: in advance tíqián tee-chyen 提前

aeroplane fēijī fay-jee 飞机

after yǐhòu yee-hoh 以后

  after you nǐ xiān qù ba nee hsyen chew bah 你先去吧

  after lunch wǔfàn hòu woo-fahn hoh 午饭后

afternoon xiàwǔ hsyah-woo 下午

  in the afternoon xiàwǔ 下午

  this afternoon jīntiān xiàwǔ

jin-tyen 今天下午

aftershave xūhòushuǐ hsyew-hoh-shway 须后水

afterwards yǐhòu yee-hoh 以后

again zài dzai 再

age niánjì nyen-jee 年纪

ago: a week ago yíge xīngqī yǐqián yee-gur hsing-chee yee-chyen 一个星期以前

an hour ago yíge xiǎoshí yǐqián yee-gur hsyow-shur 一个小时以前

agree: I agree wǒ tóngyì wor toong-yee 我同意

AIDS àizībìng ai-dzur-bing 爱滋病

air kōngqì koong-chee 空气

by air zuò fēijī dzwor fay-jee 坐飞机

air-conditioning kōngtiáo koong-tyow 空调

airmail: by airmail hángkōng(xìn) hahng-koong (-hsin) 航空信

airmail envelope hángkōng xìnfēng hsin-fung 航空信封

airplane fēijī fay-jee 飞机

airport fēijīchǎng –chahng 飞机场

to the airport, please qǐng dài wǒ dào fēijīchǎng ching dai wor dow 请带我到飞机场

airport bus jīchǎng bānchē jee-chahng bahn-chur 机场班车

alarm clock nàozhōng now-joong 闹钟

alcohol (drink) jiǔ jyoh 酒

all: all of it quánbù chew-ahn-boo 全部

that's all, thanks gòule, xièxie goh-lur hsyeh-hsyeh 够了谢谢

allergic: I'm allergic to-... wǒ duì-... guòmǐn wor dway-... gwor-min 我对 ... 过敏

allowed: is it allowed? zhè yúnxǔ-ma? jur yun-hsyew-mah 这允许吗？

all right hǎo how 好

I'm all right wǒ méi shìr wor may shur 我没事儿

are you all right? nǐ méi shìr ba? nee may-shur bah 你没事儿吧？

(greeting) ní hǎo ma? nee how 你好吗？

almost chàbuduō chah-boo-dwor 差不多

alone yíge rén yee-gur run 一个人

already yǐjing 已经

also yě yur 也

although suīrán sway-rahn 虽然

altogether yígòng yee-goong 一共

always zǒng dzoong 总

am: I am shì shur 是

a.m.: at seven a.m. shàngwǔ qī diǎn chee dyen 上午七点

amazing (surprising) méi xiǎngdào may hsyang-dow 没想到

(very good) liǎobùqǐ lyow-boo-chee 了不起

ambulance jiùhùchē jyoh-hoo-chur 救护车

call an ambulance! (kuài) jiào jiùhùchē! (kwai) jyow (快) 叫救护车

America Měiguó may-gwor 美国

American (adj) Měiguó 美国

I'm American wǒ shì Měiguó rén wor shur – run 我是美国人

among zài-... zhī zhōng dzai-... jur joong 在 ... 之中

amp: a 13-amp fuse shísān ānpéi de bǎoxiǎnsī shur-sahn ahn-pay dur bow-hsyen-sur 十三安培的保险丝

and hé hur 和

angry shēngqì shung-chee 生气

animal dòngwù doong-woo 动物

ankle jiǎobózi jyow-bor-dzur 脚脖子

annoying: how annoying! zhēn tǎoyàn! jun tow-yahn 真讨厌

another (different) lìng yíge yee-gur 另一个

(one more) yòu yíge yoh 又一个

can we have another room? wǒ xiǎng huàn lìngwài yíge fángjiān wor hsyang hwahn ling-wai 我想换另外一个房间

another beer, please qǐng zài lái yì bēi píjiǔ ching dzai lai yee 请再来一杯啤酒

antibiotics kàngjūnsù kahng-jyewn-soo 抗菌素

antique: is it a genuine antique? shì zhēn gǔdǒng ma? shur jurn goo-doong mah 是真古董吗？

antique shop wénwù shāngdiàn wun-woo shahng-dyen 文物商店

antiseptic fángfǔjì fahng-foo-jee 防腐剂

any: do you have any-...? nǐ yǒu ... ma? nee yoh ... mah

你有 … 吗？

sorry, I don't have any duìbuqǐ, wǒ méiyǒu dway-boo-chur wor may-yoh 对不起我没有

anybody shéi shay 谁

does anybody speak English? shéi huì shuō Yīngyǔ? hway shwor ying-yoo 谁会说英语？

there wasn't anybody there zàinàr shénme rén dōu méiyou zai-nar shun-mur run doh may-yoh 在那儿什么人都没有

anything shénme shun-mur 什么

anything else? hái yào shénme? hai yow
nothing else, thanks bú yào, xièxie hsyeh-hsyeh

would you like anything to drink? nǐ yào hé diǎnr shénme? hur dyenr
I don't want anything, thanks wǒ shénme dōu bú yào, xièxie wor – doh

apart from chúle-… yǐwài choo-lur 除了 … 以外
apartment dānyuán

dahn-yew-ahn 单元

aperitif kāiwèijiǔ kai-way-jyoh 开胃酒

appendicitis lánwěiyán lahn-way-yen 阑尾炎

appetizer lěngpánr lung-pahnr 冷盘儿

apple píngguǒ ping-gwor 苹果

appointment yuēhuì yew-eh-hway 约会

good morning, how can I help you? nín zǎo, wǒ néng bāng shénme máng ma? dzow wor nung bahng shun-mur mahng mah
I'd like to make an appointment wǒ xiǎng dìng ge yuèhùi hsyang ding gur
what time would you like? nín xiǎng yuē shénme shíjian yew-eh
three o'clock sān diǎn (zhōng) dyen (joong)
I'm afraid that's not possible, is four o'clock all right? duìbùqǐ sān diǎn bù xíng, sì diǎn (zhōng) xíng ma? dway-boo-chee – hsing – mah
yes, that will be fine xíng, kěyǐ kur-yee
the name was? nín guì xìng? gway

apricot xìngzi hsing-dzur 杏子

April sìyuè sur-yew-eh 四月

are: we are wǒmen shì wor-mun shur 我们是

you are (*singular*) nǐ shì 你是

(*plural*) nǐmen shì nee-mun 你们是

they are tāmen shì tah-mun 他们是

area (*measurement*) miànjì myen-jee 面积

(*region*) dìqū dee-chew 地区

arm gēbo gur-bor 胳膊

army jūnduì chewn-dway 军队

arrange: will you arrange it for us? nǐ néng tì wǒmen ānpái yí xià ma? nung tee wor-mun ahn-pai yee hsyah mah 你能替我们安排一下吗?

arrive dào dow 到

when do we arrive? wǒmen shénme shíhou dàodá? wor-mun shun-mur shur-hoh dow-dah 我们什么时候到达?

has my fax arrived yet? wǒ gěi nǐ fā de chuánzhēn dàole ma? wor gay nee fah dur chwahn-jun dow-lur mah 我给你发的传真到了吗?

we arrived today wǒmen jīntiān gāng dào jin-tyen gahng 我们今天刚到

art yìshù yee-shoo 艺术

art gallery měishùguǎn may-shoo-gwahn 美术馆

as: as big as... gēn ... yíyàng dà gun ... yee-yang dah 跟 ... 一样大

as soon as possible jǐnkuài jin-kwai 尽快

ashtray yānhuī gāng yahn-hway gahng 烟灰缸

ask (*someone to do something*) qǐng ching 请

(*a question*) wèn wun 问

could you ask him to...? nǐ néng bù néng qǐng tā ...? nung – tah 你能不能请他 ... ?

asleep: she's asleep tā shuìzháole tah shway-jow-lur 他睡着了

aspirin āsīpǐlín ah-sur-pee-lin 阿斯匹林

asthma qìchuǎn chee-chwahn 气喘

at: at my hotel zài wǒ zhú de fàndiàn dzai wor joo dur 在我住的饭店

at the railway station zài huǒchē zhàn 在火车站

at six o'clock liùdiǎn zhōng lyoh-dyen joong 六点钟

at Li Zhen's zài Lǐ Zhēn jiā jyah 在李真家

ATM zìdòng qǔkuǎnjī dzur-doong chew-kwahn-jee 自动取款机

at sign, @ xiǎo lǎoshǔ hsyow low-shoo 小老鼠
  (in email address) at at

attendant (on train) chéngwùyuán chung-woo-yew-ahn 乘务员

August bāyuè bah-yew-eh 八月

aunt (father's sister, unmarried) gūgu 姑姑
  (father's sister, married) gūmǔ 姑母
  (mother's sister, unmarried) yímǔ 姨母
  (mother's sister, married) yímā yee-mah 姨妈

Australia Àodàlìyà or-dah-lee-yah 澳大利亚

Australian (adj) Àodàlìyà 澳大利亚
  I'm Australian wǒ shì Àodàlìyà rén wor shur – run 我是澳大利亚人

automatic (adj) zìdòng dzur-doong 自动

autumn qiūtiān chyoh-tyen 秋天
  in the autumn qiūtian 秋天

average (ordinary) yíbàn yee-bahn 一般
  on average píngjūn ping-jyewn 平均

awake: is he awake? tā xǐngle ma? tah hsing-lur mah 他醒了吗？

away: is it far away? yuǎn ma? yew-ahn 远吗？

awful zāogāole dzow-gow-lur 糟糕了

B

baby yīng'ěr ying-er 婴儿

baby food yīng'ěr shíwù shur-woo 婴儿食物

baby's bottle nǎipíng 奶瓶

Travel tip While formula and nappies might be available in modern, big city super-markets, elsewhere you'll need to bring a supply (and any medication if required) – local kids don't use nappies, just pants with a slit at the back, and when baby wants to go, mummy points him at the gutter.

---

baby-sitter línshí kān xiǎoháir de lin-shur kahn hsyow-hair dur 临时看小孩儿的

back hòu hoh 后

(of body) hòubèi bay 后背

at the back zài hòumian dzai hoh-myen 在后面

can I have my money back? qǐng ba qián huán gěi wǒ ba ching bah chyen hwahn gay wor bah 请把钱还给我吧

to come back huílai hway– 回来

to go back huíqu –chew 回去

backache bèitòng bay-toong 背痛

bad huài hwai 坏

a bad headache tóu téng de lìhai toh tung dur lur-hai 头疼得利害

bag dàizi dai-dzur 袋子

(handbag) shǒutíbāo shoh-tee-bow 手提包

(suitcase) shǒutíxiāng shoh-tee-hsyang 手提箱

baggage xíngli hsing-lee 行李

baggage check (US) xíngli jìcúnchù jee-tsun-choo 行李寄存处

baggage claim xíngli tíqǔchù tee-chew-choo 行李提取处

bakery miànbāodiàn myen-bow-dyen 面包店

balcony yángtái yang-tai 阳台

a room with a balcony dài yángtái de fángjiān dur fahng-jyen 带阳台的房间

ball qiú chyoh 球

ballet bāléiwǔ bah-lay-woo 芭蕾舞

ballpoint pen yuánzhūbǐ yew-ahn-joo-bee 圆珠笔

bamboo zhúzi joo-dzur 竹子

bamboo shoots zhúsǔn joo-sun 竹笋

banana xiāngjiāo hsyang-jyow 香蕉

band (musical) yuèduì yew-eh-dway 乐队

bandage bēngdài bung-dai 绷带

Bandaid xiàngpí gāo hsyang-pee gow 橡皮膏

bank (money) yínháng yin-hahng 银行

bank account zhànghù jahng-hoo 帐户

banquet yànhuì yen-hway 宴会

bar jiǔbājiān jyoh-bah-jyen 酒吧间

a bar of chocolate yí kuàir qiǎokèlì yee kwair chyow-kur-lee 一块儿巧克力

barber's lǐfàdiàn lee-fah-dyen 理发店

how much is this? zhèi ge duōshao qián? jay gur dwor-show chyen

30 yuan sān shí kuài qián kwai chyen

that's too expensive, how about 20? tài guì le, èr shí kuài, zénme yàng? gway lur – dzun-mur

I'll let you have it for 25 èr shí wǔ kuài ba bah

can you reduce it a bit more? zài jiǎn yí diǎnr ba dzai jyen yee dyenr

OK, it's a deal hǎo ba how

basket kuāng kwahng 筐

bath xǐzǎo hshee-dzow 洗澡

can I have a bath? wǒ néng xǐ ge zǎo ma? wor nung hshee gur dzow mah 我能洗个澡吗？

bathroom yùshì yew-shur 浴室

with a private bathroom dài xízǎojiān de fángjiān dai hshee-dzow-jyen dur fahng-jyen 带洗澡间的房间

bath towel yùjīn yew-jin 浴巾

bathtub zǎopén dzow-pun 澡盆

battery diànchí dyen-chur 电池

bay hǎiwān hai-wahn 海湾

be shì shur 是

beach hǎitān hai-tahn 海滩

on the beach zài hǎitānshang dzai –shahng 在海滩上

bean curd dòufu doh-foo 豆腐

beans dòu doh 豆

French beans sìjìdòu sur-jee-doh 四季豆

broad beans cándòu tsahn-doh 蚕豆

string beans jiāngdòu jyang-doh 豇豆

soya beans huángdòu hwahng-doh 黄豆

bean sprouts dòu yár 豆芽儿

beard húzi hoo-dzur 胡子

beautiful (object) měilì may-lee 美丽

(woman) piàoliang pyow-lyang 漂亮

(view, city, building) měi 美

(day, weather) hǎo how 好

because yīnwéi yin-way 因为

because of-... yóuyú ... yoh-yew 由于

bed chuáng chwahng 床

I'm going to bed now wǒ yào shuì le wor yow shway lur 我要睡了

bedroom wòshì wor-shur 卧室

beef niúròu nyoh-roh 牛肉

beer píjiǔ pee-jyoh 啤酒

    two beers, please qǐng lái liǎng bēi píjiǔ ching lye lyang bay pee-jyoh 请来两杯啤酒

before: before-... ... yǐqián yee-chyen ... 以前

begin kāishǐ kai-shur 开始

    when does it begin? shénme shíhou kāishǐ? shun-mur shur-hoh 什么时候开始？

beginner chūxuézhě choo-yew-eh-jur 初学者

behind zài-... hòumian dzai-... hoh-myen 在 … 后面

    behind me zài wǒ hòumian wor 在我后面

believe xiāngxìn hsyang-hsin 相信

below zài-... xiàmian dzai-... hsyah-myen 在 … 下面

    (less than) zài-... yǐxià yee-hsyah 在 … 以下

belt yāodài yow-dai 腰带

bend (in road) lùwánr loo-wahnr 路弯儿

berth (on train) wòpù wor-poo 卧铺

beside: beside the-... zài-... pángbiān dzai-... pahng-byen 在 … 旁边

best zuìhǎo dzway-how 最好

better: even better gèng hǎo gung how 更好

    a bit better hǎo yì diǎnr dyenr 好一点儿

    are you feeling better? hǎo diǎnr le ma? lur mah 好点儿了吗？

between zài-... zhī jiān dzai-... jur-jyen 在 … 之间

bicycle zìxíngchē dzur-hsing-chur
自行车

big dà dah 大

   too big tài dà le lur 太大了

   it's not big enough búgòu dà
boo-goh 不够大

bill zhàngdānr jahng-dahnr
帐单儿

   (US: money) chāopiào chow-pyow
钞票

   **could I have the bill,
please?** qǐng bāng wǒ
jiézhàng, hǎo ma? ching
bahng wor jyeh-jahng how mah
请帮我结帐好吗？

bin lājī xiāng lah-jee hsyang
垃圾箱

bird niǎo nyow 鸟

birthday shēngrì shung-rur
生日

   happy birthday! zhù nǐ
shēngrì kuàilè! joo – kwai-lur
祝你生日快乐

biscuit bǐnggān bing-gahn 饼干

bit: a little bit yìdiǎnr yee-dyenr
一点儿

   a big bit yídàkuàir yee-dah-
kwair 一大块儿

   a bit expensive yǒu diǎn guì
有点贵

bite (by insect) yǎo yow 咬

bitten by a dog ràng gǒu gěi
yǎoshāng le rahng goh gay yow-
shahng 让狗给咬伤了

bitter (taste etc) kǔ 苦

black hēi hay 黑

blanket tǎnzi tahn-dzur 毯子

blind xiā hsyah 瞎

blocked dǔzhùle doo-joo-lur
堵住了

blond (adj) jīnhuángsè
jin-hwahng-sur 金黄色

blood xiě hsyeh 血

   high blood pressure gāo
xuèyā gow hsyew-eh-yah
高血压

blouse nǚchènshān nyew-chun-
shahn 女衬衫

**blow-dry: I'd like a cut
and blow-dry** wǒ xiǎng
lǐfà hé chuīfēng wor hsyang
lee-fah hur chway-fung
我想理发和吹风

blue lánsè lahn-sur 蓝色

   blue eyes lán yǎnjing lahn
yahn-jing 蓝眼睛

boarding pass dēngjì kǎ dung-
jee kah 登记卡

boat chuán chwahn 船

   (for passengers) kèchuán kur-
chwahn 客船

body shēntǐ shun-tee 身体

boiled egg zhǔ jīdàn joo jee-dahn
煮鸡蛋

boiled rice mǐfàn
mee-fahn 米饭

boiled water kāishuǐ kai-shway
开水

bone gǔ goo 骨

book (*noun*) shū 书

(*verb*) dìng 订

can I book a seat? wǒ
néng dìng ge zuòwei ma?
wor nung – gur dzwor-way mah
我能订个座位吗？

DIALOGUE

I'd like to book a table for
two/three wǒ xiǎng dìng
liǎng/sān ge rén yì zhuō de
wèizi wor hsyang – gur run
yee jwor dur way-dszur

what time would you like
it booked for? nín yào
jǐdiǎn zhōng? yow jee-dyen
joong

half past seven qī diǎn bàn

that's fine xíng hsing

and your name? nín guì
xìng? gway

bookshop, bookstore shūdiàn
shoo-dyen 书店

boot (footwear) xuēzi hsyew-eh-
dzur 靴子

(of car) xínglixiāng hsing-lee-
hsyang 行李箱

border (of country) biānjiè byen-
jyeh 边界

border region biānjìng
边境

bored: I'm bored fán sǐ le fahn
sur-lur 烦死了

boring méi jìnr may 没劲儿

**born: I was born in
Manchester** wǒ shì zài
Mànchéng shēng de-wor
shur dzai – shung dur
我是在曼城生的

I was born in 1960 wǒ shì
yí jiǔ liù líng nián-shēng de
我是一九六零年生的

borrow jiè jyeh 借

may I borrow-...? wǒ kěyǐ
jiè yíxia-... ma? wor kur-
yee jyeh yee-hsyah-... mah
我可以借一下 ... 吗？

both liǎngge dōu lyang-gur doh
两个都

**bother: sorry to bother
you** duìbuqǐ dájiǎo nín le
dway-boo-chee dah-jyow nin lur
对不起打搅您了

bottle píngzi ping-dzur 瓶子

a bottle of beer yì píng píjiǔ
一瓶啤酒

bottle-opener kāi píng qì chee 开瓶器

bottom dǐr deer 底儿

(of person) pìgu 屁股

at the bottom of the road lù de jìntóu loo dur jin-toh 路的尽头

box hézi hur-dzur 盒子

a box of chocolates yí hé qiǎokèlì hur chyow-kur-lee 一盒巧克力

box office shòupiào chù shoh-pyow 售票处

boy nán háir nahn hair 男孩儿

boyfriend nán péngyou nahn pung-yoh 男朋友

bra xiōngzhào hsyoong-jow 胸罩

bracelet shǒuzhuó shoh-jwor 手镯

brandy báilándì bai-lahn-dee 白兰地

bread (baked) miànbāo myen-bow 面包

(steamed) mántou mahn-toh 馒头

white bread bái miànbāo 白面包

brown bread hēi miànbāo hay 黑面包

wholemeal bread quánmài miànbāo chew-ahn-mai 全麦面包

break (verb) dǎpò dah-por 打破

I've broken the-... wǒ dǎpòle ... wor dah-por-lur 我打破了 ...

I think I've broken my... wǒde ... kěnéng huàile wor-dur ... kur-nung hwai-lur 我的 ... 可能坏了

breakdown gùzhàng goo-jahng 故障

breakfast zǎofàn dzow-fahn 早饭

break-in: I've had a break-in (in room) wǒde fángjiān ràng rén gěi qiàole mén le wor-dur fahng-jyen rahng run gay chyow-lur mun lur 我的房间让人给撬了门了

breast xiōng hsyoong 胸

breeze wēifēng way-fung 微风

bridge (over river) qiáo chyow 桥

brief duǎn dwahn 短

briefcase gōngwénbāo goong-wun-bow 公文包

bright (light etc) míngliàng ming-lyang 明亮

brilliant (idea, person) gāomíng gow-ming 高明

bring dàilái 带来

    I'll bring it back later wǒ guò xiē shíhou dàihuílái wor gwor hsyeh shur-hoh dai-hway-lai 我过些时侯带回来

Britain Yīngguó ying-gwor 英国

British (adj) Yīngguó 英国

    I'm British wǒ shì Yīngguó rén wor shur – run 我是英国人

brochure shuōmíng shū shwor-ming 说明书

broken (object) pòle por-lur 破了

    (leg etc) duànle dwahn-lur 断了

    (not working) huàile hwai-lur 坏了

brooch xiōngzhēn hsyoong-jun 胸针

brother xiōngdì hsyoong-dee 兄弟

    (older) gēge gur-gur 哥哥

    (younger) dìdì 弟弟

brother-in-law (elder sister's husband) jiěfū jyeh-foo 姐夫

    (younger sister's husband) mèifu may-foo 妹夫

    (wife's elder brother) nèixiōng nay-hsyoong 内兄

    (wife's younger brother) nèidì nay-dee 内弟

    (husband's elder brother) dàbó dah bor 大伯

(husband's younger brother) xiǎoshū hsyow-shoo 小叔

brown zōngsè dzoong-sur 棕色

brush shuāzi shwah-dzur 刷

bucket tǒng toong 桶

Buddha Fó for 佛

Buddhism Fójiào for-jyow 佛教

Buddhist (adj) Fójiàotú 佛教徒

buffet car cānchē tsahn-chur 餐车

building fángzi fahng-dzur 房子

    (multi-storey) dàlóu dah-loh 大楼

bunk: bottom bunk xià pù hsyah 下铺

    middle bunk zhōng pù joong 中铺

    top bunk shàng pù shahng 上铺

bureau de change wài huì duìhuàn bù hway dway-hwahn 外汇兑换部

burglary dàoqiè dow-chyeh 盗窃

Burma Miǎndiàn myen-dyen 缅甸

burn (noun) shāoshāng show-shahng 烧伤

    (verb) ránshāo rahn-show 燃烧

burnt: this is burnt (food)
shāojiāole show-jyow-lur
烧焦了

bus (public transport) gōnggòng
qìchē goong-goong chee-chur
公共汽车

(limited stop) shìqūchē shur-
chew-chur 市区车

(in suburbs) jiāoqūchē jyow-
chew-chur 郊区车

(long-distance) chángtú
qìchē chahng-too chee-chur
长途汽车

**what number bus is it
to-…?** dào … qù zuò jǐ lù chē?
dow … chew dzwor jee lu chur 到
… 去坐几路车？

**when is the next bus
to-…?** dào … qù de xià (yì)
bān chē shì jídiǎn? dow …
chew dur hsyah (yee) bahn chur
shur jee-dyen 到 … 下去的
一班车是几点？

**what time is the last
bus?** mòbānchē shì jǐ diǎn?
mor-bahn-chur shur jee dyen
末班车是几点？

does this bus go to-…?
zhèi liàng chē qù … ma? jay
lyang chur chew … mah

no, you need a number-…
bú qù, nǐ yào zuò … hào
chē chew nee yow zwor …
how chur

business shēngyi shung-yee
生意

(firm, company) gōngsī goong-sur
公司

bus station gōnggòng qìchē
zǒngzhàn goong-goong chee-chur
dzoong-jahn 公共汽车总站

bus stop gōnggòng qìchē zhàn
jahn 公共汽车站

busy (road etc) rènào rur-now
热闹

(person) hěn máng hun mahng
很忙

I'm busy tomorrow wǒ
míngtian hěn máng wor ming-
tyen hun mahng 我明天很忙

but kěshi kur-shur 可是

butcher's ròu diàn roh dyen
肉店

butter huángyóu hwahng-yoh
黄油

button niǔkòu nyoh-koh
纽扣

buy mǎi 买

where can I buy-…? zài nǎr
néng mǎidào-…? dzai nar nung

mai-dow 在哪儿能买到…？

by: by bus zuò gōnggòng qìchē dzwor 坐公共汽车

written by-... shì … xiě de shur … sheh dur 是 … 写的

by the window zài chuānghu pángbiān dzai 在窗户旁边

by the sea zài hǎibiān 在海边

by Thursday xīngqī sì zhī qián jur chyen 星期四之前

bye zàijiàn dzai-jyen 再见

C

cabbage báicài bai-tsai 白菜

cabin (on ship) chuáncāng chwahn-tsahng 船舱

cake dàngāo dahn-gow 蛋糕

cake shop gāodiǎndiàn gow-dyen-dyen 糕点店

call (verb: to phone) dǎ diànhuà dah dyen-hwah 打电话

what's it called? zhège jiào shénme? jay-gur jyow shun-mur? 这个叫什么？

he/she is called-...
(given name) tā jiào … tah jyow 他叫 …

(surname) tā xìng … hsing 他姓 …

please call the doctor qǐng bǎ yīshēng jiào lái ching bah yee-shung jyow 请把医生叫来

please give me a call at 7.30 a.m. tomorrow qǐng míngtian zǎoshàng qī diǎn bàn gěi wǒ dǎ diànhuà ching ming-tyen dzow-shahng chee dyen bahn gay wor dah dyen-hwah 请明天早上七点半给我打电话

please ask him to call me qǐng tā dǎ diànhuà gěi wǒ dah – gay 请他打电话给我

call back: I'll call back later (phone back) wǒ guò yì huìr zài dǎ lái gwor yee hwayr dzai dah 我过一回儿再打来

call round: I'll call round tomorrow wǒ míngtian lái zháo nǐ jow 我明天来找你

camcorder shèxiàngjī shur-hsyang-jee 摄相机

camera zhàoxiàngjī jow-hsyang-jee 照相机

can (noun) guàntou gwahn-toh 罐头

a can of beer yí guànr píjiǔ 一罐儿啤酒

Travel tip Many temples prohibit photography inside buildings (antiques thieves have been known to use photos to plan robberies) and you should avoid taking pictures of anything military-related, or which could be seen as having strategic value – including structures such as bridges in sensitive areas (such as along borders or in Tibet).

can: can you-...?
nǐ néng-... ma? nung-... mah
你能 … 吗？

can I have-...?
qǐng gěi wǒ ...? ching gay wor
请给我 … ？

I can't-... wǒ bù néng-...
我不能 …

Canada Jiānádà jyah-nah-dah
加拿大

Canadian (adj) Jiānádà 加拿大

I'm Canadian wǒ shì
Jiānádàrén wor shur –run
我是加拿大人

canal yùnhé yewn-hur 运河

cancel (reservation etc) tuì tway
退

candies tángguǒ tahng-gwor
糖果

candle làzhú lah-joo 蜡烛

can-opener kāiguàn dāojù kai-
gwahn dow-joo 开罐刀具

Cantonese (adj) Guǎngdōng
gwahng-doong 广东

(language) Guǎngdōnghuà –
hwah 广东话

(person) Guǎngdōng rén run
广东人

cap (hat) màozi mow-dzur 帽子

(of bottle) pínggài ping-gai 瓶盖

car xiǎo qìchē hsyow chee-chur
小汽车

by car zuò xiǎo qìchē dzwor
坐小汽车

card kǎpiàn kah-pyen 卡片

here's my (business) card
zhèi shì wǒde míngpiàn
jay shur wor-dur ming-pyen
这是我的名片

Christmas card shèngdàn kǎ
shung-dahn kah 圣诞卡

birthday card shēngrì kǎ
shung-rur kah 生日卡

cardphone cíkǎ diànhuà tsur-kah
dyen-hwah 磁卡电话

careful: be careful! xiǎoxīn!
hsyow-hsin 小心

car ferry lúndù lun-doo 轮渡

car park tíngchēchǎng ting-chur-
chahng 停车场

carpet dìtǎn dee-tahn 地毯

car rental qìchē chūzū chee-chur
choo-dzoo 汽车出租

carriage (of train) chēxiāng chur-hsyang 车厢

carrot húluóbo hoo-lwor-bor 胡萝卜

carry ná nah 拿

cash (noun) xiànqián hsyen-chyen 现钱

will you cash this for me? nǐ néng tì wǒ huàn chéng xiàn qián ma? nung tee wor hwahn chung – mah 你能替我换成现钱吗？

cash desk jiāokuǎnchù jyow-kwahn-choo 交款处

cash dispenser zìdòng qúkuǎnjī dzur-doong chew-kwahn-jee 自动取款机

cassette cídài tsur-dai 磁带

cassette recorder lùyīnjī loo-yin-jee 录音机

castle chéngbǎo chung-bow 城堡

casualty department jíjiùshì jee-jyoh-shur 急救室

cat māo mow 猫

catch (verb) zhuā jwah 抓

where do we catch the bus to-...? qù-... zài nǎr shàng chē? chew-... dzai – chur 去 … 在哪儿上车？

cathedral dà jiàotáng dah jyow-tahng 大教堂

Catholic (adj) tiānzhǔjiào tyen-joo-jyow 天主教

cauliflower càihuā tsai-hwah 菜花

cave shāndòng shahn-doong 山洞

(dwelling) yáodòng yow-doong 窑洞

cell phone shǒujī shoh-jee 机手

cemetery mùdì 墓地

centigrade shèshì shur-shur 摄氏

centimetre límǐ lee-mee 厘米

central zhōngyāng joong-yang 中央

central heating nuǎnqì nwahn-chee 暖气

centre zhōngxīn joong-hsin 中心

how do we get to the city centre? qù shì zhōngxīn zénme zǒu? chew shur joong-hsin dzun-mur dzoh 去市中心怎么走？

certainly dāngrán dahn-grahn 当然

certainly not dāngrán bù 当然不

chair yǐzi yee-dzur 椅子

Chairman Mao Máo zhǔxí mow jyew-hshee 毛主席

change (*noun*: money) língqián ling-chyen 零钱

(*verb*: money) duìhuàn dway-hwahn 兑换

can I change this for-...? nín néng bāng wǒ duìhuàn chéng ... ma? nung bahng wor dway-hwahn chung ... mah 您能帮我兑换成 ... 吗？

I don't have any change wǒ yìdiǎnr língqián yě méi yǒu wor yee-dyenr ling-chyen yur may yoh 我一点儿零钱也没有

can you give me change for a hundred-yuan note? yí bǎi kuài nín zhǎodekāi ma? kwai nin jow-dur-kai mah 一百块您找得开吗？

DIALOGUE

do we have to change (trains)? zhōngtú yào huàn chē ma? joong-too yow hwahn chur mah

yes, change at Hangzhou yào zài Hángzhōu huàn chē yow dzai

no, it's a direct train bú yòng huàn chē, zhè shì zhídáchē yoong – jur shur jur-dah-chur

changed: to get changed huàn yīfu hwahn yee-foo 换衣服

character (in Chinese writing) zì dzur 字

charge (*noun*) shōufèi shoh-fay 收费

cheap piányi pyen-yee 便宜

do you have anything cheaper? yǒu piányi diǎnr de ma? yoh pyen-yee dyenr dur mah 有便宜点儿的吗？

check: could you check the-bill, please? qǐng ba zhàngdān jiǎnchá yíxià, hǎo ma? ching bah jahng-dahn jyen-chah yee-syah how mah 请把帐单检查一下好吗？

check (US: bill) zhàngdānr jahng-dahnr 帐单儿

check in dēngjì dung-jee 登记

where do we have to check in? wǒmen yào zài nǎr dēngji? wor-men yow dzai nar 我们要在哪儿登记？

cheerio! zàijiàn! dzai-jyen 再见

cheers! (toast) gānbēi! gahn-bay 干杯

cheese nǎilào nai-low 奶酪

chemist's yàofáng yow-fahng
药房

cherry yīngtao ying-tow 樱桃

chess guójì xiàngqí gwor-jee
hsyang-chee 国际象棋

   to play chess xià qí hsyah
chee 下棋

   Chinese chess xiàngqí
hsyang-chee 象棋

chest (body) xiōng hsyoong 胸

chicken (meat) jīròu jee-roh
鸡肉

child háizi hai-dzur 孩子

child minder bǎomǔ bow-moo
保姆

chin xiàba hsyah-bah 下巴

china cíqì tsur-chee 瓷器

China Zhōngguó joong-gwor
中国

China tea Zhōngguo chá chah
中国茶

Chinese (adj) Zhōngguó joong-
gwor 中国

  (person) Zhōngguó rén run
中国人

  (spoken language) Hànyǔ hahn-
yew 汉语

  (written language) Zhōngwén
joong-wun 中文

  the Chinese Zhōngguó
rénmín run-min 中国人民

Chinese leaf báicài bai-tsai
白菜

Chinese-style Zhōngshì joong-
shur 中式

chips zhá tǔdòu tiáo jah too-doh
tyow 炸土豆条

  (US) (zhá) tǔdòupiànr too-doh-
pyenr（炸）土豆片儿

chocolate qiǎokèlì chyow-kur-lee
巧克力

  milk chocolate nǎiyóu
qiǎokèlì nai-yoh 奶油巧克力

  plain chocolate chún qiǎokèlì
纯巧克力

  a hot chocolate yì bēi rè
qiǎokèlì (yǐnliào) bay rur – (yin-
lyow) 一杯热巧克力
（饮料）

choose xuǎn hsyew-ahn 选

chopsticks kuàizi kwai-dzur
筷子

Christmas Shèngdàn jié shung-
dahn jyeh 圣诞节

  Christmas Eve
Shèngdànqiányè –chyen-yur
圣诞前夜

  Merry Christmas! Shèngdàn
kuàilè! kwai-lur 圣诞快乐

church jiàotáng jyow-tahng
教堂

cigar xuějiā hsyew-eh-jyah 雪茄

cigarette xiāngyān hsyang-yen
香烟

cinema diànyǐng yuàn dyen-ying
yew-ahn 电影院

circle yuánquān ywahn-kwahn
圆圈

(in theatre) lóutīng loh-ting 楼厅

city chéngshì chung-shur 城市

city centre shì zhōngxīn shur
joong-hsin 市中心

clean (*adj*) gānjìng gahn-jing
干净

**can you clean these
for me?** nǐ néng tì wǒ
xǐyixǐ, ma? nung tee wor
hshee-yee-hshee mah
你能替我洗一洗吗？

clear (water) qīngchè ching-chur
清澈

(speech, writing) qīngxī ching-
hshee 清晰

(obvious) míngxiǎn –hsyen
明显

clever cōngming tsoong-ming
聪明

cliff xuányá hsyew-ahn-yah 悬崖

climbing páshān pah-shahn
爬山

clinic zhénsuǒ jun-swor 诊所

cloakroom yīmàojiān yee-mow-
jyen 衣帽间

clock zhōng joong 钟

close (*verb*) guān gwahn 关

what time do you close?
nǐmen shénme shíhou guān
mén? nee-mun shun-mur
shur-hoh – mun

**we close at 8 p.m. on
weekdays and 6 p.m. on
Saturdays** zhōurì xiàwǔ
bā diǎn, xīngqī liù xiàwǔ liù
diǎn joh-rur

do you close for lunch?
chī wǔfàn de shíhou guān
mén ma? chur woo-fahn dur
shur-hoh – mah

**yes, between 1 and
3.30 p.m.** shì de, cóng yī
diǎn dào sān diǎn bàn yě
guān mén shur dur tsoong –
dow – yur

closed guānménle gwahn-mun-lur
关门了

cloth (fabric) bùliào bool-yow
布料

(for cleaning etc) mābù mah-boo
抹布

clothes yīfu yee-foo 衣服

clothes line shàiyīshéng
shai-yee-shung 晒衣绳

clothes peg yīfu jiāzi yee-foo
jyah-dzur 衣服夹子

cloudy duōyún dwor-yewn
多云

coach (bus) chángtú qìchē
chahng-too chee-chur
长途汽车

(tourist bus) lǚyóu chē
lyew-yoh chur 旅游车

(on train) kèchē kur-chur 客车

coach station chángtú
qìchēzhàn chang-too chee-chur-
jahn 长途汽车站

coach trip zuò chángtú
qìchē lǚxíng dzwor chahng-
too chee-chur lyew-hsing
坐长途汽车旅行

coast hǎibīn 海滨

coat (long coat) dàyī dah-yee 大衣

coathanger yījià yee-jyah 衣架

cockroach zhāngláng jahng-
lahng 蟑螂

code (for phoning) diànhuà
qūhào dyen-hwah chew-how
电话区号

**what's the (dialling)
code for Beijing?** Běijīng
de diànhuà qūhào shì
duōshao? dur – shur dwor-show
北京的电话区号是多
少？

coffee kāfēi kah-fay 咖啡

two coffees, please
qǐng lái liǎng bēi kāfēi ching
请来两杯咖啡

coin yìngbì ying-bee 硬币

Coke Kěkǒukělè kur-koh-kur-lur 可口可乐

cold lěng lung 冷

I'm cold wǒ juéde hěn lěng wor jyew-eh-dur hun lung 我觉得很冷

I have a cold wǒ gǎnmào le gahn-mow lur 我感冒了

collapse: he's collapsed tā kuǎle tah kwah-lur 他垮了

collar yīlǐng 衣领

collect qǔ-... chew 取

I've come to collect-... wǒ lái qǔ-... wor lai chew 我来取

collect call duìfāng fùkuǎn dway-fahng foo-kwahn 对方付款

college xuéyuàn hsyew-eh-yew-ahn 学院

colour yánsè yahn-sur 颜色

do you have this in other colours? yǒu biéde yánsè de ma? yoh byeh-dur – dur mah 有别的颜色吗？

colour film cǎisè jiāojuǎnr tsai-sur jyow-jyew-ahr 彩色胶卷儿

comb shūzi shoo-dzur 梳子

come lái 来

DIALOGUE

where do you come from?
nǐ shì cóng nǎr láide? shur tsoong nar lai-dur

I come from Edinburgh
wǒ shì cóng Àidīngbǎo lái de wor

come back huílai hway-lai 回来

I'll come back tomorrow wǒ míngtiān huílai ming-tyen 我明天回来

come in qǐng jìn ching jin 请进

comfortable shūfu shoo-foo 舒服

communism gòngchánzhǔyì goong-chahn-joo-yee 共产主义

Communist Party
Gòngchándǎng –dahng 共产党

Communist Party member
gòngchándǎngyuán –dahng-yew-ahn 共产党员

compact disc jīguāng chàngpiàn jee-gwahng chahng-pyen 激光唱片

company (business) gōngsī goong-sur 公司

compass zhǐnánzhēn jur-nahn-jun 指南针

complain mányuàn mahn-yew-ahn 埋怨

complaint bàoyuàn bow-yew-ahn 抱怨

I have a complaint to make wǒ xiǎng tí yí ge yìjiàn wor hsyang tee yee gur yee-jyen 我想提一个意见

completely wánwánquánquán wahn-wahn-chahn-chahn 完完全全

computer diànnǎo dyen-now 电脑

concert yīnyuèhuì yin-yew-eh-hway 音乐会

concussion nǎozhèndàng now-jun-dahng 脑震荡

conditioner (for hair) hùfàsù hoo-fah-soo 护发素

condom bìyùntào bee-yewn-tow 避孕套

conference huìyì hway-yee 会议

congratulations! gōngxǐ! gōngxǐ! goong-hshee 恭喜恭喜

connecting flight xiánjiē de bānjī hsyen-jyeh dur bahn-jee 衔接的班机

connection (in travelling) liányùn lyen-yewn 联运

(rail) zhōngzhuǎn joong-jwahn 中转

constipation biànbì byen-bee 便秘

consulate lǐngshìguǎn ling-shur-gwahn 领事馆

contact (verb) liánxi lyen-hshee 联系

contact lenses yīnxíng yǎnjìng yin-hsing yahn-jing 隐型眼镜

contraceptive bìyùn yòngpǐn bee-yewn yoong-pin 避孕用品

convenient fāngbiàn fahng-byen 方便

that's not convenient bù fāngbiàn 不方便

cooker lúzào loo-dzow 炉灶

cookie xiǎo bǐnggān hsyow bing-gahn 小饼干

cool liángkuai lyang-kwai 凉快

corner: on the corner jiējiǎor jyeh-jyowr 街角儿

in the corner qiángjiǎor chyang-jyowr 墙角儿

correct (right) duì dway 对

corridor zǒuláng dzoh-lahng 走廊

cosmetics huàzhuāngpǐn hwah-jwahng-pin 化妆品

cost (noun) jiàqián jyah-chyen 价钱

how much does it cost?
duōshao qián? dwor-show chyen
多少钱？

cotton miánhuā myen-hwah
棉花

cotton wool yàomián yow-myen
药棉

couchette wòpù wor-poo
卧铺

cough késou kur-soh 咳嗽

cough medicine zhǐké yào jur-kur yow 止咳药

could: could you-...? nín kěyi-... ma? kur-yee-... mah
您可以 … 吗？

I couldn't-... wǒ bù néng ... wor boo nung 我不能

country (nation) guójiā gwor-jyah
国家

(countryside) xiāngcūn hsyang-tsun 乡村

couple (two people) fūfù foo-foo
夫妇

a couple of-... liǎngge-... lyang-gur 两个 …

courier xìnshǐ hsin-shur
信使

course: of course dāngrán dahn-grahn 当然

of course not dāngrán bù
当然不

cousin (son of mother's brother: older than speaker) biǎogē byow-gur 表哥

(younger than speaker) biǎodì
表弟

(son of father's brother: older than speaker) tángxiōng tahng-hsyoong 堂兄

(younger than speaker) tángdì
堂弟

(daughter of mother's brother: older than speaker) biǎojiě byow-jyeh 表姐

(younger than speaker) biǎomèi
byow-may 表妹

(daughter of father's brother: older than speaker) tángjiě tahng-jyeh
堂姐

(younger than speaker) tángmèi
tahng-may 堂妹

cow nǎiniú nain-yoh 奶牛

crab pángxiè pahng-hsyeh
螃蟹

craft shop gōngyìpǐn shāngdiàn
goong-yee-pin shahng-dyen
工艺品商店

crash (*noun:* vehicle) zhuàng chē
jwahng chur 撞车

crazy fēng fung 疯

credit card xìnyòng kǎ hsin-yoong kah 信用卡

do you take credit cards?
shōu xìnyòng kǎ ma? show –
mah 收信用卡吗？

can I pay by credit card?
wǒ kéyǐ yòng xìnyòng kǎ
jiāo kuǎn ma? wor kur-yee
yoong hsin-yoong kah jyow
kwahn mah

**which card do you want
to use?** nín yóng de shì
shénme kǎ? dur shur shun-
mur kah

Mastercard/Visa

yes, sir kěyǐ kur-yee

what's the number?
duōshao hàomǎ? dwor-show
how-mah

and the expiry date? jǐ shí
guòqī? jee shur gwor-chee

---

credit crunch jīnróng wēijī
jin-roong way-jee 金融危机

crisps (zhá) tǔdòupiànr (jah) too-
doh-pyenr （炸）土豆片儿

crockery cānjù tsahn-jew 餐具

crossing (by sea) guòdù gwor-doo
过渡

crossroads shízì lùkǒu shur-dzur
loo-koh 十字路口

crowd rénqún run-chewn 人群

crowded yōngjǐ yoong-jee 拥挤

crown (on tooth) yáguàn yah-
gwahn 牙冠

cruise zuò chuán lǚxíng dzwor
chwahn lyew-sing 坐船旅行

crutches guǎizhàng gwai-jahng
拐杖

cry (verb) kū 哭

Cultural Revolution wénhuà dà
gémìng wun-hwah dah gur-ming
文化大革命

cup bēizi bay-dzur 杯子

**a cup of tea/coffee,
please** yì bēi chá/kāfēi bay
一杯茶／咖啡

cupboard guìzi gway-dzur 柜子

cure (verb) zhìyù jur-yew 治愈

curly juǎnqūde jwahn-chew-dur
卷曲的

current (electric) diànliú dyen-lyoh
电流
(in water) shuǐliú shway-lyoh
水流

curry gālì gah-lee 咖喱

curtains chuānglián chwahng-
lyen 窗帘

cushion diànzi dyen-dzur 垫子

custom fēngsú fung-soo 风俗

Customs hǎiguān hai-gwahn
海关

cut (noun) dāoshāng dow-shahng
刀伤

I've cut myself wǒ bǎ zìjǐ gēshāng le wor bah dzur-jee gur-shahng lur 我把自己割伤了

cutlery dāochā cānjù dow-chah tsahn-jew 刀叉餐具

cycling qí zìxíngchē chee dzur-hsing-chur 骑自行车

cyclist qí zìxíngchē de rén dur run 骑自行车的人

D

dad bàba bah-bah 爸爸

daily měi tiān may tyen 每天

damage (*verb*) sǔnhuài syewn-hwai 损坏

> **damaged** sǔnhuài le 损坏了

> **I'm sorry, I've damaged this** duìbùqǐ, wó bǎ zhèi ge nòng huài le dway-boo-chee wor bah jay gur noong hwai lur 对不起我把这个弄坏了

damn! zāole! dzow-lur! 糟了

damp (*adj*) cháoshī chow-shur 潮湿

dance (*noun*) wǔdǎo woo-dow 舞蹈

> (*verb*) tiàowǔ tyow-woo 跳舞

> **would you like to dance?** nǐ xiǎng tiàowǔ ma? hsyang – mah 你想跳舞吗？

dangerous wēixiǎn way-hsyen 危险

Danish (*adj*) Dānmài dahn-mai 丹麦

dark (*adj*) àn ahn 暗

> (colour) shēnsè shunsur 深色

> **it's getting dark** tiān hēile tyen hay-lur 天黑了

date: what's the date today? jīntiān jǐ hào? jin-tyen jee how 今天几号？

> **let's make a date for next Monday** zánmen xiàge xīngqīyī jiànmiàn zahn-mun hsyah-gur – jyen-myen 咱们下个星期一见面

daughter nǚ'ér nyew-er 女儿

daughter-in-law érxífur er-hshee-foor 儿媳妇儿

dawn límíng 黎明

> **at dawn** tiān gāng liàng tyen gahng lyang 天刚亮

day tiān tyen 天

> **the day after** dìèr tiān 第二天

> **the day after tomorrow** hòutiān hoh-tyen 后天

> **the day before** qián yì tiān chyen 前一天

> **the day before yesterday** qiántiān chyen-tyen 前天

every day měitiān may-tyen
每天

all day zhěngtiān jung-tyen
整天

in two days' time liǎng tiān
nèi nay 天内

have a nice day zhù nǐ wánr
de gāoxìng joo nee wahnr dur
gow-hsing 祝你玩儿得高兴

day trip yírìyóu yee-rur-yoh
一日游

dead sǐle sur-lur 死了

deaf ěr lóng loong 耳聋

deal (business) mǎimài buy-my 买卖

it's a deal! yì yán wéi dìng! yee
yahn way 一言为定

death sǐwáng sur-wahng 死亡

December shíèr yuè shur-er yew-
eh 十二月

decide juédìng jyew-eh-ding
决定

we haven't decided yet
wǒmen hái méi juédìng wor-
mun hai may 我门还没决定

decision juédìng 决定

deck (on ship) jiǎbǎn jyah-bahn
甲板

deep shēn shun 深

definitely yídìng 一定

definitely not yídìng bù
一定不

degree (qualification) xuéwèi
hsyew-eh-way 学位

delay (noun) wǎndiǎn wahn-dyen
晚点

deliberately gùyì goo-yee 故意

delicious hǎochī how-chur
好吃

deliver sòng soong 送

delivery (of mail) sòngxìn soong-
hsin 送信

Denmark Dānmài dahn-mai
丹麦

dentist yáyī yah-yee 牙医

dentures jiǎyá jee-ah-yah 假牙

deodorant chúchòujì choo-choh-
jee 除臭剂

department (administrative) bù 部
(academic) xì hshee 系

department store bǎihuò dàlóu
bai-hwor dah-loh 百货大楼

departure lounge hòujīshì hoh-
jee-shur 侯机室

depend: it depends on-...
nà yào kàn-... nah yow kahn
那要看 …

deposit yājīn yah-jin 押金

dessert tiánpǐn tyen-pin 甜品

destination mùdìdì 目的地

develop (film) chōngxǐ choong-
hshee 冲洗

diabetic (*noun*) tángniàobìng
rén tahng-nyow-bing run
糖尿病人

dial (*verb*) bōhào bor-how 拨号

dialling code diànhuà
qūhào dyen-hwah chew-how
电话区号

diamond zuànshí dzwahn-shur
钻石

diaper niàobù nyow-boo 尿布

diarrhoea lā dùzi lah doo-dzur
拉肚子

**do you have something
for diarrhoea?** nǐ yǒu zhì
lā dùzi de yào ma? nee yoh
jur lah doo-dzur dur yow mah
你有治拉肚子的药吗？

diary rìjì rur-jee 日记

dictionary cídiǎn tsur-dyen 词典

didn't *see* **not**

die sǐ sur 死

diet jìkǒu jee-koh 忌口

I'm on a diet wǒ zài jìkǒu wor
dzai 我在忌口

**I have to follow a
special diet** wǒ děi chī
guīdìng de yǐnshí day
chur gway-ding dur yin-shur
我得吃规定的饮食

difference bùtóng boo-toong
不同

what's the difference? yǒu
shénme bùtóng? yoh shun-mur
有什么不同？

different bùtóng 不同

difficult kùnnan kun-nahn
困难

difficulty kùnnan 困难

dining room cāntīng tsahn-ting
餐厅

dinner (evening meal) wǎnfàn
wahn-fahn 晚饭

to have dinner chī wǎnfàn
吃晚饭

direct (*adj*) zhíjiē jur-jyeh
直接
(flight) zhífēi jur-fay 直飞

is there a direct train?
yǒu zhídá huǒchē ma?
yoh jur-dah hwor-chur mah
有直达火车吗？

direction fāngxiàng fahng-hsyang
方向

which direction is it? zài nǎige fāngxiàng? dzai nay-gur 在哪个方向？

is it in this direction? shì zhèige fāngxiàng ma? shur jay-gur – mah 是这个方向吗？

director zhǔrén joo-run 主任

dirt wūgòu woo-goh 污垢

dirty zāng dzahng 脏

disabled cánfèi tsahn-fay 残废

is there access for the disabled? yǒu cánjirén de tōngdào ma? you tsahn-jee–run dur toong-dow mah 有残疾人的通道吗？

disaster zāinàn dzai-nahn 灾难

disco dísīkē dee-sur-kur 迪斯科

discount jiǎnjià jyen-jyah 减价

is there a discount? néng jiǎnjià ma? nung – mah 能减价吗？

disease jíbìng 疾病

disgusting ěxīn ur-hsin 恶心

dish (meal) cài tsai 菜

(bowl) diézi dyeh-dzur 碟子

disk (for computer) ruǎnpán rwahn-pahn 软盘

disposable nappies/ diapers (yícìxìng) niàobù (yee-tsur-hsing) nyow-boo （一次性）尿布

distance jùlí 距离

in the distance zài yuǎnchù dzai yew-ahn-choo 在远处

The Rough Guide Mandarin Chinese Phrasebook > **ENGLISH→CHINESE**

district dìqū dee-chew 地区

disturb dárǎo dah-row 打扰

divorced líhūn lee-hun 离婚

dizzy: I feel dizzy wǒ tóuyūn wor toh-yewn 我头晕

do (*verb*) zuò dzwor 作

what shall we do? nǐ xiǎng zuò shénme? hsyang – shun-mur 你想作什么？

how do you do it? gāi zěnme zuò? dzun-mur 该怎么做？

will you do it for me? máfan nǐ bāng wǒ zuò yíxià, hǎo ma? mah-fahn nee bahng wor dzwor yee-hsyah how mah 麻烦你帮我做一下好吗？

how do you do? nín hǎo? how

nice to meet you jiàn dào nín zhēn gāoxìng jyen dow nin jun gow-hsing

what do you do? (work) nǐ shì zuò shénme gōngzuò de? shur – goong-dzwor dur

I'm a teacher, and you? wǒ shì jiàoshī, nǐ ne? wor – nur

I'm a student wǒ shì xuésheng

what are you doing this evening? nǐ jīnwǎn zuò shénme? jin-wahn

we're going out for a drink, do you want to join us? wǒmen chū qù hē jiǔ, nǐ xiǎng gēn wǒmen yí kuàir qù ma? wor-mun choo chew hur jyoh nee hsyang gun – kwair chew mah

do you want more rice? nǐ hái yào fàn, ma? yow fahn

I do, but she doesn't wǒ yào, tā bú yào wor yow tah

doctor yīshēng yee-shung 医生

please call a doctor qǐng nǐ jiào ge yīshēng ching nee jyow gur 请你叫个医生

where does it hurt? nǎr téng? tung

right here jiù zài zhèr jyoh dzai jer

does that hurt now? xiànzài hái téng ma? hsyahn-dzai – mah

yes hái téng

take this prescription to the chemist ná zhèi gè yàofāng dào yàodiàn qù pèi yào nah jay gur yow-fahng dow yow-dyen chew pay yow

document wénjiàn wun-jyen
文件

dog gǒu goh 狗

domestic flight guónèi
hángbān gwor-nay hahng-bahn
国内行班

don't! búyào! boo-yow 不要

  don't do that! bié zhème zuò
byeh jur-mur zwor 别这么做

  see **not**

door mén mun 门

doorman bǎménrde bah-munr-
dur 把门儿的

double shuāng shwahng 双

double bed shuāngrén chuáng
–run chwahng 双人床

double room shuāngrén
fáng(jiān) fahng(jyen)
双人房（间）

down xià hsyah 下

  down here jiù zài zhèr jyoh
dzai jer 就在这儿

  put it down over there gē zài
nàr 搁在那儿

  **it's down there on the
right** jiù zài yòubian yoh-byen
就在右边

  it's further down the road
zài wǎng qián wahng chyen
再往前

download (*verb*) xiàzǎi hsyah-dzai
下载

downstairs lóuxià loh-hsyah
楼下

dozen yì dá dah 一打

  half a dozen bàn dá bahn
半打

dragon lóng loong 龙

draught beer shēng píjiǔ shung
pee-jyoh 生啤酒

draughty: it's draughty
zhèr tōngfēng jer toong-fung
这儿通风

drawer chōutì choh-tee 抽屉

drawing huìhuà hway-hwah
绘画

dreadful zāotòule dzow-toh-lur
糟透了

dress (*noun*) liányīqún lyen-yee-
chewn 连衣裙

dressed: to get dressed chuān
yīfu chwahn 穿衣服

dressing gown chényī chun-yee
晨衣

drink (*noun*: alcoholic) jiǔ jyoh 酒
(non-alcoholic) yǐnliào yin-lyow
饮料
(*verb*) hē hur 喝

  a cold drink yì bēi léngyǐn yee
bay lung-yin 一杯冷饮

can I get you a drink?
hēdiǎnr shénme ma?
dyenr shun-mur mah
喝点儿什么吗？

what would you like (to drink)? nǐ xiǎng hē diǎnr shénme? hsyang
你想喝点儿什么？

no thanks, I don't drink
xièxie, wǒ bú huì hē jiǔ hsyeh-hsyeh wor boo hway hur jyoh
谢谢我不会喝酒

I'll just have a drink of water wǒ hē diǎnr shuǐ ba
shway bah 我喝点儿水吧

drinking water yǐnyòngshuǐ yin-yoong-shway 饮用水

is this drinking water?
zhè shuǐ kěyǐ hē ma?
jur shway kur-yee hur ma
这水可以喝吗？

drive (*verb*) kāichē kai-chur
开车

we drove here wǒmen kāichē lái de wor-mun kai-chur lai dur
我们开车来的

I'll drive you home wǒ kāichē sòng nǐ huíjiā wor kai-chur soong nee hway-jyah 我开车送你回家

driver sījī sur-jee 司机

driving licence jiàshǐ zhízhào jyah-shur jur-jow 驾驶执照

drop: just a drop, please (of drink) zhēn de yì diǎnr, xièxie jun dur yee dyen hsyeh-hsyeh 真的一点儿谢谢

drugs (narcotics) dúpǐn doo-pin 毒品

drunk (*adj*) hēzuìle hur-dzway-lur 喝醉了

dry (*adj*) gān gahn 干

dry-cleaner gānxǐdiàn gahn-hshee-dyen 干洗店

duck (meat) yā yah 鸭

due: he was due to arrive yesterday tā yīnggāi shì zuótiān dào tah ying-gai dzwor-tyen dow 他应该昨天到

when is the train due?
huǒchē jǐ diǎn dào? hwor-chur jee shur 火车几点到？

dull (pain) yǐnyǐn zuòtòng dzwor-toong 隐隐作痛

(weather) yīntiān yin-tyen 阴天

during zài... de shíhou dzai-... dur shur-hoh 在 ... 的时候

dust huīchén hway-chun 灰尘

dustbin lājīxiāng lah-jee-hsyang 垃圾箱

Dutch (*adj*) Hélán hur-lahn 荷兰

duty-free (goods) miǎnshuì myen-shway 免税

duty-free shop miǎnshuì shāngdiàn shahng-dyen 免税商店

DVD DVD dee-way-dee DVD盘

dynasty cháodài chow-dai 朝代

E

each (every) měi may 每

how much are they each? yí ge yào duōshao qián? yee gur yow dwor-show chyen 一个要多少钱？

ear ěrduo er-dwor 耳朵

earache: I have earache wó ěrduo téng wor – tung 我耳朵疼

early zǎo dzow 早

early in the morning yì zǎo 一早

I called by earlier wǒ zǎo xiē shíhou láiguo wor – hsyeh shur-hoh lai-gwor 我早些时候来过

earrings ěrhuán er-hwahn 耳环

east dōng doong 东

in the east dōngbiān doong-byen 东边

East China Sea Dōng Hǎi 东海

easy róngyì roong-yee 容易

eat chī chur 吃

we've already eaten, thanks xièxie, wǒmen yǐjing chīle hsyeh-hsyeh wor-mun –chur-lur 谢谢我们已经吃了

economy class jīngjìcāng –tsahng 经济舱

egg jīdàn jee-dahn 鸡蛋

either: either-... or-... huòzhe-... huòzhe-... hwor-jur 或者 ... 或者 ...

either of them něi liǎngge dōu kěyǐ nay lyang-gur doh kur-yee 那两个都可以

elastic band xiàngpíjīnr hsyahng– 橡皮筋儿

elbow gēbozhǒur gur-bor-johr 胳膊肘儿

electric diàn dyen 电

electric fire diàn lúzi loo-dzur 电炉子

electrician diàngōng dyen-goong 电工

electricity diàn dyen 电

elevator diàntī dyen-tee 电梯

else: something else biéde dōngxi byeh-dur doong-hshee 别的东西

somewhere else biéde dìfāng
dee-fahng 别的地方

DIALOGUE

**would you like anything
else?** hái yào biéde ma?
yow – mah

no, nothing else, thanks
bú yào le, xièxie lur hsyeh-
hsyeh

email (*noun*) diànzi yóujiàn dyen-
dzur yoh-jyen 电子邮件 (*verb*)
fāyóujiàn fah-yoh-jyen 发邮件

embassy dàshíguǎn dah-shur-
gwahn 大使馆

embroidery cìxiù tsur-hsyoh
刺绣

emergency jǐnjí qíngkuàng
ching-kwahng 紧急情况

this is an emergency!
jiùmìng! jyoh-ming 救命

emergency exit ānquánmén
ahn-choo-en-mun 安全门

emperor huángdì hwahng-dee
皇帝

empress huánghòu 皇后

empty kōng koong 空

end (*noun*) mòduān mor-dwahn
末端

at the end of the street zhèi
tiáo jiē de jìntóu jay tyow jyeh
dur jin-toh 这条街的尽头

when does it end?
shénme shíhou jiéshù?
shun-mur shur-hoh jyeh-shoo
什么时候结束？

engaged (toilet) yǒurén yoh-run
有人

(phone) zhànxiàn jahn-hsyen
占线

(to be married) dìnghūnle ding-
hun-lur 定婚了

England Yīngguó ying-gwor
英国

English (*adj*) Yīngguó ying-gwor
英国

(language) Yīngyǔ ying-yew
英语

I'm English wǒ shì Yīngguó
rén wor shur – run 我
是英国人

do you speak English?
ni huìbuhuì shuō Yīngyǔ?
hway-boo-hway shwor
你会不会说英语？

enjoy: to enjoy oneself wánr
de hěn kāixīn wahnr dur hun kai-
hsin 玩儿得很开心

DIALOGUE

how did you like the film?
nǐ juéde diànyǐng zěnme
yàng? jyew-eh-dur dyen-ying
dzun-mur yang

enjoyable lìng rén yúkuàide run yew-kwai-dur 令人愉快的

enormous dàjíle dah-jee-lur 大极了

enough: that's enough gòule goh-lur 够了

there's not enough bú gòu 不够

it's not big enough bú gòu dà 不够大

entrance (noun) rùkǒuchù roo-koh-choo 入口处

envelope xìnfēng hsin-fung 信封

equipment shèbèi shur-bay 设备

(for climbing, sport etc) qìxiè chee-hsyeh 器械

especially tèbié tur-byeh 特别

essential zhòngyào joong-yow 重要

it is essential that–...
... shì juéduì bìyào de shur jyew-eh-dway bee-yow dur ... 是决对必要的

Europe Ōuzhōu oh-joh 欧洲

European (adj) Ōuzhōu 欧洲

even shènzhì shun-jur 甚至

even if–... jìshǐ–... yě jee-shur–... yur 即使 ... 也

evening wǎnshang wahn-shahng 晚上

this evening jīntiān wǎnshang jin-tyen 今天晚上

in the evening wǎnshang 晚上

evening meal wǎnfàn wahn-fahn 晚饭

eventually zuìhòu dzway-hoh 最后

ever céngjīng tsung-jing 曾经

have you ever been to the Great Wall? nǐ qùguo Chángchéng ma? chew-gwor – mah

yes, I was there two years ago qùguo, liǎng nián qián qùguo chew-gwor lyang nyen chyen chew-gwor

every měige may-gur 每个

every day měitiān may-tyen 每天

everyone měige rén may-gur run 每个人

everything měijiàn shìr may-jyen chur 每件的事儿

(objects) suǒyǒu de dōngxi
swor-yoh dur doong-hshee
所有西

everywhere měige dìfang may-
gur dee-fahng 每个地方

exactly! duìjíle! dway-jee-lur
对极了

exam kǎoshì kow-shur 考试

example lìzi lee-dzur 例子

for example lìrú 例如

excellent hǎojíle how-jee-lur
好极了

except chúle-… yǐwài choo-lur
除了…以外

excess baggage chāozhòng
xíngli chow-joong hsing-lee
超重行李

exchange rate duìhuàn lǜ
dway-hwahn lyew 兑换率

exciting (day) cìji tsur-jee 刺激

excuse me (to get past) láojià low-
jyah 劳驾

(to get attention) láojià, qǐng
wèn-… ching wun 劳驾请问

(to say sorry) duìbuqǐ dway-boo-
chee 对不起

exhausted (tired) lèisǐle lay-sur-lur
累死了

exhibition (of paintings etc)
zhǎnlǎn jan-lan 展览

(trade fair etc) jiāoyì huì jyow-yee
hway 交易会

exit chūkǒu choo-koh 出口

where's the nearest exit?
zuì jìn de chūkǒu zài nǎr?
dzway jin dur choo-koh dzai
最近的出口在哪儿？

expensive guì gway 贵

experienced yǒu jīngyàn yoh
jing-yen 有经验

explain jiěshì jyeh-shur 解释

can you explain that?
nǐ néng jiěshì yíxià ma?
nung – yee-syah mah
你能解释一下吗？

express (mail) kuàidì kwai-dee
快递

(train) kuàichē kwai-chur 快车

extension (telephone) fēnjī fun-jee
分机

extension 221, please qǐng
guà èr èr yāo ching gwah er er
yow 请挂二二一

**extra: can we have an extra
one?** qǐng zài lái yíge? dzai lai
yee-gur 请再来一个？

**do you charge extra for
that?** hái yào qián ma? hai yow
chyen mah 还要钱吗？

extremely fēicháng fay-chahng
非常

eye yǎnjīng yahn-jing 眼睛

will you keep an eye on my suitcase for me? máfan nín bāng wǒ kān yíxià tíbāo, hǎo ma? mah-fahn nin bahng wor kahn yee-hsyah tee-bow how mah 麻烦您帮我看一下提包好吗？

eyeglasses yǎnjìng yahn-jing 眼镜

F

face liǎn lyen 脸

factory gōngchǎng goong-chahng 工厂

Fahrenheit huáshì hwah-shur 华氏

faint (verb) yūn yewn 晕

she's fainted tā yūndǎole tah yewn-dow-lur 她晕倒了

I feel faint wǒ juéde yǒu diǎn (tóu) yūn wor jyew-eh-dur yoh dyen (toh) yūn 我觉得有点（头）晕

fair (adj) gōngpíng goong-ping 公平

fake màopái mow-pai 冒牌

fall (verb: person) shuāidǎo shwai-dow 摔倒

she's had a fall tā shuāile

yì jiāo tah shwai-lur yee jyow 她摔了一交

fall (US) qiūtiān chyoh-tyen 秋天

in the fall qiūtiān 秋天

false jiǎ jyah 假

family jiātíng jyah-ting 家庭

famous yǒumíng yoh-ming 有名

fan (electrical) fēngshàn fung-shahn 风扇

(hand-held) shànzi shahn-dzur 扇子

(sports) qiúmí chyoh-mee 球迷

fantastic (wonderful) tàihǎole tai-how-lur 太好了

far yuǎn yew-ahn 远

DIALOGUE

is it far from here? lí zhèr yuǎn ma? jer – mah

no, not very far bú tài yuǎn

well, how far? duō yuǎn ne? dwor – nur

it's about 20 kilometres èr shí gōnglǐ zuǒyòu goong-lee dzor-yoh

fare chēfèi chur-fay 车费

Far East Yuǎndōng yew-ahn-doong 远东

farm nóngchǎng noong-chahng 农场

fashionable shímáo shur-mow
时髦

fast kuài kwai 快

fat (person) pàng pahng 胖

(on meat) féiròu fay-roh 肥肉

father fùqīn foo-chin 父亲

father-in-law yuèfù yew-eh-foo
岳父

faucet shuǐlóngtóu shway-loong-
toh 水龙头

fault cuò tswor 错

  sorry, it was my fault
  duìbuqǐ shì wǒde cuò dway-
  boo-chee shur wor-dur tswor
  对不起是我的错

  it's not my fault bú shì wǒde
  cuò 不是我的错

faulty yǒu máobìng yoh mow-bing
有毛病

favourite zuì xǐhuan de dzway
hshee-hwahn dur 最喜欢的

fax (*noun*) chuánzhēn chwahn-jun
传真

  to send a fax fā chuánzhēn
  fah 发传真

February èryuè er-yew-eh 二月

feel gǎnjué gahn-jyew-eh 感觉

  I feel hot wǒ juéde hěn rè
  wor jyew-eh-dur hun rur
  我觉得很热

I feel unwell wǒ juéde bú
tài shūfu –dur – shoo-foo
我觉得不太舒服

I feel like going for a walk
wǒ xiǎng qù zǒuzǒu hsyahng
chew dzoh-dzoh 我想去走走

how are you feeling?
nǐ juéde zěnme yàng le?
nee jyew-eh-dur dzun-mur – lur
你觉得怎么样了？

I'm feeling better
wǒ hǎo diǎnr le how dyenr
我好点儿了

fence zhàlan jah-lahn 栅栏

ferry bǎidù 摆渡

festival jiérì jyeh-ree 节日

fetch qǔ chew 取

  I'll fetch him wǒ qù jiào tā lái
  wor – jyow tah 我去叫他来

  **will you come and fetch
  me later?** děng huìr nǐ lái jiē
  wǒ, hǎo ma? dung hwayr – jyeh
  等会儿你来接我好吗？

feverish fāshāo fah-show 发烧

few: a few yì xiē yee-hsyeh 一些

  a few days jǐ tiān tyen 几天

fiancé wèihūnfū way-hun-foo
未婚夫

fiancée wèihūnqī way-hun-chee
未婚妻

field tiándì tyen-dee 田地

(paddy) dàotián dow-tyen 稻田

file (*noun*) wénjiàn wun-jyen 文件

fill in tián tyen 填

    do I have to fill this in? wǒ
    yào tián zhèi zhāng biǎo ma?
    wor yow tyen jay jahng byow mah
    我要填这张表吗？

filling (in cake, sandwich) xiànr
hsyenr 馅儿

    (in tooth) bǔ yá byew yah 补牙

film (movie) diànyǐng dyen-ying
电影

    (for camera) jiāojuǎnr jyow-jew-
ahnr 胶卷儿

filthy zāng dzahng 脏

find (*verb*) zhǎodào jow-dow 找到

    I can't find it wǒ zhǎobúdào
    wor jow-boo-dow 我找不到

    I've found it zhǎodàole jow-
    dow-lur 找到了

find out zhǎochū jow-choo 找出

    **could you find out for
    me?** nǐ néng tì wǒ diàochá
    yíxià ma? nung tee wor
    dyow-chah yee-hsyah mah
    你能替我调查一下吗？

fine (weather) qínglǎng ching-lang
晴朗

    (punishment) fákuǎn fah-kwahn
罚款

    how are you? nǐ hǎo ma?
    how mah

    I'm fine, thanks hěn hǎo,
    xièxie hun how hsyeh-hsyeh

    is that OK? zhèyàng xíng
    ma? jur-yang hsing mah

    that's fine, thanks xíng,
    xièxie

finger shóuzhǐ shoh-jur 手指

finish (*verb*) zuò wán dzwor wahn
作完

    I haven't finished yet wǒ
    hái méi nòng wán wor hai may
    noong wahn 我还没弄完

    when does it finish? shénme
    shíhou néng wán? shun-mur
    shur-hoh nung 什么时候能
    完？

fire huǒ hwor 火

    (blaze) huǒzāi hwor-dzai 火灾

    fire! zháohuǒle! jow-hwor-lur
    着火了

    can we light a fire here?
    zhèr néng diǎn huǒ ma?
    jer nung dyen hwor mah
    这儿能点火吗？

fire alarm huǒjǐng hwor-jing
火警

fire brigade xiāofángduì hsyow-
fahng-dway 消防队

fire escape tàipíngtī 太平梯

fire extinguisher mièhuǒqì
myeh-hwor-chee 灭火器

first dìyī 第一

    I was first wǒ dìyī wor
    我第一

    first of all shǒuxiān shoh-hsyen
    首先

    at first qǐchū chee-choo
    起初

    the first time dìyí cì tsur
    第一次

    first on the left zuǒbian
    dì yīge zwor-byen – gur
    左边第一个

first aid jíjiù jee-jyoh 急救

first-aid kit jíjiùxiāng –hsyahng
急救箱

first class (travel etc) yīděng yee-
dung 一等

first floor èr lóu er loh 二楼
(US) yī lóu 一楼

first name míngzi ming-dzur
名子

fish (noun) yú yew 鱼

fit: it doesn't fit me zhè duì wǒ
bù héshì jur dway wor boo hur-
shur 这对我不合适

fitting room shì yī shì shur yee
shur 试衣室

fix: can you fix this? (repair) nǐ
néng bǎ zhège xiū hǎo ma?
nung bah jay-gur hsyoh how mah
你能把这个修好吗？

fizzy yǒuqìde yoh-chee-dur
有气的

flag qí chee 旗

flannel (xǐliǎn) máojīn (hshee-lyen) mow-jin 洗脸毛巾

flash (for camera) shǎnguāngdēng shahn-gwahng-dung 闪光灯

flat (noun: apartment) dānyuán dahn-yew-ahn 单元

(adj) píngtǎn ping-tahn 平坦

I've got a flat tyre wǒde chētāi biěle wor-dur chur-tai byeh-lur 我的车胎瘪了

flavour wèidao way-dow 味道

flea tiàozǎo tyow-dzow 跳蚤

flight hángbān hahng-bahn 航班

flight number hángbān hào how 航班号

flood hóngshuǐ hoong-shway 洪水

floor (of room: wooden) dìbǎn 地板

(storey) lóu loh 楼

(in hotel etc) céng tsung 层

on the floor zài dìshang dzai dee-shahng 在地上

florist huādiàn hwah-dyen 花店

flower huā hwah 花

flu liúgǎn lyoh-gahn 流感

fluent: he speaks fluent Chinese tā Hànyǔ jiǎngde hěn liúlì tah hahn-yew jyang-dur hun lyoh-lee 他汉语讲得很流利

fly (noun) cāngying tsahng-ying 苍蝇

(verb) fēi fay 飞

can we fly there? dào nàr yǒu fēijī ma? dow nar yoh fay-jee mah 到那儿有飞机吗？

fog wù 雾

foggy: it's foggy yǒu wù yoh 有雾

folk dancing mínjiān wǔdǎo min-jyen woo-dow 民间舞蹈

folk music mínjiān yīnyuè yin-yew-eh 民间音乐

food shíwù shur-woo 食物

(in shops) shípǐn shur-pin 食品

food poisoning shíwù zhòngdú joong-doo 食物中毒

food shop, food store shípǐn diàn shur-pin dyen 食品店

foot (measurement) yīngchǐ ying-chur 英尺

(of person) jiǎo jyow 脚

to go on foot bùxíng boo-hsing 步行

football (game) zúqiúsài dzoo-chyoh-sai 足球赛

(ball) zúqiú dzoo-chyoh 足球

for: do you have something for-...? (illness) nǐ yǒu zhì... de yào ma? yoh –jur yow mah 你有治 … 的药吗？

who are the dumplings for? zhèi xiē jiǎozi shì shéi (jiào) de? jay hsyeh jyow-dzur shur shay (jyow) dur

that's for me shì wǒ de shur wor

and this one? zhèi gè ne? jay gur nur

that's for her shì tā de shur tah

where do I get the bus for Beijing? qù Běijīng zài nár zuò chē? chew – dzai nar dzwor chur

the bus for Beijing leaves from Donglu Street qù Běijīng de chē zài Dōnglù kāi chew – dur chur dzai

how long have you been here? nǐ lái zhèr duō cháng shíjiān le? jer dwor chahng shur-jyen lur

I've been here for two days, how about you? wǒ láile liǎng tiān le, nǐ ne? wor lai-lur lyang tyen lur nee nur

I've been here for a week wǒ láile yígé xīngqī le yee-gur hsing-chee lur

Forbidden City Gùgōng goo-goong 故宫

foreign wàiguó wai-gwor 外国

foreigner wàiguó rén run 外国人

forest sēnlín sun-lin 森林

forget wàng wahng 忘

I forget, I've forgotten wǒ wàngle wor –lur 我忘了

fork (for eating) chā chah 叉

(in road) chàlù chah-loo 岔路

form (document) biǎo byow 表

formal (dress) zhèngshì jung-shur 正式

fortnight liǎngge xīngqī lyang-gur hsing-chee 两个星期

fortunately xìngkuī hsing-kway 幸亏

forward: could you forward my mail? nín néng bāng wǒ zhuǎn yíxià xìn ma? nung bahng wor jwahn yee-hsyah hsin mah 您能帮我转一下信吗？

forwarding address zhuǎnxìn dìzhǐ jwahn-hsin dee-jur 转信地址

fountain pēnquán pun-chew-ahn
喷泉

foyer xiūxītīng hsyoh-see-ting
休息厅

fracture (*noun*) gǔzhé gyew-jur
骨折

France Fǎguó fah-gwor 法国

free zìyóu dzur-yoh 自由

(no charge) miǎn fèi myen fay
免费

is it free (of charge)?
miǎn fèi de ma? dur mah
免费的吗？

French (*adj*) Fǎguó fah-gwor
法国

(language) Fáyǔ fah-yew 法语

French fries zhá tǔdòu tiáo jah
too-doh tyow 炸土豆条

frequent jīngcháng jing-chahng
经常

**how frequent is the bus
to the Forbidden City?** dào
Gùgōng qù de gōnggòng qìchē
duōcháng shíjian kāi yì bān?
dow goo-goong chew dur goong-
goong chee-chur dwor-chahng
shur-jyen kai yee bahn
到故宫去的公共汽车
多长时间开一班？

fresh (weather, breeze) qīngxīn
ching-hsin 清新

(fruit etc) xiān hsyen 鲜

fresh orange juice xiān júzhī
jyew-jur 鲜桔汁

Friday xīngqī wǔ hsing-chee-woo
星期五

fridge bīngxiāng –hsyahng 冰箱

fried (shallow-fried) jiānde jyen-dur
煎的

(deep-fried) zháde jah-dur 炸

(stir-fried) chǎode chow-dur 炒

fried egg jiān jīdàn jyen jee-dahn
煎鸡蛋

fried noodles chǎomiàn chow-
myen 炒面

fried rice chǎofàn chow-fahn
炒饭

friend péngyou pung-yoh 朋友

friendly yǒuhǎo yoh-how 友好

friendship yǒuyì yoh-yee 友谊

friendship store yǒuyì
shāngdiàn yoh-yee shahng-dyen
友谊商店

from cóng tsoong 从

how far is it from here? lí
zhèr duō yuǎn? jer dwor ywahn
离这儿多远？

**when does the next train
from Suzhou arrive?** cóng
Sūzhōu lái de xià yì bān
huǒchē jǐdiǎn dàodá? tsoong

soo-joh lai dur hsyah yee bahn
hwor-chur jee-dyen dow-dah

从苏州来的下一班火
车几点到达？

from Monday to Friday cóng
xīngqī yī dào xīngqī wǔ tsoong
hsing-chee-yee dow hsing-chee

从星期一到星期五

from next Thursday cóng
xià xīngqī sì qǐ hsyah – sur chee

从下星期四起

where are you from?
nǐ shì nǎr de rén? shur nar-
duh run

I'm from Slough wǒ shì
Slough láide rén wor shur
– lai-dur

front qiánmian chyen-myen
前面

in front, at the front zài
qiánbianr dzai chyen-byenr
在前边儿

in front of the hotel zài
fàndiàn qiánmian dzai fahn-dyen
chyen-myen 在饭店前面

frozen bīngdòngde bing-doong-
dur 冰冻的

fruit shuǐguǒ shway-gwor 水果

fruit juice guǒzhī gwor-jur 果汁

full mǎn mahn 满

it's full of-… lǐmian dōu
shì … lee-myen doh shur
里面都是 …

I'm full wǒ bǎole wor bow-lur
我饱了

full board shí zhù quán bāo shur
joo choo-en bow 食住全包

fun: it was fun hěn hǎo wánr
hun how wahnr 很好玩儿

funeral zànglǐ dzahng-lee 葬礼

funny (strange) qíguài chee-gwai
奇怪

(amusing) yǒu yìsi yoh yee-sur
有意思

(comical) huájī hwah-jee
滑稽

furniture jiājù jyah-jyew 家具

**further: it's further down the
road** zài wǎng qián zǒu dzai
wahng chyen soh 再往前走

**how much further is it to
the Forbidden City?** dào
Gùgōng hái yǒu duōshao
lù? dow – yoh dwor-show

about 5 kilometres dàyuē
wǔ gōnglǐ (lù) dah-yew-eh
woo goong-lee

future jiānglái jyang-lai 将来

in future jiānglái 将来

G

game (cards etc) yóuxì yoh-hshee
游戏

(match) bǐsài 比赛

(meat) yěwèi yur-way 野味

garage (for fuel) jiāyóu zhàn jyah-yoh jahn 加油站

(for repairs) qìchē xiūlíchǎng
chee-chur hsyoh-lee-chahng
汽车修理厂

(for parking) chēkù chur-koo
车库

garden huāyuán hwah-yew-ahn
花园

garlic dàsuàn dah-swahn
大蒜

gas méiqì may-chee 煤气

gasoline qìyóu chee-yoh 气油

gas station jiāyóu zhàn jyah-yoh
jahn 加油站

gate dàmén dah-mun 大门

(at airport) dēngjīkǒu dung-jee-koh 登机口

gay tóngxìngliàn toong-hsing-lyen
同性恋

general (adj) yì bān yee bahn
一般

gents' toilet nán cèsuǒ nahn tsur-swor 男厕所

genuine (antique etc) zhēnzhèng
jun-jung 真正

German (adj) Déguó dur-gwor
德国

(language) Déyǔ dur-yew 德语

Germany Déguó 德国

get (fetch) qǔ chew 取

could you get me another one, please? qǐng nǐ zài gěi wǒ yí ge hǎo ma? ching nee dzai gay wor yee gur how mah
请你再给我一个好吗？

how do I get to-...? qù-... zěnme zǒu? chew-... dzun-mur dzoh 去 … 怎么走？

do you know where I can get them? nǐ zhīdao wǒ zài nǎr néng mǎi dào ma? jee-dow wor dzai nar nung mai dow mah
你知道我在哪儿能买到吗？

can I get you a drink? hē diǎnr shénme ma? hur dyenr shun-mur mah

no, I'll get this one, what would you like? zhèi huí wǒ lái mǎi, nǐ xiǎng hē shénme? jay hway wor – hsyahng hur

a glass of Maotai (lái) yì bēi Máotáijiǔ bay

get back huílai hway-lai 回来

get in (arrive) dàodá dow-dah
到达

**get off: where do I get
off?** wǒ zài nár xià chē?
wor dzai nar hsyah chur
我在哪儿下车？

get on (to train etc) shàng chē
shahng chur 上车

get out (of car etc) xià chē hsyah-
chur 下车

get up (in the morning) qǐchuáng
chee-chwahng 起床

gift lǐwù lee-woo 礼物

gift shop lǐwù shāngdiàn shahng-
dyen 礼物商店

ginger shēngjiāng shung-jyang
生姜

girl nǚ háir nyew 女孩儿

girlfriend nǚ péngyou pung-yoh
女朋友

give gěi gay 给

**can you give me some
change?** qǐng gěi wǒ
líng qián, hǎo ma? ching
gay wor ling chyen how mah
请给我零钱好吗？

I gave... to him wǒ bǎ ...
sòng gěi tā wor bah ... soong gay
tah 我把 ... 送给他

will you give this to-...?
qǐng bǎ zhèige sònggěi ...?
ching bah jay-gur soong-gay
请把这个送给 ... ？

give back huán hwahn 还

glad gāoxìng gow-sing 高兴

glass (material) bōli bor-lee
玻璃

(for drinking) bōli bēi bay
玻璃杯

a glass of wine yì bēi jiǔ
一杯酒

glasses yǎnjìng yahn-jing 眼镜

gloves shǒutào shoh-tow 手套

glue jiāoshuǐr jyow-shwayr
胶水儿

go qù chew 去

**we'd like to go to the
Summer Palace** wǒmen
xiǎng qù Yíhéyuán wor-mun
hsyahng 我们想去颐和园

where are you going? nǐ qù
nǎr? 你去哪儿？

where does this bus go?
zhèi liàng chē qù nǎr? jay lyang
chur 这辆车去哪儿？

let's go! wǒmen zǒu ba! wor-
mun dzoh bah 我们走吧

she's gone tā yǐjing zǒule tah
yee-ying zoh-lur 她已经走了

where has he gone?
tā dào nǎr qù le? dow
他到哪儿去了？

I went there last week
wǒ shì shàng xīngqī qù nàr
de wor shur shahng hsing-chee
我是上星期去那儿的

go away líkāi 离开

go away! zǒu kāi! dzoh 走开

go back (return) huí hway 回

go down (the stairs etc) xià
hsyah 下

go in jìn 进

go out (in the evening) chūqu choo-
chew 出去

**do you want to go out
tonight?** nǐ jīntiān wǎnshang
xiǎng chūqù ma? jin-tyen
wahn-shahng hsyahng – mah
你今天晚上想出去吗？

go through chuān chwahn 穿

go up (the stairs etc) shàng shahng
上

God shàngdì 上帝

gold (metal) huángjīn hwahng-jin
黄金

(colour) jīnsè jin-sur 金色

good hǎo how 好

good! hǎo! how 好

it's no good bù hǎo 不好

goodbye zàijiàn dzai-jyen 再见

good evening nǐ hǎo how 你好

good morning nǐ zǎo zow 你早

good night wǎnān wahn-ahn
晚安

goose é ur 鹅

gorge xiá hsyah 峡

got: we've got to leave wǒmen
déi zǒu le wor-mun day zoh lur
我们得走了

have you got any-…?
nǐ yǒu … ma? yoh … mah
你有 … 吗？

government zhèngfǔ jung-foo
政府

gradually jiànjiàn de jyen-jyen dur
渐渐地

grammar yǔfǎ yew-fah 语法

gram(me) kè kur 克

granddaughter (daughter's
daughter) wàisūnnǚr wai-sun-
nyewr 外孙女儿

(son's daughter) sūnnǚr 孙
女儿

grandfather (maternal) wàigōng
wai-goong 外公

(paternal) yéye yur-yur 爷爷

grandmother (maternal) wàipó
wai-por 外婆

(paternal) nǎinai 奶奶

grandson (daughter's son) wài sūnzi sun-dzur 外孙子
(son's son) sūnzi 孙子

grapefruit pútáoyòu poo-tow-yoh 葡萄柚

grapes pútáo poo-tow 葡萄

grass cǎo tsow 草

grateful gǎnjī gahn-jee 感激

great (excellent) hǎojíle how-jee-lur 好极了

   a great success jùdà chéngjiù joo-dah chung-jyoh 巨大成就

greedy (for money etc) tānxīn tahn-hsin 贪心
(for food) chán chahn 馋

green lǜsè(de) lyew-sur(-dur) 绿色的

greengrocer's càidiàn tsai-dyen 菜店

grey huīsè(de) hway-sur(-dur) 灰色的

grilled kǎo kow 烤

grocer's záhuòdiàn dzah-hwor-dyen 杂货店

ground: on the ground zài dì shàng dzai dee shahng 在地上

ground floor yī lóu loh 一楼

group (tourist etc) cānguāntuán tsahn-gwahn-twahn 参观团

(study, work etc) xiǎozǔ hsyow-dzew 小组

guarantee (*noun*) bǎozhèng bow-jung 保证

   is it guaranteed? bǎo bù bǎoxiū? bow – hsyoh 保不保修？

guest kèrén kur-run 客人

guesthouse bīnguǎn bing-wahn 宾馆

guide (tour guide) dǎoyóu dow-yoh 导游

guidebook dǎoyóu shǒucè shoh-tsur 导游手册

guided tour yǒu dǎoyóu de yóulǎn yoh – dur yoh-lahn 有导游的游览

guitar jítā jee-tah 吉他

gum (in mouth) chǐyín chur-yin 齿龈

gym tǐyùguǎn tee-yoo-gwahn 体育馆

H

hair tóufa toh-fah 头发

haircut lǐfà lee-fah 理发

hairdresser's lǐfàdiàn dyen 理发店

hairdryer diànchuīfēng dyen-chway-fung 电吹风

hair spray pēnfàjì pun-fah-jee
喷发剂

half (*adj*) bàn bahn 半

(*noun*) yí bàn 一半

half an hour bàn xiǎoshí
hsyow-shur 半小时

half a litre bàn shēng shung
半升

about half that nàme
duō yí bàn nah-mur dwor
那么多一半

half board bàn shísù shur-soo
半食宿

half-bottle bàn píng 半瓶

half fare bànfèi bahn-fay 半费

half price bànjià bahn-jyah 半价

ham huǒtuǐ hwor-tway 火腿

hamburger hànbǎobāo hahn-
bow-bow 汉堡包

hand shǒu shoh 手

handbag shǒutíbāo shoh-tee-bow
手提包

handkerchief shǒujuànr shoh-
jwahnr 手绢儿

hand luggage shǒutí xíngli
shoh-tee hsing-lee 手提行李

happen fāshēng fah-shung 发生

what's happening? zěnme
huí shìr? dzun-mur hway shur
怎么回事儿？

what has happened?
fāshēng le shénme shìr la?
fah-shung lur shun-mur lah
发生了什么事儿啦？

happy kuàilè kwai-lur 快乐

I'm not happy about this
wǒ duì zhèige bù mǎnyì wor
dway jay-gur boo mahn-yee
我对这个不满意

harbour gángkǒu gahng-koh
港口

hard yìng 硬

(difficult) nán nahn 难

hardly: hardly ever hěn shǎo
hun show 很少

hard seat yìngxí ying-hshee
硬席

hardware shop wǔjīn (shāng) diàn woo-jin (shahng) dyen 五金（商）店

hat màozi mow-dzur 帽子

hate (*verb*) hèn hun 恨

have yǒu yoh 有

  can I have a-...? (asking for something) qǐng gěi wǒ-... hǎo ma? ching gay wor-... how 请给我 … 好吗？

  (ordering food) qǐng lái-..., hǎo ma? ching 请来 … 好吗？

  (in shop) wǒ xiǎng mǎi-... wor hsyahng 我想买 …

  do you have-...? nǐmen yǒu-... ma? nee-mun yoh-... mah 你们有 … 吗？

  what'll you have? nǐ xiǎng hē shénme? hsyahng hur shun-mur 你想喝什么？

  I have to leave now wǒ děi zǒu le wor day dzoh lur 我得走了

  do I have to-...? wǒ děi-... ma? 我得 … 吗？

hayfever huāfěnrè hwah-fun-rur 花粉热

he tā tah 他

head tóu toh 头

headache tóuténg toh-tung 头疼

hear tīngjian ting-jyen 听见

  can you hear me? nǐ néng tīngjiàn ma? nung ting-jyen mah

  I can't hear you, could you repeat that? duìbuqǐ, tīngbujiàn, nǐ néng zài shuō yí biàn ma? dway-boo-chee ting-boo-jyen – dzai shwor yee byen

hearing aid zhùtīngqì joo-ting-chee 助听器

heart xīnzàng hsin-dzahng 心脏

heart attack xīnzàngbìng –bing 心脏病

heat rè rur 热

heater sànrèqì sahn-rur-chee 散热器

heating nuǎnqì nwahn-chee 暖器

heavy zhòng joong 重

heel (of foot) jiǎogēn jyow-gun 脚跟

  (of shoe) xié hòugēn hsyeh 鞋后跟

  could you heel these? qǐng gěi wǒ dǎ hòugēn, hǎo ma? ching gay wor dah – how mah 请给我打后跟好吗？

heelbar xiūxiépù hsyoh-hsyeh-poo 修鞋铺

helicopter zhíshēng fēijī jur-shung fay-jee 直升飞机

hello nǐ hǎo nee how 你好

(answer on phone) wéi way 喂

help bāngzhù bahng-joo 帮助

help! jiùmìng! jyoh-ming 救命

can you help me? nǐ néng bù néng bāngbāng wǒ? nung bahng-bahng wor 你能不能帮帮我？

thank you very much for your help xièxie nǐde bāngmáng hsyeh-hsyeh nee-dur 谢谢你的帮忙

helpful bāngle bú shǎo máng bahng-lur boo show mahng 帮了不少忙

hepatitis gānyán gah-nyen 肝炎

her tā tah 她

that's her towel nà shì tāde máojīn nah shur tah-dur mow-jin 那是她的毛巾

herbs (for cooking) zuóliào dzwor-lyow 作料

(medicinal) cǎoyào tsow-yow 草药

here zhèr jer 这儿

here is/are-... zhèr shì ... shur 这儿是 …

here you are gěi nǐ gay 给你

hers tāde tah-dur 她的

that's hers zhè shì tāde jur shur 这是她的

hey! hēi! hay 嘿

hi! (hello) nǐ hǎo! how 你好

high gāo gow 高

hill shān shahn 山

him tā tah 他

hip túnbù tun-boo 臀部

hire (bike, car) zū dzoo 租

(guide, interpreter) gù 顾

for hire chūzū choo-dzoo 出租

where can I hire a bike? zài nǎr néng zū dào zìxíngchē? dzai nar nung zoo dow dzi-hsing-chur 在哪儿能租到自行车？

his tāde tah-dur 他的

hit (verb) dǎ dah 打

hitch-hike dā biànchē byen-chur 搭便车

hobby shìhào shur-how 嗜好

hole dòng doong 洞

holiday (public) jiàqī jyah-chee 假期

(festival) jiérì jyeh-ree 节日

on holiday dùjià doo-jyah 度假

home jiā 家

at home (in my house etc) zài jiā dzai 在家

we go home tomorrow (to country) wǒmen míngtian huí guó wor-mun ming-tyen hway gwor 我们明天回国

honest chéngshí chung-shur 诚实

honey fēngmì fung-mee 蜂蜜

honeymoon mìyuè mee-yew-eh 蜜月

Hong Kong Xiānggǎng hsyahng-gahng 香港

hope xīwàng hshee-wahng 希望

  I hope so wǒ xīwàng shì zhèi yàng wor – shur jay yang 我希望是这样

  I hope not wǒ xīwàng bú shì zhèi yàng 我希望不是这样

hopefully xīwàng rúcǐ hshee-wahng roo-tsur 希望如此

horrible kěpà kur-pah 可怕

horse mǎ mah 马

horse riding qí mǎ chee 骑马

hospital yīyuàn yee-yew-ahn 医院

hospitality hàokè how-kur 好客

  thank you for your hospitality xièxie nínde

shèngqíng kuǎndài hsyeh-hsyeh nin-dur shung-ching kwahn-dai 谢谢您的盛情款待

hot rè rur 热

  (spicy) là lah 辣

  I'm hot wǒ juéde hěn rè wor jyew-eh-dur hun rur 我觉得很热

  it's hot today jīntiān hěn rè jin-tyen 今天很热

hotel (small) lǚguǎn lyew-gwahn 旅馆

  (luxury) fàndiàn fahn-dyen 饭店

hour xiǎoshí hsyow-shur 小时

house fángzi fahng-dzur 房子

how zěnme dzun-mur 怎么？

  how many? (if answer is likely to be more than ten) duōshao? dwor-show 多少？

  (if answer is likely to be ten or less) jǐge? jee-gur 几个？

  how do you do? nǐ hǎo how 你好？

how are you? nǐ hǎo ma? mah

fine, thanks, and you? hěn hǎo, nǐ ne? hun – nur

how much is it? duōshao qián? chyen

17 yuan shí qī kuài shur chee kwai

I'll take it wǒ mǎi wor

humid cháoshī chow-shur 潮湿

hungry è ur 饿

are you hungry? nǐ èle ma? ur-lur mah 你饿了吗？

hurry: I'm in a hurry wǒ hěn jí de wor hun jee dur 我很急的

there's no hurry mànmàn lái mahn-mahn 慢慢来

hurry up! kuài diǎnr! kwai dyenr 快点儿

hurt (verb) téng tung 疼

it really hurts zhēn téng jun tung 真疼

husband zhàngfu jahng-foo 丈夫

I wǒ wor 我

ice bīng 冰

with ice jiā bīngkuàir jyah bing-kwair 加冰块儿

no ice, thanks bù jiā bīngkuàir, xièxie boo jyah bing-kwair hsyeh-hsyeh 不加冰块儿谢谢

ice cream bīngqílín bing-chee-lin 冰淇淋

ice-cream cone dànjuǎnr bīngqílín dahn-jyew-ahnr 蛋卷儿冰淇淋

ice lolly bīnggùnr bing-gunr 冰棍儿

idea zhǔyi joo-yee 主意

idiot shǎguā shah-gwah 傻瓜

if rúguǒ roo-gwor 如果

ill bìngle bing-lur 病了

I feel ill wǒ juéde bù shūfu wor jyew-eh-dur 我觉得不舒服

illness jíbìng jee-bing 疾病

imitation (leather etc) fǎng fahng 仿

immediately mǎshàng mah-shahng 马上

important zhòngyào joong-yow 重要

it's very important hěn zhòngyào hun joong-yow 很重要

it's not important bú zhòngyào 不重要

impossible bù kěnéng kur-nung 不可能

impressive (building, view) xióngwěi hsyoong-way 雄伟

improve tígāo tee-gow 提高

I want to improve my Chinese wǒ xiǎng tígāo wǒde Hànyǔ shuǐpíng wor hsyahng – wor-dur hah-yew shway-ping 我想提高我的汉语水平

in: it's in the centre zài zhōngjiān dzai joong-jyen 在中间

in my car zài wǒde chē lǐ wor-dur chur lee 在我的车里

in London zài Lúndūn 在伦敦

in two days from now liǎng tiān zhī hòu tyen jur hoh 两天之后

in five minutes wǔ fēn zhōng (zhī) nèi fun joong (jur) nay 五分钟（之）内

in May zài wǔyuè 在五月

in English yòng Yīngyǔ 用英语

in Chinese yòng Hànyǔ 用汉语

is Mr Li in? Lǐ xiānsheng zài ma? hsyahng-shung dzai mah 李先生在吗？

inch yīngcùn ying-tsun 英寸

include bāokuò bow-kwor 包括

does that include meals? zhè bāokuò fàn qián

ma? jur – fahn chyen mah 这包括饭钱吗？

is that included? nèige yě bāokuò zài nèi ma? nay-gur yur 那个也包括在内吗？

inconvenient bù fāngbiàn fahng-byen 不方便

India Yìndù yin-doo 印度

Indian (adj) Yìndù 印度

indigestion xiāohuà bù liáng hsyow-hwah boo lyang 消化不良

Indonesia Yìndùníxīyà yin-doo-nee-hshee-yah 印度尼西亚

indoor pool shìnèi yóuyǒngchí shur-nay yoh-yoong-chur 室内游泳池

indoors shìnèi shur-nay 室内

inexpensive piányi pyen-yee 便宜

infection gǎnrǎn gahn-rahn 感染

infectious chuánrǎn chwahn-rahn 传染

inflammation fāyán fah-yen 发炎

informal (clothes) suíbiàn sway-byen 随便

(occasion) fēi zhèngshì fay jung-shur 非正式

information xiāoxi hsyow-hshee
消息

do you have any information about-...?
nǐ yǒu guānyú ... de xiāoxi ma? nee yoh gwahn-yew dur – mah 你有关于 … 的消息吗？

information desk wènxùnchù wun-hsyewn-choo 问讯处

injection dǎzhēn dah-jun 打针

injured shòushāng shoh-shahng 受伤

she's been injured
tā shòushāng le tah – lur 她受伤了

inner tube (for tyre) nèitāi nay– 内胎

innocent wúgū 无辜

insect kūnchóng kun-choong 昆虫

insect bite chóngzi yǎo de choong-dzur yow dur 虫子咬的

do you have anything for insect bites? yǒu zhì chóng yǎo de yào ma? yoh jur choong yow dur yow mah 有治虫咬的药吗？

insect repellent qūchóngjì chew-choong-jee 驱虫剂

inside zài-... lǐ dzai-... lee 在 … 里

inside the hotel zài lǚguǎn lǐmiàn 在旅馆里面

let's sit inside wǒmen jìnqù zuò ba wor-mun jin-chew dzwor bah 我们进去坐吧

insist: I insist wǒ jiānchí wor jyen-chur 我坚持

instant coffee sùróng kāfēi soo-roong kah-fay 速溶咖啡

insulin yídǎosù yee-dow-soo 胰岛素

insurance bǎoxiǎn bow-hsyen 保险

intelligent cōngming tsoong-ming 聪明

interested: I'm interested in-... wǒ duì-... hěn gǎn xìngqù wor dway-... hun gahn hsing-chew 我对 … 很感兴趣

interesting yǒu yìsi yoh yee-sur 有意思

that's very interesting hěn yǒu yìsi hun 很有意思

international guójì gwor-jee 国际

Internet hùliánwǎng hoo-lyen-wahng 互联网

interpreter fānyì fahn-yee 翻译

intersection (US) shízi lùkǒu
shur-dzur loo-koh 十字路口

interval (at theatre) mùjiān
xiūxi moo-jyen hsyoh-hshee
幕间休息

into: I'm not into-… wǒ duì
… bù gǎn xìngqù wor dway …
boo gahn hsing-chew 我对 …
不感兴趣

introduce jièshào jyeh-show
介绍

　may I introduce-…? wǒ lái
　jièshào yíxià, zhèi wèi shì-…
　wor – yee-hsyah jay-way shur
　我来介绍一下这位是 …

invitation yāoqǐng yow-ching
邀请

invite yāoqǐng 邀请

Ireland Àiěrlán ai-er-lahn
爱尔兰

Irish Àiěrlán ai-er-lahn 爱尔兰

　I'm Irish wǒ shì Àiěrlán
　rén wor shur ai-er-lahn run
　我是爱尔兰人

iron (for ironing) yùndǒu yewn-doh
熨斗

　can you iron these for
　me? qǐng nǐ bāng wǒ
　yùnyùn zhè xié yīfu, hǎo ma?
　ching nee bahng wor yun-yun
　jur hsyeh yee-foo how mah

请你帮我熨熨这些衣
服好吗？

is shì shur 是

island dǎo dow 岛

it tā tah 它

　it is-…, it was-… shì-… shur
　是 …

　is it-…? shì-… ma? mah 是
　… 吗？

　where is it? zài nǎr? dzai
　在哪儿？

Italian (adj) Yìdàlì yee-dah-lee
意大利

Italy Yìdàlì 意大利

itch: it itches yǎng 痒

J

jacket jiākè jyah-kur 茄克

jade yù yew 玉

jam guǒjiàng gwor-jyang 果酱

January yīyuè yee-yew-eh 一月

Japan Rìběn ree-bun 日本

jar guànzi gwahn-dzur 罐子

jasmine tea mòlìhuā chá mor-lee
hwah chah 茉莉花茶

jaw xiàba hsyah-bah 下巴

jazz juéshì yuè jyeweh-shur yeweh
爵士乐

jealous jìdù 忌妒

jeans niúzǎikù nyoh-dzai-koo
牛仔裤

jetty mǎtóu mah-toh 码头

jeweller's zhūbǎo (shāng)
diàn joo-bow (shahng-)dyen
珠宝（商）店

jewellery zhūbǎo 珠宝

Jewish Yóutàirén de yoh-tai-run
dur 犹太人的

job gōngzuò goong-dzwor 工作

jogging pǎobù pow-boo 跑步

　to go jogging qù pǎobù chew
　去跑步

joke wánxiào wahn-hsyow 玩笑

journey lǚxíng lyew-sing 旅行

　have a good journey!
　yílù shùnfēng! shun-fung
　一路顺风

jug guàn gwahn 罐

　a jug of water yí guànr shuǐ
　一罐儿水

July qīyuè chee-yew-eh 七月

jumper tàoshān tow-shahn 套衫

junction (road) jiāochākǒu jyow-
chah-koh 交叉口

June liùyuè lyoh-yew-eh 六月

just (only just) jǐnjǐn 仅仅

　(with numbers) zhǐ jur 只

　just two zhǐ yào liǎngge yow
　只要两个

just for me jiù wǒ yào jyoh wor
就我要

just here jiù zài zhèr dzai jer
就在这儿

not just now xiànzài
bùxíng hsyen-dzai boo-hsing
现在不行

we've just arrived wǒmen
gāng dào wor-mun gahng dow
我们刚到

K

keep liú lyoh 留

　keep the change búyòng
　zhǎo le boo-yoong jow lur
　不用找了

　can I keep it? wǒ kěyi liúzhe
　ma? wor kur-yee lyoh-jur mah
　我可以留着吗？

　please keep it qǐng liúzhe ba
　ching – bah 请留着吧

kettle shuǐhú shway-hoo 水壶

key yàoshi yow-shur 钥匙

　the key for room 201,
　please qǐng gěi wǒ èr líng yāo
　fáng de yàoshi ching gay wor
　er ling yow fahng dur yow-shur
　请给我二零一房的钥匙

keyring yàoshi quān yow-shur
choo-en 钥匙环

kidneys (in body) shènzàng shun-dzahng 肾脏

(food) yāozi yow-dzur 腰子

kill shā shah 杀

kilo gōngjīn goong-jin 公斤

kilometre gōnglǐ goong-lee 公里

how many kilometres is it to-...? qù … yǒu duōshao gōnglǐ? chew … yoh dow-show 去 … 有多少公里？

kind (type) zhǒng joong 种

that's very kind nǐ zhēn hǎo nee jun how 你真好

which kind do you want? nǐ yào nǎ yí zhǒng? yow nah

I want this/that kind wǒ yào zhèi/nèi yì zhǒng wor yow jay/nay

king guówáng gwor-wahng 国王

kiosk shòuhuòtíng shoh-hwor-ting 售货亭

kiss wěn wun 吻

kitchen chúfáng choo-fahng 厨房

Kleenex zhǐjīn jur-jin 纸巾

knee xīgài hshee-gai 膝盖

knickers sānjiǎokù sahn-jyow-koo 三角裤

knife dāozi dow-dzur 刀子

knock (verb) qiāo chyow 敲

knock over (object) dǎ fān dah fahn 打翻

(pedestrian) zhuàng dǎo jwahng dow 撞倒

know (somebody) rènshi run-shur 认识

(something, a place) zhīdao jur-dow 知道

I don't know wǒ bù zhīdao 我不知道

I didn't know that nà wǒ bù zhīdao nah 那我不知道

do you know where I can buy-...? nǐ zhīdao wǒ zài nǎr néng mǎi dào …? wor dzai nar nung mai dow 你知道我在哪儿能买到 … ？

Korean (adj) Cháoxiān chow-hsyen 朝鲜

L

lacquerware qīqì chee-chee 漆器

ladies' room, ladies' toilets nǚ cèsuǒ nyew tsur-swor 女厕所

ladies' wear nǚzhuāng nyew-jwahng 女装

lady nǚshì nyew-shur 女士

lager píjiǔ pee-jyoh 啤酒

lake hú hoo 湖

lamb (meat) yángròu yang-roh 羊肉

lamp dēng dung 灯

lane (motorway) chēdào chur-dow 车道

　　(small road) hútòng hoo-toong 胡同

language yǔyán yew-yen 语言

language course yǔyán kè kur 语言课

Laos Lǎowō low-wor 老挝

laptop shǒutí diànnǎo shoh-tee dyen-now 手提电脑

large dà dah 大

last (final) zuìhòu dzway-hoh 最后

　　last week shàng xīngqī shahng hsing-chee 上星期

　　last Friday shàng xīngqī wǔ 上星期五

　　last night zuótiān wǎnshang dzwor-tyen wahn-shahng 昨天晚上

　　what time is the last train to Beijing? qù Běijīng de zuìhòu yì bān huǒchē jǐ diǎn kāi? chew – dur dzway-hoh yur bahn hwor-chur jee dyen

去北京的最后一班火车几点开？

late (at night) wǎn wahn 晚

　　(delayed) chí chur 迟

　　sorry I'm late duìbuqǐ, wǒ lái wǎnle dway-boo-chee wor lai wahn-lur 对不起我来晚了

　　the train was late huǒchē lái wǎnle hwor-chur 火车来晚了

　　we must go – we'll be late wǒmen děi zǒule láibujíle wor-mun day dzoh-lur lai-boo-jee-lur 我们得走了来不及了

　　it's getting late bù zǎole dzow-lur 不早了

later hòulái hoh-lai 后来

　　I'll come back later wǒ guò yìhuǐr zài lái wor gwor yee-hwayr dzai 我过一会儿再来

　　see you later huítóujiàn hway-toh-jyen 回头见

　　later on hòulái 后来

latest zuìhòu dzway-hoh 最后

　　(most recent) zuìjìn dzway-jin 最近

　　by Wednesday at the latest zuìwǎn xīngqīsān 最晚星期三

laugh (verb) xiào hsyow 笑

laundry (clothes) xǐyī hshee-yee 洗衣

(place) xǐyīdiàn –dyen 洗衣店

lavatory cèsuǒ tsur-swor 厕所

law fǎlǜ fah-lyew 法律

lawyer lǜshī lyew-shur 律师

laxative xièyào hsyeh-hyow 泄药

lazy lǎn lahn 懒

**lead: where does this road
  lead to?** zhè tiáo lù tōng nǎr
  qù? jur tyow loo toong nar chew
  这条路通哪儿去？

leak: the roof leaks
  wūdǐng lòule woo-ding loh-lur
  屋顶漏了

learn xuéxí hsyew-eh-hshee 学习

least: not in the least yìdiǎnr
  dōu bù yee-dyenr doh bu
  一点儿都不

  at least zhìshǎo jee-show
  至少

leather pígé pee-gur 皮革

leave (depart) zǒu dzoh 走

  I am leaving tomorrow wǒ
  míngtian zǒu wor ming-tyen
  我明天走

  **when does the bus for
  Beijing leave?** qù Běijīng
  de qìchē jǐ diǎn kāi? chew
  – dur chee-chur jee dyen
  去北京的汽车几点开？

may I leave this here?
wǒ néng bǎ zhèige liú zài
zhèr ma? wor nung bah
jay-gur lyoh dzai jer mah
我能把这个留在这儿
吗？

he left yesterday tā
shì zuótiān líkāi de tah
shur dzwor-tyen lee-kai dur
他是昨天离开的

I left my coat in the bar
wǒ bǎ wǒde dàyī liú zài
jiǔbājiān bah wor-dur dah-
yee lyoh dzai jyoh-bah-jyen
我把我的大衣留在酒
吧间

there's none left shénme
dōu búshèng shun-mur doh boo-
shung 什么都不剩

left zuǒ dzwor 左

on the left zài zuǒbiānr dzai
dzwor-byenr 在左边儿

to the left wǎng zuǒ wahng
往左

turn left wǎng zuǒ guǎi gwai
往左拐

left-handed zuópiězi dzwor-pyeh-
dzur 左撇子

left luggage (office) xíngli
jìcúnchù hsing-lee jee-tsun-choo
行李寄存处

leg tuǐ tway 腿

lemon níngméng ning-mung
柠檬

lemonade níngméng qìshuǐr
chee-shwayr 柠檬汽水儿

lemon tea níngméngchá
–chah 柠檬茶

lend jiè jyeh 借

will you lend me your-...?
qǐng bǎ nǐde ... jiè gěi wǒ ching
bah nee-dur ... jyeh gay wor
请把你的 ... 借给我？

lens (of camera) jìngtóu jing-toh
镜头

less shǎo show 少

less than... bǐ ... shǎo
比 ... 少

less expensive than... bǐ ...
piányi pyen-yee 比 ... 便宜

lesson kè kur 课

let: will you let me know?
nǐ dào shíhou gàosu wǒ,
hǎo ma? dow shur-hoh
gow-soo wor how mah
你到时候告诉我好吗？

I'll let you know wǒ
dào shíhou gàosu nǐ
我到时候告诉你

**let's go for something to
eat** chīfàn, ba chur-fahn bah
吃饭吧

**let off: will you let me off
at-…?** wǒ zài-… xià, xíng ma?
dzai-… hsyah hsing 我在 …
下行吗？

letter xìn hsin 信

**do you have any letters for
me?** yǒu xìn, ma? yoh hsin mah
有信吗？

letterbox xìnxiāng hsin-hsyahng
信箱

library túshūguǎn too-shoo-gwahn
图书馆

lid gàir gair 盖儿

lie (tell untruth) shuōhuǎng shwor-
hwahng 说谎

lie down tǎng tahng 躺

life shēnghuó shung-hwor 生活

lifebelt jiùshēngquān jyoh-shung-
choo-en 救生圈

lifeguard jiùshēngyuán jyoh-
shung-yew-ahn 救生员

life jacket jiùshēngyī jyoh-shung-
yee 救生衣

lift (in building) diàntī dyen-tee
电梯

could you give me a lift?
nǐ néng bù néng ràng wǒ
dāge chē? nung – rahng wor
dah-gur chur 你能不能让
我搭个车？

light (noun) dēng dung 灯

(not heavy) qīng ching 轻

do you have a light? (for
cigarette) nǐ yǒu huǒ ma? nur
yoh hwor mah 你有火吗？

light bulb dēngpào dung-pow
灯泡

I need a new light bulb
wǒ xūyào yíge xīn dēngpào
wor hsyoo-yow yee-gur hsin
我需要一个新灯泡

lighter (cigarette) dǎhuǒjī dah-
hwor-jee 打火机

lightning shǎndiàn shahn-dyen
闪电

like xǐhuan hshee-hwahn 喜欢

I like it wǒ xǐhuan wor
我喜欢

I don't like it wǒ bù xǐhuan
我不喜欢

I like you wǒ xǐhuan nǐ
我喜欢你

do you like-…? nǐ xǐhuan-…
ma? mah 你喜欢 … 吗？

I'd like a beer wǒ xiǎng hē
yìpíng píjiǔ hsyahng hur yee-ping
我想喝一瓶啤酒

I'd like to go swimming
wǒ xiǎng qù yóuyǒng 我想
去游泳

would you like a drink?
nǐ xiǎng hē diǎnr shénme

ma? hur dyenr shun-mur

你想喝点儿什么吗？

**would you like to go for a
walk?** nǐ xiǎng bu xiǎng qù
zǒuyizǒu? chew dzoh-yee-dzoh

你想不想去走一走？

what's it like? tā xiàng
shénme? tah shang-shen-mur 它象什么？

I want one like this wǒ yào
tónglèide yow toong-lay-dur

我要同类的

line xiàn hsyen 线

**could you give me an
outside line?** qǐng gěi wǒ
wàixiàn, hǎo ma? ching gay
wor wai-hsyen how dzwaymah

请给我外线好吗？

lips zuǐchún dzway 嘴唇

lip salve chúngāo chun-gow
唇膏

lipstick kǒuhóng koh-hoong
口红

listen tīng 听

litre shēng shung 升

little xiǎo hsyow 小

just a little, thanks jiù
yìdiǎnr, xièxie jyoh yee-dyenr
hsyeh-hsyeh 就一点儿谢谢

a little milk yìdiǎnr níunǎi
nyoh-nai 一点儿牛奶

a little bit more duō yìdiǎnr
dwor yee-dyenr 多一点儿

live (verb) zhù joo 住

we live together wǒmen zhù
zài yìqǐ wor-mun joo dzai yee-
chee 我们住在一起

DIALOGUE

where do you live? nǐ zhù
zài nǎr? joo dzai

I live in London wǒ zhù zài
Lúndūn wor

lively (person) huópo hwor-por
活泼

(town) rènao rur-now 热闹

liver (in body, food) gān gahn
肝

lobby (in hotel) qiántīng chyen-ting
前厅

lobster lóngxiā loong-hsyah
龙虾

local dìfāngde dee-fahng-dur
地方的

lock suǒ swor 锁

it's locked suǒshang le swor
shahng lur 锁上了

**lock out: I've locked
myself out** wǒ bǎ zìjǐ suǒ
zài ménwài le wor bah dzur-
jee swor dzai mun-wai lur

我把自己锁在门外了

looker (for luggage etc) xiǎochúguì

hsyow-choo-gway 小橱柜

London Lúndūn 伦敦

long cháng chahng 长

how long does it take?
yào duōcháng shíjian?
yow dwor-chahng shur-jyen?
要多长时间？

**how long will it take to fix
it?** bǎ zhèige dōngxi xiūlǐ hǎo
yào duōcháng shíjian? bah jay-
gur doong-hshee hsyoo-lee hao
把这个东西修理好要
多长时间？

a long time hěn cháng shíjian
hun 很长时间

one day/two days longer
yí/liǎng tiān duō tyen dwor
一／两天多

long-distance call chángtú
diànhuà chahng-too dyen-hwah
长途电话

look: I'm just looking, thanks
wǒ zhǐshi kànyikàn, xièxie wor
jur-shur kahn-yee-kahn hsyeh-
hsyeh 我只是看一看谢谢

you don't look well kànqǐlái,
nǐ shēntǐ bù shūfu kahn-chee-
lai nee shun-tee boo shoo-foo
看起来你身体不舒服

look out! xiǎoxīn! hsyow-hsin
小心

can I have a look? kěyi
kànkan ma? kur-yee kahn-kahn
mah 可以看看吗？

look after zhàokàn jow-kahn
照看

look at kàn kahn 看

look for zhǎo jow 找

I'm looking for-... wǒ zhǎo
... wor jow 我找 ...

look forward to pànwàng pahn-
wahng 盼望

I'm looking forward to it wǒ
pànwàng wor 我盼望

loose (handle etc) sōng soong 松

lorry kǎchē kah-chur 卡车

lose diū dyoh 丢

I'm lost wǒ mílùle wor mee-
loo-lur 我迷路了

I've lost my bag wǒ bǎ dàizi
diūle bah dai-dzur dyoh-lur
我把带子丢了

lost property (office) shīwù
zhāolǐng chù shur-woo jow-ling
choo 失物招领处

lot: a lot, lots hěnduō hun-dwor
很多

not a lot bù duō 不多

a lot of people hěnduō rén
run 很多人

a lot bigger dà de duō dah dur
大得多

I like it a lot wǒ hén xǐhuan wor hun hshee-hwahn
我很喜欢

loud dàshēng de dah-shung dur
大声的

lounge (in house) kètīng kur-ting
客厅

(in hotel) xiūxìshì hsyoh-hshee-shur
休息室

love (*noun*) liànài lyen-ai 恋爱

(*verb*) ài 爱

I love China wǒ ài Zhōngguó
wor ai joong-gwor 我爱中国

lovely (person) kěài kur-ai 可爱

(thing) hěn hǎo hun how
很好

low (bridge) dī 低

(prices) piányide pyen-yee-dur
便宜的

luck yùnqi yewn-chee 运气

good luck! zhù nǐ shùnlì! joo nee shun-lee 祝你顺利

luggage xíngli hsing-lee 行李

luggage trolley xínglichē –chur
行李车

lunch wǔfàn woo-fahn 午饭

luxurious háohuá how-hwah
豪华

luxury (comfort etc) gāojí gow-jee
高级

(extravagance) shēchǐ shur-chee
奢侈

lychee lìzhī lee-jur 荔枝

M

machine jīqì jee-chee 机器

magazine zázhì dzah-jur 杂志

maid (in hotel) nǚ fúwùyuán nyew
foo-woo-yew-ahn 女服务员

mail (*noun*) yóujiàn yoh-jyen 邮件

(*verb*) jì 寄

is there any mail for me?
yǒu wǒde xìn ma? yoh wor-dur
hsin mah 有我的信吗？

mailbox xìnxiāng hsin-hsyahng
信箱

main zhǔyào de joo-yow dur
主要的

main course zhǔcài joo-tsai
主菜

main post office dà yóujú
dah yoh-joo 大邮局

main road dàlù dah-loo 大路

make (brand name) pái 牌

(*verb*) zhìzào jur-dzow 制造

I make it 10 yuan, OK? wǒ
suàn shí kuài qián, hǎo ma? wor
swahn shur kwai chyen how mah
我算十块钱好吗？

what is it made of? zhè shì yòng shénme zào de? jur shur yoong shun-mur dzow dur 这是用什么造的？

make-up huàzhuāngpǐn hwah-jwahng-pin 化妆品

Malaysia Mǎláixīyà mah-lai-hshee-yah 马来西亚

man nánrén nahn-run 男人

manager jīnglǐ 经

can I see the manager? kěyǐ jiànjian jīnglǐ ma? kur-yee jyen-jyen – mah 可以见见经理吗？

Mandarin Pǔtōnghuà poo-toong-hwah 普通话

mandarin orange gānzi gahn-dzur 柑子

many hěn duō hun dwor 很多

not many bù duō 不多

map dìtú 地图

March sānyuè sahn-yew-eh 三月

margarine rénzào huángyóu run-zow hwahng-yoh 人造黄油

market shìchǎng shur-chahng 市场

married: I'm married wǒ jiéhūnle wor jyeh-hun-lur 我结婚了

are you married? nǐ jiéhūnle ma? nee jyeh-hun-lur mah 你结婚了吗？

martial arts wǔshù 武术

mascara jiémáogāo jyeh-mow-gow 睫毛膏

match (sport) bǐsài 比赛

football match zúqiú sài dzoo-chyoh 足球赛

matches huǒchái hwor- 火柴

material (fabric) bù 布

matter: it doesn't matter méi guānxi may gwahn-hshee 没关系

what's the matter? zěnmele? dzun-mur-lur 怎么了？

mattress chuángdiàn chwahng-dyen 床垫

May wǔyuè woo-yew-eh 五月

may: may I have another one? qǐng zài lái yīge ching dzai lai yee-gur 请再来一个

may I come in? wǒ néng jìnlái ma? wor nung jin-lai mah 我能进来吗？

may I see it? wǒ néng kàn ma? kahn 我能看吗？

may I sit here? wǒ néng zuò zhèr ma? zwor jer 我能坐这儿吗？

maybe kěnéng kur-nung 可能

me wǒ wor 我

that's for me zhè shì wǒde jer shur wor-dur 这是我的

send it to me qǐng sòng gěi wǒ ching soong gay 请送给我

me too wǒ yě yur 我也

meal fàn fahn 饭

did you enjoy your meal? chīde hái hǎo ma? chur-dur hai how mah

it was excellent, thank you hěn hǎo, xièxie hun how hsyeh-hsyeh

mean: what do you mean? nǐ zhǐde shì shénme? nee jur-dur shur shun-mur 你指的是什么？

what does this word mean? zhèige cír shì shénme yìsi? jay-gur tsur – yee-sur

it means-… in English yòng yīngwen shì … de yìsi yoong ying-wun – dur

meat ròu roh 肉

medicine (Western) xīyào hshee-yow 西药

(Chinese) zhōngyào joong-yow 中药

medium (adj: size) zhōngděng joong-dung 中等

medium-rare (steak) bànshēng de bahn-shung dur 半生的

medium-sized zhōnghào joong-how 中号

meet pèngjiàn pung-jyen 碰见

nice to meet you jiàndào nǐ hěn gāoxìng jyen-dow nee hun gow-hsing 见到你很高兴

where shall I meet you? wǒ zài nǎr jiàn nǐ? wor dzai-nar jyen 我在哪儿见你？

meeting huì(yì) (hway-yee 会（议）

melon guā gwah 瓜

memory stick shǎnpán shahn-pahn 闪盘

men nánde nahn-dur 男的

mend (machine, bicycle) xiūlǐ hsyoh-lee 修理

(clothes) féngbǔ fung-boo 缝补

could you mend this for me? qǐng gěi wǒ xiūlǐ yíxià hǎo ma? ching gay wor – yee-hsyah how mah 请给我修理一下好吗？

men's room nán cèsuǒ nahn tsur-swor 男厕所

menswear nánzhuāng nahn-jwahng 男装

mention shuōdào shwor-dow 说到

don't mention it búyòng kèqi boo-yoong kur-chee 不用客气

menu càidānr tsai-dahnr 菜单儿

may I see the menu, please? qǐng lái càidānr, hǎo ma? ching lai tsai-dahnr - how mah 请来菜单儿好吗？

see menu reader

message xìnr hsinr 信儿

are there any messages for me? yǒu wǒde xìn shénmede ma? yoh wor-dur hsin shun-mur-dur mah 有我的信什么的吗？

I want to leave a message for-... wǒ xiǎng gěi ... liúge xìnr hsyahng gay ... lyoh-gur 我想给 ... 留个信儿

metal jīnshǔ jin-shoo 金属

metre mǐ 米

midday zhōngwǔ joong-woo 中午

at midday zhōngwǔ 中午

middle: in the middle zài zhōngjiān dzai joong-jyen 在中间

in the middle of the night yèli yur-lee 夜里

the middle one zhōngjiānde joong-jyen-dur 中间的

midnight bànyè bahn-yur 半夜

at midnight bànyè bahn-yur 半夜

might: I might... yěxǔ ... yur-hsoo 也许

I might not... yěxǔ bù ... 也许不 ...

mild (taste) wèidàn wei-dahn 味淡

(weather) nuǎnhuo nwahn-hwor 暖和

mile yīnglǐ 英里

milk niúnǎi nyoh-nai 牛奶

millimetre háomǐ how-mee 毫米

mind: never mind méi guānxi may gwahn-hshee 没关系

I've changed my mind wǒ gǎibiàn zhǔyì le wor gai-byen joo-yee lur 我改变主意了

do you mind if I open the window? wǒ kāi chuāng, xíngbùxíng? chwahng hsing-boo-hsing

no, I don't mind xíng hsing

miss: I missed the bus wǒ méi gǎnshàng chē wor may gahn-shahng chur 我没赶上车

missing: my-… is missing wǒde … diūle wor-dur … dyoh-lur 我的 … 丢了

there's a suitcase missing yíge yīxiāng diūle yee-gur yee-hsyahng dyoh-lur 一个衣箱丢了

mist wù 雾

mistake cuò(wù) tswor– 错（误）

I think there's a mistake zhèr yǒuge cuòr jer yoh-gur tswor-ur 这儿有个错儿

sorry, I've made a mistake dùibùqǐ, wǒ nòngcuòle dway-boo-chee wor noong-tswor-lur 对不起我弄错了

misunderstanding wùhuì woo-hway 误会

mobile phone shǒujī shoh-jee 手机

modern xiàndài hsyen-dai 现代

moisturizer cāliǎnyóu tsah-lyen-yoh 擦脸油

moment: I won't be a moment jiù yìfēn zhōng jyoh yee-fun joong 就一分钟

mine: it's mine shì wǒde shur wor-dur 是我的

mineral water kuàngquánshuǐr kwahng-choo-en-shwayr 矿泉水儿

Ming Tombs shísānlíng shur-sahn-ling 十三陵

minute fēn(zhōng) fun(-joong) 分（钟）

in a minute yìhuǐr yee-hwayr 一会儿

just a minute děng yìhuǐr dung 等一会儿

mirror jìngzi jing-dzur 镜子

Miss xiǎojiě hsyow-jyeh 小姐

monastery (*Buddhist*) sìyuàn sur-yew-ahn 寺院

Monday xīngqīyī hsing-chee-yee 星期一

money qián chyen 钱

Mongolia Ménggǔ mung-goo 蒙古

Mongolian (*adj*) Ménggǔ 蒙古

monk sēng sung 僧

month yuè yew-eh 月

monument jìniànbēi jin-yen-bay 纪念碑

moon yuèliang yew-eh-lyang 月亮

more gèng duō gung dwor 更多

  can I have some more water, please? qǐng zài lái diǎnr shuǐ? ching dzai lai shway 请再来点儿水？

  more expensive gèng guì gung gway 更贵

  more interesting than... bǐ ... gèng yǒu xìngqù yoh hsing-chew 比 ... 更有兴趣

  more than 50/100 wǔshí/yìbǎi duō 五十／一百多

  more than that one bǐ nèige duō nay-gur 比那个多

  a lot more duōde duō dwor-dur 多得多

  would you like some more? nǐ hái yào diǎnr shénme ma? yow dyenr shun-mur mah

  no, no more for me, thanks búyào, xièxie boo-yow hsyeh-hsyeh

  how about you? nǐ ne? nee-nur

  I don't want any more, thanks wǒ bú zàiyàole, xièxie wor boo dzai-yow-lur

morning zǎoshang dzow-shahng 早上

  this morning jīntiān zǎoshang jin-tyen dzow-shahng 今天早上

  in the morning zǎoshang dzow-shahng 早上

mosquito wénzi wun-dzur 蚊子

mosquito net wénzhàng wun-jahng 蚊帐

mosquito repellent qūwénjì chew-wun-jee 驱蚊剂

most: I like this one most of all wǒ zuì xǐhuān zhèige wor dzway hshee-hwahn jay-gur 我最喜欢这个

  most of the time dàbùfen shíjiān dah-boo-fun shur-jyen 大部分时间

most tourists dà duōshù lǚyóuzhě dah dwor-shoo 大多数旅游者

mostly dàduō dah-dwor 大多

mother mǔqīn moo-chin 母亲

mother-in-law pópo por-por 婆婆

motorbike mótuōchē mor-twor-chur 摩托车

motorboat qìtǐng chee-ting 汽艇

mountain shān shahn 山

  in the mountains zài shānlǐ dzai shahn-lee 在山里

mountaineering dēngshān dung-shahn 登山

mouse (computer) shǔbiāo shoo-byow

  (animal) láoshǔ low-shoo 老鼠

moustache xiǎo húzi hsyow hoo-dzur 小胡子

mouth zuǐ dzway 嘴

move: he's moved to another room tā bāndào lìngwài yí jiān qùle tah bahn-dow ling-wai yee jyen choo-lur 他搬到另外一间去了

could you move it? qǐng nín nuó yíxià, hǎo ma? ching nin nwor yee-hsyah how mah 请您挪一下好吗？

could you move up a little? qǐng wǎng qián nuó yíxià, hǎo ma? wahng chyen nwor yee-hsyah 请往前挪一下好吗？

movie diànyǐng dyen-ying 电影

movie theater diànyǐng yuàn dyen-ying yew-ahn 电影院

MP3 format MP sān géshi em-pee sahn gur-shur MP3格式

Mr xiānsheng hsyen-shung 先生

Mrs fūren foo-run 夫人

Ms nǚshì nyew-shur 女士

much duō dwor 多

  much better/worse hǎo/huài de duō dur 好／坏得多

  not (very) much bù hěn duō 不很多

  I don't want very much wǒ búyào tài dūo wor boo-yow 我不要太多

mug (for drinking) bēi bay 杯

  I've been mugged wǒ gěi rén qiǎngle gay run chyang-lur 我给人抢了

mum māma mah-mah 妈妈

museum bówùguǎn bor-woo-gwahn 博物馆

mushrooms mógu mor-goo 蘑菇

music yīnyuè yin-yew-eh 音乐

Muslim (*adj*) mùsīlín moo-sur-lin 穆斯林

must: I must wǒ bìxū wor bee-hsyew 我必须

I mustn't drink alcohol wǒ búhuì hē jiǔ wor-boo-hway hur jyoh 我不会喝酒

my wǒde wor-dur 我的

myself: I'll do it myself wǒ zìjǐ lái wor dzur-jee 我自己来

by myself wǒ yíge rén yee-gur run 我一个人

N

nail (finger) zhǐjiǎ jur-jyah 指甲
(metal) dīngzi ding-dzur 钉子

nail varnish zhǐjiǎ yóu jur-jyah yoh 指甲油

name míngzi ming-dzur 名子

my name's John wǒde míngzi jiào John wor-dur – jyow 我的名子叫John

what's your name? nǐ jiào shénme? nee – shun-mur 你叫什么？

what is the name of this street? zhèi tiào lù jiào shénme? jay tyow 这条路叫什么？

napkin cānjīn tsahn-jin 餐巾

nappy niàobù nyow-boo 尿布

narrow (street) zhǎi jai 窄

nasty (person) ràng rén tǎoyàn rahng run tow-yen 让人讨厌
(weather, accident) zāotòule dzow-toh-lur 糟透了

national (state) guójiā gwor-jyah 国家
(nationwide) quánguó choo-en-gwor 全国

nationality guójí gwor-jee 国籍
(for Chinese minorities) shǎoshù mínzú show-shoo min-dzoo 少数民族

natural zìrán dzur-rahn 自然

near jìn 近

near the ... lí-... hěnjìn hun-jin 离 ... 很近

is it near the city centre? lí-shì zhōngxīn jìn ma? shur joong-hsin jin mah 离市中心近吗？

do you go near the Great Wall? nǐ zài-Chángchéng fùjìn tíngchē ma? nee dzai chahng-chung foo-jin ting-chur mah 你在长城附近停车吗？

where is the nearest-...? zuìjìn de-... zài nǎr? dzway-jin dur-... dzai nar 最近的 ... 在哪儿？

nearby fùjìn foo-jin 附近

nearly chàbuduō chah-boo-dwor
差不多

necessary bìyào(de) bee-yow
(-dur) 必要（的）

neck bózi boh-dzur 脖子

necklace xiàngliàn hsyahng-lyen
项链

necktie lǐngdài 领带

need: I need-... wǒ xūyào-...
wor hsyew-yow 我需要

do I need to pay? wǒ yīnggāi
fùqián ma? foo-chyen mah
我应该付钱吗？

needle zhēn jun 针

neither: neither (one) of them
liǎngge dōu bù lyang-gur doh
两个都不

Nepal Níbóěr nee-bor-er
尼泊尔

Nepali (*adj*) Níbóěr 尼泊尔

nephew zhízi jur-dzur 侄子

net (in sport) wǎng wahng 网

network map jiāotōngtú jyow-
toong-too 交通图

never (not ever) cónglái bù tsoong-
lai 从来不

(not yet) hái méiyou may-yoh
还没有

DIALOGUE

**have you ever been to
Beijing?** nǐ qùguo Běijīng
méiyou? chew-gwor – may-
yoh

**no, never, I've never been
there** cónglái méiqù tsoong-
lai may-chew

new xīn hsin 新

news (radio, TV etc) xīnwén hsin-
wun 新闻

newspaper bào(zhǐ) bow(-jur)
报（纸）

New Year xīnnián hsin-nyen
新年

Chinese New Year chūnjié
chun-jyeh 春节

Happy New Year! xīnnián
hǎo! how 新年好

(Chinese) gōnghè xīnxǐ! goong-
hur hsin-hshee 恭贺新禧

**New Year's Eve: Chinese New
Year's Eve** chúxī choo-hshee
除夕

New Zealand Xīnxīlán hsin-see-
lahn 新西兰

**New Zealander: I'm a New
Zealander** wǒ shì xīnxīlánrén
–run 我是新西兰人

next xià yīge hsyah yee-gur
下一个

the next street on the left zuǒbiānr díyī tiáo lù dzwor-byenr dee-yee tiao 左边儿第一条路

at the next stop xià yízhàn hsyah yee-jahn 下一站

next week xià(ge) xīngqī hsyah(-gur) hsing-chee 下（个）星期

next to... zài-... pángbiān dzai-... pahng-byen 在 ... 旁边

nice (food) hǎochī how-chur 好吃

(looks, view etc) hǎokàn how-kahn 好看

(person) hǎo how 好

niece zhínǚ jin-yew 侄女

night yè yur 夜

at night yèli yur-lee 夜里

good night wǎn ān wahn ahn 晚安

do you have a single room for one night? yǒu yìtiān de dānrén jiān ma? yoh yee-tyen dur dahn-run jyen mah

yes, madam yǒu yoh

how much is it per night? yìwǎn yào duōshaoqián? yee-wahn yow dwor-show-chyen

it's 30 yuan for one night yìwǎn yào sānshí kuài qián sahn-shur – chyen

thank you, I'll take it xíng hsing

nightclub yèzǒnghuì yur-dzoong-hway 夜总会

no bù 不

I've no change wǒ méiyou líng qián wor may-yoh – chyen 我没有零钱

no way! bù xíng! hsing 不行

oh no! (upset) tiān na! tyen nah 天哪

nobody méirén may-run 没人

there's nobody there méirén zài nàr dzai 没人在那儿

noise zàoyīn dzow-yin 噪音

noisy: it's too noisy tài chǎole chow-lur 太吵了

non-alcoholic bù hán jiǔjīng de hahn jyoh-jing dur 不含酒精的

none shénme yě méiyou shun-mur yur may-yoh 什么也没有

noon zhōngwǔ joong-woo 中午

at noon zhōngwǔ 中午

no-one méirén may-run 没人

nor: nor do I wǒ yě bù
wor yur 我也不

normal zhèngcháng(de) jung-
chahng(-dur) 正常（的）

north běi bay 北

  in the north běibian bay-byen
北边

  to the north wǎng běi wahng
往北

  north of Shanghai
Shànghǎi běi 上海北

northeast dōngběi doong-bay
东北

northern běibiān bay-byen 北边

Northern Ireland Běi Àiěrlán
bay ai-er-lahn 北爱尔兰

North Korea Běi Cháoxiān bay
chow-hsyen 北朝鲜

northwest xīběi hshee-bay 西北

Norway Nuówēi nwor-way
挪威

Norwegian (*adj*: language)
Nuówēiyǔ 挪威语

nose bízi bee-dzur 鼻子

not bù 不

  no, I'm not hungry wǒ búè
wor bway 我不饿

  I don't want any, thank you
búyào, xièxie boo-yow hsyeh-
hsyeh 不要谢谢

it's not necessary búbìyào
不必要

I didn't know that wǒ
bù zhīdao wor boo jur-dow
我不知道

not that one, this one búyào
nèige, yào zhèige nay-gur yow
jay-gur 不要那个要这个

note (banknote) chāopiào chow-
pyow 钞票

notebook bǐjìběn bee-jee-bun
笔记本

nothing méiyou shénme may-yoh
shun-mur 没有什么

  nothing for me, thanks wǒ
shénme dōu bú yào, xièxie
wor – doh boo yow hsyeh-hsyeh
我什么都不要谢谢

  nothing else, thanks qítade
búyào, xièxie chee-tah-dur boo-
yow 其他的不要谢谢

novel (*noun*) xiǎoshuō hsyow-
shwor 小说

November shíyīyuè shur-yee-
yew-eh 十一月

now xiànzài hsyen-dzai 现在

number hàomǎ how-mah 号码
(figure) shùzì shoo-dzur 数字

  I've got the wrong number
wǒ dǎcuòle wor dah-tswor-lur
我打错了

what is your phone number? nǐde diànhuà hàomǎ shì duōshao? nee-dur dyen-hwah shur dwor-show 你的电话号码是多少？

number plate chēpái chur-pai 车牌

nurse hùshi hoo-shur 护士

nut (for bolt) luósī lwor-sur 螺丝

nuts (chestnuts) lìzi lee-dzur 栗子

(hazelnuts) zhēnzi jun-dzur 榛子

(walnuts) hétao hur-tow 核桃

O

occupied (toilet) yǒurén yoh-run 有人

o'clock diǎnzhōng dyen-joong 点钟

October shíyuè shur-yew-eh 十月

odd (strange) qíguài chee-gwai 奇怪

of de dur 的

off (lights, machine) guān shangle gwahn shahng-lur 关上了

it's just off... (street etc) lí ... bùyuán boo-ywahn 离 ... 不远

we're off tomorrow wǒmen míngtian zǒu wor-mun ming-tyen dzoh 我们明天走

office (place of work) bàngōngshì bahn-goong-shur 办公室

often jīngcháng jing-chahng 经常

not often bù jīngcháng boo jing-chahng 不经常

how often are the buses? yíge zhōngtóu duōshao qìchē? yee-gur joong-toh dwor-show chee-chur 一个钟头多少汽车？

oil (for car) yóu yoh 油

vegetable oil càiyóu tsai-yoh 菜油

oily (food) yóunì yoh-nee 油腻

ointment yàogāo yow-gow 药膏

OK hǎo how 好

are you OK? hái hǎo ma? mah 还好吗？

I feel OK hěn hǎo hun 很好

is that OK with you? xíng bù xíng? hsing 行不行？

is it OK to-...? wǒ kěyi ...? wor kur-yee 我可以 ... ？

that's OK, thanks xíngle xièxie hsing-lur hsyeh-hsyeh 行了谢谢

is this train OK for-...?
zhè liè huǒchē qù … ma? jer
lyeh hwor-chur chew … mah
这列火车去 … 吗？

old (person) lǎo low 老

(thing) jiù jyoh 旧

how old are you? nín
duō dà niánlíng? dwor dah
nyen-ling

(to an old person) nín duō dà
niánjì le? dwor dah nyen-jee
lur

(to a child) nǐ jǐsuì le?
jee-sway lur

I'm 25 wǒ èrshíwǔ suì
wor – sway

and you? nǐ ne? nur

old-fashioned guòshí(de) gwor-
shur(-dur) 过时（的）

(person) shǒujiù(de) shoh-jyoh(-
dur) 守旧（的）

old town (old part of town)
jiùchéng jyoh-chung 旧城

omelette chǎojīdàn chow-jee-
dahn 炒鸡蛋

on: on... (on top of) zài-…
shàngmian dzai-… shahng-myen
在 … 上面

on the street zài-lùshàng
在路上

on the beach zài-hǎitān
shàng 在海滩上

is it on this road?
zài-zhètíaolù ma? jur-tyow-loo
mah 在这条路吗？

on the plane zài-fēijī shàng
在飞机上

on Saturday xīngqī liù lyoh
星期六

on television zài diànshìshang
在电视上

I haven't got it on me
wǒ méi dài zài shēnshang
wor may dai dzai shun-shahng
我没带在身上

this one's on me (drink)
wǒ fùqián wor foo-choo-en
我付钱

the light wasn't on dēng méi
kāi dung may 灯没开

what's on tonight? jīntiān
wǎnshang yǒu shénme
huódòng? jin-tyen wahn-
shahng you shun-mur hwor-dong
今天晚上有什么活动？

once (one time) yícì yee-tsur 一次

at once (immediately) mǎshàng
mah-shahng 马上

one yī yee 一

the white one báisè de bai-sur
dur 白色的

one-way ticket dānchéng piào dahn-chung pyow 单程票

onion yángcōng yang-tsoong 洋葱

online (book, check) zàixiàn dzai-hsyen 在线

only zhǐ yǒu jur yoh 只有

    only one zhǐ yǒu yíge yee-gur 只有一个

    it's only 6 o'clock cái liùdiǎn tsai lyoh-dyen 才六点

    I've only just got here wǒ gāng dào le wor gahng dow lur 我刚到了

on/off switch kāiguān kai-gwahn 开关

open (adj) kāi(de) kai(-dur) 开（的）

    (verb) kāi 开

    when do you open? nǐmen shénme shíhou kāiménr? nee-mun shun-mur shur-hoh kai-munr 你们什么时候开门儿？

    I can't get it open wǒ dǎbukāi wor dah-boo--kai 我打不开

    in the open air zài shìwài dzai shur-wai 在室外

opening times yíngyè shíjiān ying-yur shur-jyen 营业时间

opera gējù gur-jyew 歌剧

> **Travel tip** Chinese opera is a unique combination of song, dance, acrobatics and mime. It's highly stylized, with every aspect of the performance, from costumes and make-up to movements, imbued with a specific symbolic meaning. The main barrier to appreciation for the uninitiated is the percussive din of the accompanying orchestra.

operation (medical) shǒushù shoh-shoo 手术

operator (telephone) zǒngjī dzoong-jee 总机

opposite: the opposite direction xiāngfǎn de fāngxiàng hsyahng-fahn dur fahng-hsyahng 相反的方向

    the bar opposite zài duìmianr de jiǔba dzai dway-myenr dur 在对面儿的酒吧

    opposite my hotel zài wǒ fàndiàn duìmianr 在我饭店对面儿

optician yǎnjìngdiàn yen-jing-dyen 眼镜店

or (in statement) huòzhě hwor-jur 或者

    (in question) háishi hai-shur 还是

orange (fruit) júzi joo-dzur 橘子

(colour) júhuángsè jyew-sur
橘黄色

orange juice (fresh) xiānjúzhī
hsyen-jyew-jur 鲜橘汁

(fizzy) júzi qìshuǐ jyew-dzur chee-
shway 橘子汽水

(diluted) júzishuǐr jyew-dzur-
shwayr 橘子水儿

order: can we order now? (in
restaurant) wǒmen kěyǐ diǎncài
ma? wor-mun kur-yee dyen-tsai
mah 我们可以点菜吗？

**I've already ordered,
thanks** yǐjīng diǎn le, xièxie
yee-jing dyen lur hsyeh-hsyeh
已经点了谢谢

I didn't order this wǒ
méiyǒu diǎn zhèige cài wor
may-yoh dyen jay-gur tsai
我没有点这个菜

out of order huàile hwai-lur
坏了

ordinary pǔtōng poo-toong 普通

other qítā chee-tah 其他

the other one lìng yíge yee-
gur 另一个

the other day zuìjìn dzway-jin
最近

I'm waiting for the others
wǒ děngzhe qíyúde wor dung-jer
chee-yoo-dur 我等着其余的

do you have any others?
(other kinds) hái yǒu biéde
ma? yoh byeh-dur mah
还有别的吗？

otherwise yàobùrán yow-boor-
ahn 要不然

our/ours wǒmende wor-mun-dur
我们的

out: he's out tā chūqule tah
choo-chew-lur 他出去了

**three kilometres out of
town** lí shìqū sān gōnglǐ
shur-chew – goong-lee
离市区三公里

outdoors lùtiān loo-tyen 露天

outside wàimian wai-myen 外面

can we sit outside?
wǒmen kěyǐ dào wàimian
qù zuò ma? wor-mun kur-yee
dow wai-myen chew dzwor
mah 我们可以到外面
去坐吗？

oven kǎoxiāng kow-syang 烤箱

over: over here zài zhèr dzai jer
在这儿

over there zài nàr 在那儿

over 500 wǔbǎi duō dwor
五百多

it's over wánle wahn-lur 完了

overcharge:
you've overcharged me

nǐ duōshōule wǒde qián

dwor-shoh-lur wor-dur chyen

你多收了我的钱

overland mail lùshang yóudì

loo-shahng yoh-dee

陆上邮递

overnight (travel) guòyè gwor-yur

过夜

overtake chāoguò chow-gwor

超过

**owe: how much do I owe
you?** yígòng duōshao qián?

yee-goong dwor-show chyen

一共多少钱？

own: my own-... wǒ zìjǐde-...

wor dzur-jur-dur 我自己的 ...

are you on your own? jiù nǐ
yíge rén ma? jyoh nee yee-gur run
mah 就你一个人吗？

I'm on my own jiù wǒ yíge
rén jyoh wor yee-gur run 就我
一个人

P

pack (verb) shōushi shoh-shur

收拾

package (parcel) bāoguǒ bow-
gwor 包裹

packed lunch héfàn hur-fahn

盒饭

packet: a packet of cigarettes

yìbāo yān yee-bow yen

一包烟

paddy field dàotián dow-tyen

稻田

page (of book) yè yur 页

could you page Mr-...?

nǐ néng jiào yíxia-...
xiānsheng ma? nung jyow
yee-hsyah-... hsyen-shung
mah 你能叫一下 ...
先生吗？

pagoda tǎ tah 塔

pain téng tung 疼

I have a pain here wǒ zhèr
téng wor jer 我这儿疼

painful téng 疼

painkillers zhǐténgyào jur-tung-
yow 止疼药

painting huà hwah 画

(oil) yóuhuà yoh-hwah 油画

(Chinese) guóhuà gwor-hwah
国画

pair: a pair of-... yíduìr-... yee-
dwayr 一对儿 ...

Pakistani (adj) Bājīsītǎn bah-jee-
sur-tahn 巴基斯坦

palace gōngdiàn goong-dyen
宫殿

pale cāngbái tsahng-bai 苍白

pale blue dàn lánsè dahn lahn-sur 淡蓝色

panda dà xióngmāo dah hsyoong-mow 大熊猫

pants (underwear: men's) kùchǎ koo-chah 裤衩

(women's) xiǎo sānjiǎokù hsyow sahn-jyow-koo 小三角裤

(US: trousers) kùzi koo-dzur 裤子

pantyhose liánkùwà lyen-koo-wah 连裤袜

paper zhǐ jur 纸

(newspaper) bàozhǐ bow-jur 报纸

a piece of paper yìzhāng zhǐ yee-jahng jur 一张纸

paper handkerchiefs zhǐjīn jur-jin 纸巾

parcel bāoguǒ bow-gwor 包裹

pardon (me)? (didn't understand/hear) nǐ shuō shénme? shwor shun-mur 你说什么？

parents fùmǔ 父母

park (*noun*) gōngyuán goong-yew-ahn 公园

(*verb*) tíngchē ting-chur 停车

can I park here? wǒ néng zài zhèr tíngchē ma? wor nung dzai-jer ting-chur mah 我能在这儿停车吗？

parking lot tíngchē chǎng ting-chur chahng 停车场

part (*noun*) bùfen 部分

partner (boyfriend, girlfriend etc) bànr bahnr 伴儿

party (group) tuántǐ twahn-tee 团体

(celebration) wǎnhuì wahn-hway 晚会

passenger chéngkè chung-kur 乘客

passport hùzhào hoo-jow 护照

password mìmǎ mee-mah 密码

past: in the past guòqu gwor-chew 过去

just past the information office gāng jīngguò wènxùnchù gahng jing-gwor wun-hsun-choo 刚经过问讯处

path xiǎolù hsyow-loo 小路

pattern tú'àn too-ahn 图案

pavement rénxíng dào run-hsing dow 人行道

pavilion tíngzi ting-dzur 亭子

pay (*verb*) fù qián foo(-chyen) 付钱

can I pay, please? suànzhàng ba? swahn-jahng bah 算帐吧？

it's already paid for
zhèige yǐjīng fùqián le jay-
gur yee-jing foo-chyen lur
这个已经付钱了

who's paying? shúi fùqián?
shway foo-chyen

I'll pay wǒ fùqián wor foo-
chyen

**no, you paid last time, I'll
pay** bù, nǐ shì zuìhòu yícì
fùde, wǒ fùqián shur dzway-
hoh yee-tsur foo-dur

payphone jìfèi diànhuà jee-fay
dyen-hwah 计费电话

peaceful ānjìng ahn-jing 安静

peach táozi tow-dzur 桃子

peanuts huāshēng hwah-shung
花生

pear lí lee 梨

peculiar (taste, custom) guài
gwai 怪

pedestrian crossing rénxíng
héngdào run-hsing hung-dow
人行横道

Peking Opera Jīngjù jing-jew
京剧

pen gāngbǐ gahng-bee 钢笔

pencil qiānbǐ chyen-bee 铅笔

penfriend bǐyǒu bee-yoh 笔友

penicillin pánníxīlín pahn-nee-
see-lin 盘尼西林

penknife qiānbǐdāo chyen-bee-
dow 铅笔刀

pensioner lǐng yǎnglǎojīn
de rén yang-low-jin dur run
领养老金的人

people rénmín run-min 人民

**the other people in the
hotel** fàndiàn li de qítā kèrén
lee dur chee-tah ker-run 饭
店里的其他客人

too many people rén tài duō
le run tai dwor-lur 人太多了

People's Republic of China
Zhōnghuá Rénmín Gònghéguó
joong-hwah run-min goong-hur-
gwor 中华人民共和国

pepper (spice) hújiāo hoo-jyow
胡椒

(vegetable, red) shìzijiāo shur-
dzur-jyow 柿子椒

per: per night měi wǎn may
wahn 每晚

how much per day?
yìtiān yào duōshao qián?
yee-tyen yow dwor-show chyen
一天要多少钱？

... per cent bǎifēn zhī-... bai-
fun jur 百分之 ...

perfect wánměi wahn-may 完美

perfume xiāngshuǐr hsyahng-shwayr 香水儿

perhaps kěnéng kur-nung 可能

perhaps not kěnéng bù 可能不

period (of time) shíqī shur-chee 时期

(menstruation) yuèjīng yew-eh-jing 月经

permit (noun) xǔkě zhèng hsyew-kur jung 许可证

person rén run 人

personal stereo fàngyīnjī fahng-yin-jee 放音机

petrol qìyóu chee-yoh 汽油

petrol can yóutǒng yoh-toong 油桶

petrol station jiāyóu zhàn jyah-yoh jahn 加油站

pharmacy yàodiàn yow-dyen 药店

Philippines Fēilǜbīn fay-lew-bin 菲律宾

phone (noun) diànhuà dyen-hwah 电话

(verb) dǎ diànhuà dah 打电话

phone book diànhuà bù dyen-hwah 电话簿

phone box diànhuàtíng 电话亭

phonecard diànhuàkǎ dyen-hwah-kah 电话卡

phone charger shǒujī chōngdiànqì shoh-jee choong-dyen-chee 手机充电器

phone number diànhuà hàomǎ how-mah 电话号码

photo zhàopiàn jow-pyen 照片

could you take a photo of us, please? qǐng gěi wǒ zhàozhāng xiàng ching gay-wor jow-jahng hsyahng 请给我照张相

phrasebook duìhuà shǒucè dway-hwah shoh-tsur 对话手册

piano gāngqín gahng-chin 钢琴

pickpocket páshǒu pah-shoh 扒手

pick up: will you be there to pick me up? nǐ lái jiē wǒ hǎo ma? ni lai jyeh wor how mah 你来接我好吗？

picnic (noun) yěcān yur-tsahn 野餐

picture (painting) huà hwah 画

(photo) zhàopiàn jow-pyen 照片

piece kuàir kwair 块儿

a piece of-... yíkuàir-... yee-kwair 一块儿 ...

pig zhū joo 猪

pill bìyùnyào bee-yewn-yow
避孕药

I'm on the pill wǒ chī
bìyùnyào wor chur bee-yew-nyow
我吃避孕药

pillow zhèntou jun-toh 枕头

pillow case zhěntào jun-tow
枕套

pin (*noun*) biézhēn byeh-jun 别针

pineapple bōluó bor-lwor 菠萝

pineapple juice bōluózhī bor-
lwor-jur 菠萝汁

pink fěnhóng fun-hoong 粉红

pipe (for smoking) yāndǒu yen-doh
烟斗

(for water) guǎnzi gwahn-dzur
管子

pity: it's a pity zhēn kěxī jun kur-
hshee 真可惜

place (*noun*) dìfāng dee-fahng
地方

at your place zài nǐde jiā dzai
nee-dur jyah 在你的家

plane fēijī fay-jee 飞机

by plane zuò fēijī dzwor fēijī
坐飞机

plant zhíwù jur-woo 植物

plasters xiàngpí gāo syang-pee
gow 橡皮膏

plastic sùliào soo-lyow 塑料

plastic bag sùliàodài 塑料袋

plate pánzi pahn-dzur 盘子

platform zhàntái jahn-tai 站台

**which platform is it for
Beijing?** wǎng Běijīng de
huǒchē cóng jǐhào zhàntái
kāichū? wahng – dur hwor-chur
tsoong jee-how jahn-tai kai-choo
往北京的火车从几号
站台开出？

play (*verb*) wánr wahnr 玩儿

(*noun*: in theatre) huàjù hwah-jew
话剧

pleasant lìngrén yúkuài ling-run
yew-kwai 令人愉快

please qǐng ching 请

yes, please hǎo, xièxie how
hsyeh-hsyeh 好谢谢

could you please-...? qǐng
nín-..., hǎo ma? mah 请您 …
好吗？

please don't qǐng nín-bù
请您不

**pleased: pleased to meet
you** hěn gāoxìng jiàndào
nǐ hun gow hsing jyen dow
很高兴见到你

pleasure: my pleasure méi shìr
may shur 没事儿

plenty: plenty of-... xǔduō-...
hsyew-dwor 许多

there's plenty of time hǎo duō shíjian how dwor shur-jyen 好多时间

that's plenty, thanks gòule, xièxie goh-lur hsyeh-hsyeh 够了谢谢

plug (electrical) chātóu chah-toh 插头

(in sink) sāizi sai-dzur 塞子

plum lǐzi lee-dzur 李子

plumber guǎnzigōng gwahn-dzur-goong 管子工

p.m. xiàwǔ hsyah-woo 下午

pocket kǒudàir koh-dair 口袋儿

point: two point five èr diǎn wǔ dyen 二点五

there's no point bù zhíde jur-dur 不值得

poisonous yǒudúde yoh-doo-dur 有毒的

police jǐngchá jing-chah 警察

call the police! kuài jiào jǐngchá! kwai jyow jing-chah 快叫警察

policeman jǐngchá jing-chah 警察

police station pàichūsuǒ pai-choo-swor 派出所

polish (for shoes) xiéyóu hsyeh-yoh 鞋油

polite kèqi kur-chee 客气

polluted wūrǎnle de woo-rahn-lur dur 污染了的

pool (for swimming) yóuyǒngchí yoh-yoong-chur 游泳池

poor (not rich) qióng chyoong 穷 (quality) lièzhì lyeh-jur 劣质

pop music liúxíng yīnyuè lyoh-hsing yin-yew-eh 流行音乐

pop singer liúxíng gēshǒu gur-shoh 流行歌手

pork zhūròu joo-roh 猪肉

port (for boats) gǎngkǒu gahng-koh 港口

porter (in hotel) ménfáng mun-fahng 门房

possible kěnéng kur-nung 可能

is it possible to-...? kěyǐ... ma? yoh 可以 ... 吗？

as-... as possible jǐn kěnéng 尽可能

post (noun: mail) yóujiàn yoh-jyen 邮件

(verb) jì jee 寄

could you post this letter for me? qǐng bāng wǒ bǎ zhèifēng xìn jìzǒu, hǎo ma? ching bahng wor bah jay-fung hsin jee-dzoh how mah 请帮我把这封信寄走好吗？

postbox xìnxiāng hsin-hsyahng
信箱

postcard míngxìnpiàn ming-hsin-pyen 名信片

poster zhāotiē jow-tyeh 招贴

poste restante dàilǐng yóujiàn yoh-jyen 待领邮件

post office yóujú yoh-jew 邮局

potato tǔdòu too-doh 土豆

potato chips (US) zhá tǔdòupiànr jah too-doh-pyenr 炸土豆片儿

pound (money) yīngbàng ying-bahng 英镑

(weight) bàng bahng 磅

power cut tíngdiàn ting-dyen 停电

power point diànyuán chāzuò dyen-yew-ahn chah-dzwor 电源插座

practise: I want to practise my Chinese wǒ xiǎng liànxí jiǎng Zhōngwén wor hsyahng lyen-hshee jyang joong-wun 我想练习讲中文

prawn crackers xiābǐng hsyah-bing 虾饼

prawns duìxiā dway-hsyah 对虾

prefer: I prefer-... wǒ gèng xǐhuan-... wor gung see-hwahn 我更喜欢 …

pregnant huáiyùn hwai-yewn
怀孕

prescription (for medicine) yàofāng yow-fahng 药方

present (gift) lǐwù 礼物

president (of country) zóngtǒng dzoong-toong 总统

pretty piàoliang pyow-lyang
漂亮

it's pretty expensive tài guìle gway-lur 太贵了

price jiàgé jyah-gur 价格

prime minister shǒuxiàng shoh-hsyahng 首相

printed matter yìnshuāpǐn yin-shwah-pin 印刷品

prison jiānyù jyen-yew 监狱

private sīrén(de) sur-run(-dur)
私人（的）

private bathroom sīrén(de)yùshì –yoo-shur 私人（的）浴室

probably dàgài dah-gai 大概

problem wèntí wun-tee
问题

no problem! méi wèntí! may
没问题

programme (theatre) jiémùdānr jyeh-moo-dahnr 节目单儿

pronounce: how is this pronounced? zhège zì zěnme

fāyīn? jay-gur dzur dzun-mur fah-yin 这个字怎么发音？

Protestant xīnjiàotú hsin-jyow-too 新教徒 **public convenience** gōnggòng cèsuǒ goong-goong tsur-swor 公共厕所

public holiday gōngjià goong-jyah 公假

pull lā lah 拉

pullover tàoshān mow-bay-hsin 套衫

puncture (*noun*) pǎoqì pow-chee 跑气

purple zǐ dzur 紫

purse (for money) qiánbāo chyen-bow 钱包

(US: handbag) shǒutíbāo shoh-tee-bow 手提包

push tuī tway 推

put fàng fahng 放

where can I put-...? wǒ bǎ-... fàng zai nǎr? wor bah--dzai 我把 ... 放在哪儿？

could you put us up for the night? wǒmen kěyi zài zhèr guò yíyè ma? wor-mun kur-yee – jer gwor yee-yur mah 我们可以在这儿过一夜吗？

pyjamas shuìyī shway-yee 睡衣

Q

quality zhìliàng jur-lyang 质量

quarter sì fēn zhī yī sur fun jur yee 四分之一

question wèntí wun-tee 问题

queue (*noun*) duì dway 队

quick kuài kwai 快

that was quick zhēn kuài jun kwai 真快

what's the quickest way there? něitiáo lù zuì jìn? nay-tyow loo zway 哪条路最近？

quickly hěn kuài di hun kwai 很快的

quiet (place, hotel) ānjìng ahn-jing 安静

quite (fairly) xiāngdāng hsyahng-dahng 相当

that's quite right duì jíle dway-jee-lur 对极了

quite a lot xiāngdāng duō hsyahng-dahng dwor 相当多

R

rabbit (meat) tùzi too-dzur 兔子

race (for runners, cars) bǐsài bee-sai 比赛

racket (tennis, squash) qiúpāi chyoh-pai 球拍

radiator (in room) nuǎnqì nwahn-chee 暖器

(of car) sànrèqì sahn-rur-chee 散热器

radio shōuyīnjī shoh-yin-jee 收音机

on the radio zài shōuyīnjīlǐ dzai – lee 在收音机里

rail: by rail zuò huǒchē dzwor hwor-chur 坐火车

railway tiělù tyeh-loo 铁路

rain (*noun*) yǔ yew 雨

in the rain zài yǔli dzai yew-lee 在雨里

it's raining xià yǔ le hsyah yew lur 下雨了

raincoat yǔyī yew-yee 雨衣

rape (*noun*) qiángjiān chyang-jyen 强奸

rare (uncommon) xīyǒu hshee-yoh 稀有

(steak) nèn diǎnr nun dyenr 嫩点儿

rash (on skin) pízhěn pee-jun 皮疹

rat láoshǔ low-shoo 老鼠

rate (for changing money) duìhuànlǜ dway-hwahn-lyew 兑换率

rather: it's rather good búcuò boo-tswor 不错

I'd rather-... wǒ nìngkě... wor ning-kur 我宁可 ...

razor (wet) tìxúdāo tee-hsyew-dow 剃须刀

(electric) diàntìdāo dyen-tee-dow 电剃刀

razor blades tìxú dāopiàn tee-hsyew dow-pyen 剃须刀片

read (book) kànshū kahn-shoo 看书

(newspaper) kànbào kahn-bow 看报

ready zhǔnbèi hǎole jun-bay how-lur 准备好了

are you ready? zhǔnbèi hǎole ma? mah 准备好了吗？

I'm not ready yet wǒ hái méi hǎo ne wor hai may how nur 我还没好呢

real (genuine) zhēn de jun dur
真的

really zhēnde jun-dur 真的

I'm really sorry zhēn duìbuqǐ
jun dway-boo-chee 真对不起

that's really great bàngjíle
bahng-jee-lur 棒极了

really? (doubt) shì ma? shur mah
是吗？

(polite interest) zhēnde ma? mah
真的吗？

reasonable (prices etc) hélǐ hur-
lee 合理

receipt shōujù shoh-jyew 收据

recently zuìjìn dzway-jin 最近

reception (in hotel) fúwùtái foo-
wnn-tai 服务台

(for guests) zhāodàihuì jow-dai-
hway 招待会

reception desk zǒng fúwùtái
dzoong foo-woo-tai 总服务台

receptionist fúwùyuán foo-woo-
yew-ahn 服务员

recognize rènshi run-shur 认识

**recommend: could you
recommend-...?** qǐng
nín tuījiàn-..., hǎo ma?
ching nin tway-jyen-... how
mah**v**请您推荐 … 好吗？

red hóngsède hoong-sur-dur
红色的

red wine hóng pútaojiǔ hoong
poo-tow-jyoh 红葡萄酒

refund (noun) tuìkuǎn tway-kwahn
退款

can I have a refund?
qǐng nín ba qián tuì gěi
wǒ hǎo ma? ching nin bah
chyen tway gay wor how mah
请您把钱退给我好吗？

region dìqū dee-chew 地区

**registered: by registered
mail** guàhàoxìn gwah-how-hsin
挂号信

registration number chēhào
chur-how 车号

religion zōngjiào dzoong-jyow
宗教

remember: I don't remember
wǒ jìbudé le wor jee-boo-dur lur
我记不得了

I remember wǒ jìdé wor jee-dur 我记得

do you remember? nǐ jìde ma? nee jee-dur mah 你记得吗？

rent (noun: for apartment etc) fángzū fahng-dzoo 房租

(verb: car etc) chūzū choo-dzoo 出租

to rent chūzū 出租

I'd like to rent a bike wǒ xiǎng zū yīliàng zìxíng chē wor hsyahng dzoo yee-lyang dzur-hsing chur 我想租一辆自行车

repair (verb) xiūlǐ hsyoh-lee 修理

can you repair it? nǐ kěyi xiūxiu ma? kur-yee hsyoh-hsyoh mah 你可以修修吗？

repeat chóngfù choong-foo 重复

could you repeat that?
qǐng nǐ zài shuō yíbiàn, hǎo ma? ching nee dzai shwor yee-byen how mah 请你再说一遍好吗？

reservation yùdìng yew-ding 预订

I'd like to make a reservation for a train ticket

wǒ xiǎng yùdìng huǒchēpiào wor hsyahng yew-ding hwor-chur-pyow 我想预订火车票

I have a reservation wǒ yǐjing yùdìng le yee-jing –lur

yes sir, what name, please? hǎo, nín guì xìng? how nin gway hsing

reserve (verb) yùdìng yew-ding 预订

can I reserve a table for tonight? wǒ kěyi dìng ge jīntiān wǎnshang de zuò ma? kur-yee ding gur jin-tyen wah-shahng dur dzwor mah

yes madam, for how many people? hǎo, yígòng jǐge rén? how yee-goong jee-gur run

for two liǎngge rén lyang-gur run

and for what time? jǐdiǎn zhōng? jee-dyen joong

for eight o'clock bā diǎn zhōng bah dyen

and could I have your name, please? hǎo, nín guì xìng? how nin gway hsing

rest: I need a rest wǒ xūyào xiūxi yíxià wor hsyew-yow

hsyoh-hshee yee-hsyah

我需要休息一下

the rest of the group tāmen
biéde rén tah-mun byeh-dur 他
们别的人

restaurant cāntīng tsahn-ting
餐厅

(big) fàndiàn fahn-dyen 饭店

(small) fànguǎnr fahn-gwahnr
饭馆儿

(Western-style) xīcāntīng hshee-
tsahn-ting 西餐厅

restaurant car cānchē tsahn-chur
餐车

rest room cèsuǒ tsur-swor 厕所

retired: I'm retired wǒ tuìxiūle
wor tway-hsyoh-lur 我退休了

return: a return to-... dào-...
de láihuí piào dow-... dur lai-
hway pyow 到 ... 的来回票

return ticket láihuí piào
来回票

reverse charge call duìfāng
fùkuǎn dway-fahng foo-kwahn
对方付款

revolting ràng rén ěxīn rahng run
ur-hsin 让人恶心

rice (cooked) mǐfàn mee-fahn
米饭

(uncooked) dàmǐ dah-mee
大米

rice bowl fànwǎn fahn-wahn
饭碗

rice field dàotián dow-tyen 稻田

rice wine mǐjiǔ mee-jyoh 米酒

rich (person) yǒuqián yoh-chyen
有钱

ridiculous kěxiàode kur-hsyow-
dur 可笑的

right (correct) duì dway 对

(not left) yòu(biānr) yoh(-byenr)
右（边儿）

you were right nǐ duìle nee
dway-lur 你对了

that's right duì le 对了

this can't be right zhè búduì
jur boo-dway 这不对

right! duì! 对

is this the right road for-...?
qù-..., zhème zǒu duì ma?
chew-... jur-mur dzoh dway mah?
去 ... 这么走对吗？

on the right zài yòubiānr dzai
在右边儿

turn right wǎng yòu guǎi
wahng yoh gwai 往右拐

ring (on finger) jièzhi jyeh-jur
戒指

I'll ring you wǒ géi nǐ dǎ
diànhuà wor gay nee dah dyen-
hwah 我给你打电话

ring back zài dǎ diànhuà dzai

再打电话

ripe (fruit) shú shoo 熟

rip-off: it's a rip-off zhè shì

qiāozhúgàng jur shur chyow-joo-

gahng 这是敲竹杠

rip-off prices qiāozhúgàng

de jiàr chyow-joo-gahng dur jyahr

敲竹杠的价儿

risky màoxiǎn mow-hsyen 冒险

river hé hur 河

RMB rénmínbì run-min-bee

人民币

road lù 路

is this the road for-…? zhèi

tiáo lù wǎng … qù?

jay tyow loo wahng … chew

这条路往 … 去？

rob: I've been robbed wǒ bèi

rén qiǎngle wor bay run chyang-

lur 我被人抢了

Travel tip Flashing expensive jewellery, watches or
cash on the street will attract
unwanted attention. Not
looking obviously wealthy
also helps you avoid being
ripped off by street traders
and taxi drivers, as does
telling them you're a student
– the Chinese have huge
respect for education.

---

rock yánshí yen-shur 岩石

(music) yáogǔn yuè yow-gun

yew-eh 摇滚乐

on the rocks (with ice) jiā

bīngkuàir jyah bing-kwair

加冰块儿

roll (bread) miànbāo juǎnr myen-

bow jyew-ahnr 面包卷儿

roof fángdǐng fahng-ding 房顶

room (hotel) fángjiān fahng-jyen

房间

(space) kōngjiān koong-jyen

空间

in my room zài wǒ fángjiānli

dzai 在我房间里

room service sòngfàn fúwù

soong-fahn foo-woo 送饭服务

rope shéngzi shung-dzur 绳子

roughly (approximately) dàyuē dah-

yew-eh 大约

round: it's my round gāi wǒ mǎi

le gai wor mai lur 该我买了

round trip ticket láihuí piào lai-

hway pyow 来回票

route lùxiàn loo-hsyen 路线

what's the best route?

něitiáo lùxiàn zuì hǎo? nay-

tyow loo-hsyen dzway how

哪条路线最好？

rubber (material) xiàngjiāo

hsyahng-jyow 橡胶

(eraser) xiàngpí hsyahng-pee
橡皮

rubbish (waste) lājī lah-jee 垃圾

(poor-quality goods) fèiwù fay-woo
废物

rubbish! (nonsense) fèihuà! fay-hwah 废话

rucksack bèibāo bay-bow 背包

rude bù lǐmào lee-mow 不礼貌

ruins fèixū fay-hsyew 废墟

rum lángmǔjiǔ lahng-moo-jyoh
朗姆酒

rum and Coke kěkǒukělè
jiā lángmǔjiǔ kur-koh-
kur-lur jyah lahng-moo-jyoh
可口可乐加朗姆酒

run (verb: person) pǎo pow 跑

how often do the buses run? gōnggòng qìchē duóchang shíjian yítàng? goong-goong chee-chur dwor-chahng shur-jyen yee-tahng
公共汽车多长时间一趟？

Russia Éguó ur-gwor 俄国

Russian (adj) Éguó 俄国

S

saddle (for horse) ānzi ahn-dzur
鞍子

safe (not in danger) píng'ān
平安

(not dangerous) ānquán ahn-choo-en 安全

safety pin biézhēn byeh-jun
别针

sail (noun) fān fahn 帆

salad shālà shah-lah 沙拉

salad dressing shālà yóu yoh
沙拉油

sale: for sale chūshòu choo-shoh
出售

salt yán yahn 盐

same: the same yíyàng yee-yang
一样

the same as this gēn zhèige yíyàng gun jay-gur yee-yang
跟这个一样

the same again, please qǐng zài lái yíge ching dzai lai yee-gur
请再来一个

it's all the same to me wǒ wú suǒwèi wor woo swor-way
我无所谓

sandals liángxié lyang-hsyeh
凉鞋

sandwich sānmíngzhì sahn-ming-jur 三明治

sanitary napkins/towels
wèishēngjīn way-shung-jin

卫生巾

Saturday xīngqīliù hsing-chee-lyoh 星期六

say (*verb*) shuō shwor 说

how do you say-…-in Chinese? yòng Zhōngwén zěnme shuō-…? yoong joong-wun dzun-mur shwor 用中文怎么说…？

what did he say? tā shuō shénme? tah – shun-mur 他说什么？

he said tā shuō tah 他说

could you say that again? qǐng zài shuō yíbiàn ching dzai – yee-byen 请再说一遍

scarf (for neck) wéijīn way-jin 围巾

(for head) tóujīn toh-jin 头巾

scenery fēngjǐng fung-jing 风景

schedule (US: train) lièchē shíkèbiǎo lyeh-chur shur-kur byow 列车时刻表

scheduled flight bānjī bahn-jee 班机

school xuéxiào hsyew-eh-hsyow 学校

scissors: a pair of scissors yìbǎ jiǎnzi yee-bah jyen-dzur 一把剪子

scotch wēishìjì way-shur-jee

威士忌

Scotch tape tòumíng jiāodài toh-ming jyow-dai 透明胶带

Scotland Sūgélán 苏格兰

Scottish Sūgélán soo-gur-lahn 苏格兰

I'm Scottish wǒ shi Sūgélánren wor shur –run 我是苏格兰人

scrambled eggs chǎo jīdàn chow jee-dahn 炒鸡蛋

sea hǎi 海

by the sea zài hǎibiānr dzai hai-byenr 在海边儿

seafood hǎiwèi hai-way 海味

seal (for printing name) túzhāng too-jahng 图章

seasick: I feel seasick wǒ yūnchuánle wor yewn-chwahn-lur 我晕船了

I get seasick wǒ yūnchuán wor yewn-chwahn 我晕船

seat zuòwei dzor-way 座位

is this seat taken? yǒu rén ma? yoh run mah 有人吗？

second (*adj*) dièrge dee-er-gur 第二个

(of time) miǎo myow 秒

just a second! zhè jiù dé!

jur jyoh dur 这就得

second class (travel etc) èr děng
er dung 二等

(hard sleeper) yìngwò ying-wor
硬卧

second-hand jiù(de) jyoh(-dur)
旧（的）

see kànjian kahn-jyen 看见

  can I see? wǒ kěyi kànkan
  ma? wor kur-yee kahn-kahn mah
  我可以看看吗？

  have you seen-…? nǐ
  kàndàole-…ma? kahn-dow-lur
  mah 你看到了…吗？

  I saw him this morning
  wǒ jīntian zǎoshang kànjian
  tā le wor jin-tyen dzow-
  shahng kahn-jyen tah lur
  我今天早上看见他了

  see you! zàijiàn! dzai-jyen
  再见

  I see (I understand) wǒ míngbai
  le wor ming-bai lur 我明白了

self-service zìzhù dzur-joo
自助

sell mài 卖

  do you sell-…? nǐ mài bu
  mài-…? 你卖不卖…？

Sellotape tòumíng jiāobù toh-
ming jyow-boo 透明胶布

send sòng soong 送

(by post) jì 寄

**I want to send this to
England** wǒ xiǎng ba zhèige jì
dào Yīngguó qù wor syahng bah
jay-gur jee dow ying-gwor chew
我想把这个寄到英国去

senior citizen lǎoniánren low-
nyen-run 老年人

separate fēnkāi fun-kai 分开

separately (pay, travel) fēnkāi de
分开地

September jiǔyuè jyoh-yew-eh
九月

serious (problem, illness)
yánzhòng(de) yen-joong(-dur)
严重（的）

service charge (in restaurant)
xiǎofèi hsyow-fay 小费

serviette cānjīn tsahn-jin 餐巾

set menu fènrfàn funr-fahn
份儿饭

several jǐge jee-gur 几个

sew féng fung 缝

  **could you sew this-…-back
  on?** qǐng nín bāng wǒ bǎ
  zhèige-…-fénghuíqu, hǎo
  ma? ching nin bahng wor bah
  jay-gur … fung-hway-chew how
  mah 请您帮我把这个…
  缝回去好吗？

sex (male/female) xìnghié hsingbyeh 性别

sexy xìnggǎn hsing-gahn 性感

shade: in the shade zài yīnliáng chù dzai yin-lyang 在阴凉处

shake: let's shake hands wǒmen wòwo shǒu ba wor-mun wor-wor shoh bah 我们握握手吧

shallow (water) qiǎn chyen 浅

shame: what a shame! zhēn kěxī! jun kur-hshee 真可惜

shampoo (*noun*) xǐfàqì hshee-fah-chee 洗发剂

share (*verb*: room, table etc) héyòng hur-yoong 合用

sharp (knife) jiānruì jyen-rway 尖锐

(pain) ruì rway 锐

shaver diàndòng tìxū dāo dyen-doong tee-hsyew dow 电动剃须刀

shaving foam guā hú pàomò gwah hoo pow-mor 刮胡泡沫

shaving point diàntìdāo chāxiāo dyen-tee-dow chah-hsyow 电剃刀插销

she tā tah 她

is she here? tā zài ma? dzai mah 她在吗？

sheet (for bed) bèidān bei-dahn 被单

shelf jiàzi jyah-dzur 架子

shellfish bèilèi bay-lay 贝类

ship chuán chwahn 船

by ship zuò chuán dzwor 坐船

shirt chènyī chun-yee 衬衣

shock: I got an electric shock from the-... wǒ pèngzhe...-ér chùdiàn wor pung-jur – dyen 我碰着 … 而触电

shocking jīngrénde jing-run-dur 惊人的

shoe xié hsyeh 鞋

a pair of shoes yìshuāng xié yee-shwahng 一双鞋

> **Travel tip** Before entering someone's home, always remember to first remove your shoes, even if your host says it's not necessary. If your hosts take their shoes off and leave them outside the door, it means you should too.

shoelaces xiédài hsyeh-dai 鞋带

shoe polish xiéyóu hsyeh-yoh 鞋油

shoe repairer xiūxiéjiàng hsyoh-hsyeh-jyang 修鞋匠

shop shāngdiàn shahng-dyen 商店

shopping: I'm going shopping
wǒ qù mǎi dōngxi wor chew mai doong-hshee 我去买东西

shore (of sea, lake) àn ahn 岸

short (person) ǎi 矮

(time, journey) duǎn dwahn 短

shorts duǎnkù dwahn-koo 短裤

should: what should I do? wǒ gāi zěnme bàn? wor gai dzun-mur bahn 我该怎么办？

you should-…-nǐ yīnggāi-… -ying-gai 你应该 …

you shouldn't-…-nǐ bù yīnggāi-… 你不应该 …

he should be back soon guò yíhuìr, tā yīng zài huílai gwor yee-hwayr tah ying dzai hway-lai 过一回儿他应再回来

shoulder jiānbǎng jyen-bahng 肩膀

shout (verb) hǎn hahn 喊

show (in theatre) biǎoyǎn byow-yahn 表演

could you show me? nǐ néng ràng wǒ kànkan ma? nung rahng wor kahn-kahn mah 你能让我看看吗？

shower (of rain) zhènyǔ jun-yew 阵雨

(in bathroom) línyù lin-yew 淋浴

with shower dài línyù 带淋浴

shrine shénkān shun-kahn 神龛

shut (verb) guān gwahn 关

when do you shut?
nǐmen jídiǎn guānménr? nee-mun jee-dyen gwahn-munr 你们几点关门儿？

when does it shut?
jídiǎn guānménr? jee-dyen 几点关门儿？

they're shut guānménr le lur 关门儿了

I've shut myself out wǒ bǎ zìjǐ guān zài wàitou le wor bah dzur-jee gwahn dzai wai-toh lur 我把自己关在外头了

shut up! zhù zuǐ! joo dzway 住嘴

shy hàixiū hai-hsyoh 害羞

sick (ill) yǒubìng yoh-bing 有病

I'm going to be sick (vomit) wǒ yào ǒutù wor yow oh-too 我要呕吐

side: the other side of the street zài jiē duìmian dzai jyeh dway-myen 在街对面

sidewalk rénxíng dào run-hsing dow 人行道

sight: the sights of-…-…-de fēngjǐng fung-jing … 的风景

sightseeing: we're going sightseeing wǒmen qù yóulǎn wor-mun chew yoh-lahn 我们去游览

silk sīchóu sur-choh 丝绸

Silk Road sīchóu zhī lù jur 丝绸之路

silly chǔn 蠢

silver (noun) yín(zi) yin-dzur 银（子）

similar xiāngjìn de hsyahng-jin dur 相近

simple (easy) jiǎndān jyen-dahn 简单

since: since last week zìcóng shàngge xīngqī yǐlái dzur-tsoong shahng-gur hsing-chee yee-lai 自从上个星期以来

since I got here zìcóng wǒ lái yǐhòu dzur-tsoong wor lai yee-hoh 自从我来以后

sing chànggē chahng-gur 唱歌

Singapore Xīnjiāpō hsin-jyah-por 新加坡

singer gēchàngjiā gur-chahng-jyah 歌唱家

single: a single to-...- yìzhāng qù-...-de dānchéngpiào yee-jahng chew-...-dur dahn-chung-pyow 一张去…的单程票

I'm single wǒ shì dúshēn wor shur dahn-shun 我是独身

single bed dānrén chuáng dahn-run chwahng 单人床

single room dānrén jiān jyen 单人间

single ticket (dānchéng) piào pyow （单程）票

sink (in kitchen) shuǐchí shway-chur 水池

sister (elder) jiějie jyeh-jyeh 姐姐

(younger) mèimei may-may 妹妹

sit: can I sit here? wǒ kěyi zuò zhèr ma? wor kur-yee dzwor jer mah 我可以坐这儿吗？

is anyone sitting here? yǒu rén zài zhèr ma? yoh run zai jer mah 有人在这儿吗？

sit down zuòxià dzwor-hsyah 坐下

sit down! qǐng zuò! ching 请坐

size chǐcùn chur-tsun 尺寸

skin (human) pífu 皮肤

(animal) pí 皮

skinny shòu shoh 瘦

skirt qúnzi chewn-dzur 裙子

sky tiān tyen 天

sleep (*verb*) shuìjiào shway-jyow 睡觉

did you sleep well? nǐ shuì
de hǎo ma? shway dur how mah
你睡得好吗？

sleeper (on train) wòpù wor-poo
卧铺

(soft) ruǎnwò rwahn-wor 软卧

(hard) yìngwò ying-wor 硬卧

sleeping bag shuìdài shway-dai
睡袋

sleeping car wòpù chēxiāng
wor-poo chur-hsyahng
卧铺车厢

sleeve xiùzi hsyoh-dzur 袖子

slide (photographic) huàndēngpiānr
hwahn-dung-pyenr 幻灯片儿

slip (garment) chènqún chun-
chewn 衬裙

slow màn mahn 慢

slow down! màn diǎnr! dyenr!
慢点儿

slowly màn 慢

very slowly hěn màn hun
很慢

small xiǎo hsyow 小

smell: it smells (bad) yǒu wèir le
yoh wayr lur 有味儿了

smile (verb) xiào hsyow 笑

smoke (noun) yān yahn 烟

do you mind if I smoke? wǒ
kěyǐ zài zhèr chōu yān ma? wor

kur-yee dzai jer choh yahn mah
我可以在这儿抽烟吗？

I don't smoke wǒ bú huì
chōu yān hway 我不会抽烟

do you smoke? nǐ chōu yān
ma? 你抽烟吗？

snack diǎnxīn dyen-hsin 点心

sneeze (noun) dǎ pēntì da pun-tee
打喷嚏

snow (noun) xuě hsyew-eh 雪

so: it's so good nàme hǎo nah-
mur how 那么好

it's so expensive nàme guì
那么贵

not so much méi nàme duō
may – dwor 没那么多

not so bad méi nàme huài
没那么坏

so-so búguò rúcǐ
boo-gwor roo-tsur 不过如此

soap féizào fay-dzow 肥皂

soap powder xǐyīfěn hshee-yee-
fun 洗衣粉

sock duǎnwà dwahn-wah 短袜

socket chāzuò chah-dzwor 插座

soda (water) sūdá soo-dah 苏打

sofa shāfā shah-fah 沙发

soft (material etc) ruǎn rwahn 软

soft drink qìshuǐr chee-shwayr
汽水儿

soft seat ruǎnzuò rwahn-dzwor
软座

sole (of shoe) xiédǐ hsyeh-dee
鞋底

(of foot) jiáodǐ jyow-dee 脚底

**could you put new soles on
these?** qǐng nín huàn shuāng
xīn xiédǐ, hǎo ma? ching nin
hwahn shwahng hsin – how mah
请你换双新鞋底好吗？

**some: can I have some
water?** qǐng lái yídiǎnr
shuǐ, hǎo ma? ching lai
yee-dyenr – how mah
请来一点儿水好吗？

can I have some apples?
qǐng lái yíxiē píngguǒ, hǎo

ma? yee-hsyeh 请来一
些苹果好吗？

somebody, someone mǒurén
moh-rın 某人

something mǒushì moh-shur
某事

I want something to eat
wǒ xiǎng chī diǎn dōngxī wor
hsyahng chur dyen doong-hshee
我想吃点东西

sometimes yǒushíhhou yoh-
shur-hoh 有时候

somewhere mǒudì moh-dee
某地

I need somewhere to stay
wǒ yào zhǎoge zhùchù wor yow
jow-gur 我要找个住处

son érzi er-dzur 儿子

song gē gur 歌

son-in-law nǚxu nyoo-hsoo
女婿

soon (after a while) yìhuǐr yee-
hwayr 一会儿

(quickly) kuài kwai 快

I'll be back soon wǒ yìhuǐr
jiù huílai wor yee-hwayr jyoh
hway-lai 我一会儿就回来

as soon as possible yuè
kuài yuè hǎo yew-eh – how
越快越好

sore: it's sore téng tung 疼

sore throat sǎngzitēng sahng-dzur-tung 嗓子疼

sorry: (I'm) sorry duìbuqǐ dway-boo-chee 对不起

sorry? (didn't understand) nǐ shuō shénme? shwor shun-mur 你说什么？

sort: what sort of-…? shénme yàng de-…? dur 什么样的 … ？

soup tāng tahng 汤

sour (taste) suān swahn 酸

south nán nahn 南

in the south nánfāng nahn-fahng 南方

South Africa Nánfēi nahn-fay 南非

South African (adj) Nánfēi 南非

I'm South African wǒ shì Nánfēirén wor shur –run 我是南非人

South China Sea Nánhǎi nahn-hai 南海

southeast dōngnán doong-nahn 东南

southern nánde nahn-dur 南的

South Korea nán Cháoxiān nahn chow-hsyen 南朝鲜

southwest xīnán hsin-ahn 西南

souvenir jìniànpǐn jin-yen-pin

纪念品

soy sauce jiàngyóu jyahn-gyoh 酱油

Spain Xībānyá hshee-bahn-yah 西班牙

Spanish (adj) Xībānyáde hshee-bahn-yah-dur 西班牙的

speak: do you speak English?

nín huì jiǎng Yīngyǔ ma? hway jyang ying-yew mah 您会讲英语吗？

I don't speak-…-wǒ búhuì jiǎng-…-wor boo-hway 我不会讲 …

can I speak to-…? (in person) máfan nín zhǎo yíxia … hǎo ma? mah-fahn nin jow yee-hsyah-…-how 麻烦您找一下 … 好吗？

can I speak to Mr Wang?

Wáng xiānsheng zàibúzài? hsyahng-shung dzai-boo-dzai

who's calling? nǐ shì nawéi? shur nar-way

it's Patricia wǒ shì Patricia wor

I'm sorry, he's not in, can I take a message? duìbuqǐ, tā búzài, yàobúyào liú gexìn? dway-boo-chee tah boo-dzai yow-boo-yow lyoh gur-hsin

no thanks, I'll call back later xièxie, guò yìhuìr wǒ zài dǎ hsyeh-hsyeh gwor yee-hwayr wor dzai dah

please tell him I called qǐng gàosu tā wǒ dǎ le diànhuà ching gow-soo tah wor dah lur dyen-hwah

spectacles yǎnjìng yenjing 眼镜

spend huāfèi hwah-fay 花费

spoke (in wheel) fútiáo foo-tyow 辐条

spoon sháozi show-dzur 勺子

sport yùndòng yewn-doong 运动

sprain: I've sprained my-... -wǒde ... niǔ le wor-dur-... nyoh lur 我的 ... 扭了

spring (season) chūntian chun-tyen 春天

in the spring chūntian 春天

square (in town) guǎngchǎng gwahng-chahng 广场

stairs lóutī loh-tee 楼梯

stamp (*noun*) yóupiào yoh-pyow 邮票

a stamp for England, please mǎi yìzhāng jì

Yīngguó de yóupiào mai yee-jahng jee ying-gwor dur

what are you sending? nǐ jì shénme? shun-mur

this postcard zhèizhāng míngxìnpiàn jay-jahng ming-hsin-pyen

star xīngxing hsing-hsing 星星

start kāishǐ kai-shur 开始

when does it start? jǐdiǎn kāishǐ? jee-dyen 几点开始？

the car won't start chē fādòngbùqǐlái chur fah-doong-boo-chee-lai 车发动不起来

starter (food) lěngpánr lung-pahnr 冷盘儿

station (train) huǒchē zhàn hwor-chur jahn 火车站

(city bus) qìchē zǒng zhàn chee-chur dzoong 汽车总站

(long-distance bus) chángtú qìchēzhàn chahng-too chee-chur-jahn 长途汽车站

(underground) dì tiě zhàn tyeh jahn 地铁站

statue sùxiàng soo-hsyahng 塑像

stay: where are you staying? nǐmen zhù zài nǎr? nee-mun joo dzai nar 你们住在哪儿？

I'm staying at-... wǒ zhù
zài-... -wor joo dzai 我住在 …

**I'd like to stay another
two nights** wǒ xiǎng zài
zhù liǎng tiān syahng dzai joo
我想再住两天

steak niúpái nyoh-pai 牛排

steal tōu toh 偷

my bag has been stolen
wǒde bāo bèi tōule wor-dur bow
bay toh-lur 我的包被偷了

steamed zhēng jung 蒸

steamed roll huājuǎnr hwah-
jwahnr 花卷儿

steep (hill) dǒu doh 陡

step: on the steps zài táijiē
shang dzai tai-jyeh shahng
在台阶上

stereo lìtǐshēng lee-tee-shung
立体声

Sterling yīngbàng ying-bahng
英镑

steward (on plane) fúwùyuán
nahn foo-woo-yew-ahn 服务员

stewardess kōngzhōng xiǎojiě
koong-joong hsyow-jyeh 空中
小姐

still: I'm still here wǒ hái zài wor
hai dzai 我还在

is he still there? tā hái zài
ma? tah – mah 他还在吗？

keep still! bié dòng! byeh
doong 别动

sting: I've been stung wǒ gěi
zhēle wor gay jur-lur 我给螫了

stockings chángtǒngwà chahng-
toong-wah 长统袜

stomach wèi way 胃

stomach ache wèiténg way-tung
胃疼

stone (rock) shítou shur-toh 石头

stop (verb) tíng 停

please, stop here (to
taxi driver etc) qǐng tíng
zài zhèr ching ting dzai jer
请停在这儿

do you stop near-...?
zài-...-fùjìn tíng ma? mah
在 … 附近停吗？

stop it! tíngzhǐ! ting-jur 停止

storm bàofēngyǔ bow-fung-yew
暴风雨

straight (whisky etc) chún 纯

it's straight ahead yìzhí
cháoqián yee-jur chow-chyen
一直朝前

straightaway mǎshàng mah-
shahng 马上

strange (odd) qíguài de chee-gwai
dur 奇怪的

stranger shēngrén shun-grun
生人

strap dàir 带儿

strawberry cǎoméi tsow-may
草莓

stream xiǎoxī hsyow-hshee 小溪

street jiē(dào) jyeh(-dow)
街（道）

   on the street zài jiēshang dzai
   jyeh-shahng 在街上

streetmap jiāotōngtú jyow-toong-
too 交通图

string shéngzi shung-dzur 绳子

strong (person) qiángzhuàng
chyang-jwahng 强壮

   (material) jiēshi jyeh-shur 结实

   (drink, taste) nóng noong 浓

stuck: it's stuck kǎle kah-lur
卡了

student xuésheng hsyew-eh-
shung 学生

stupid bèn bun 笨

suburb jiāoqū jyow-chew 郊区

subway (US) dìtiě dee-tyeh 地铁

suddenly tūrán too-rahn 突然

sugar táng tahng 糖

suit (*noun*) tàozhuāng tow-jwahng
套装

   it doesn't suit me (jacket etc)
   wǒ chuān bù héshì wor chwahn
   boo hur-shur 我穿不合适

   it suits you nǐ chuān héshì

你穿合适

suitcase shǒutíxiāng shoh-tee-
hsyahng 手提箱

summer xiàtian hsyah-tyen 夏天

   in the summer xiàtian 夏天

sun tàiyáng 太阳

sunbathe shài tàiyáng 晒太阳

sunblock (cream) fángshàirǔ
fahng-shai-roo 防晒乳

sunburn rìzhì rur-shur 日炙

Sunday xīngqītiān hsing-chee-
tyen 星期天

sunglasses tàiyángjìng tai-yang-
jing 太阳镜

sunny: it's sunny yángguāng
chōngzú yang-gwahng choong-
dzoo 阳光充足

sunset rìluò rur-lwor 日落

sunshine yángguāng yang-
gwahng 阳光

sunstroke zhòngshǔ joong-shoo
中暑

suntan lotion fángshài jì fahng-
shai 防晒剂

suntan oil fángshàiyóu –yoh
防晒油

super hǎojíle how-jee-lur
好极了

supermarket chāojí shìchǎng
chow-jee shur-chahng

超级市场

supper wǎnfàn wahn-fahn 晚饭

supplement (extra charge) fùjiāfèi foo-jyah-fay 附加费

sure: are you sure? zhēnde ma? jun dur mah 真的吗？

  sure! dāngrán! dahn-grahn 当然

surname xìng hsing 姓

swearword zāngzìr dzahng-dzur 脏字儿

sweater máoyī mow-yee 毛衣

sweatshirt (chángxiù) hànshān chahng-hsyoh hahn-shahn （长袖）汗衫

Sweden Ruìdiǎn rway-dyen 瑞典

Swedish (adj) Ruìdiǎnyǔ 瑞典语

sweet (taste) tián tyen 甜

  (noun: dessert) tiánshí tyen-shur 甜食

sweets tángguǒ tahng-gwor 糖果

swim (verb) yóuyǒng yoh-yoong 游泳

  I'm going for a swim wǒ qù yóuyǒng wor chew yoh-yoong 我去游泳

  let's go for a swim zánmen qù yóuyǒng ba zahn-mun

咱们去游泳吧

swimming costume yóuyǒngyī yoh-yoong-yee 游泳衣

swimming pool yóuyǒng chí chur 游泳池

swimming trunks yóuyǒngkù yoh-yoong-koo 游泳裤

switch (noun) kāiguān kai-gwahn 开关

switch off guān gwahn 关

switch on kāi kai 开

swollen zhǒng joong 肿

T

table zhuōzi jwor-dzur 桌子

  a table for two liǎngrén zhuō lyang-run 两人桌

tablecloth zhuōbù jwor-boo 桌布

table tennis pīngpāngqiú ping-pahng-chyoh 乒乓球

tailor cáifeng tsai-fung 裁缝

Taiwan Táiwān tai-wahn 台湾

Taiwanese (adj) Táiwān(de) –dur 台湾（的）

take ná nah 拿

  (somebody somewhere) lǐng 领

  (something somewhere) dài 带

(accept) jiēshòu jyeh-shoh
接受

can you take me to the-...?
qǐng dài wǒ dào-...? ching dai
wor dow 请带我到 … ？

do you take credit cards?
nǐ shòu xìnyòngkǎ ma?
shoh hsin-yoong-kah mah
你受信用卡吗？

fine, I'll take it hǎo, xíngle
how hsing-lur 好行了

can I take this? (leaflet
etc) kěyǐ ná ma? kur-yee nah
可以拿吗？

how long does it take?
yào duōcháng shíjiān?
yow dwor-chahng shur-jyen
要多长时间？

it takes three hours yào
sānge zhōngtóu yow sahng-gur
joong-toh 要三个钟头

is this seat taken? zhèr
yǒu rén ma? jer yoh run mah
这儿有人吗？

talk (verb) shuōhuà shwor-hwah
说话

tall gāo gow 高

tampons wèishēngjīn way-shung-
jin 卫生巾

tap shuǐlóng tóu shway-loong toh
水龙头

tape (cassette) cídài tsur-dai 磁带

taste (noun) wèir wayr 味儿

can I taste it? kěyǐ
chángchang ma? kur-
yee chahng-chahng mah
可以尝尝吗？

taxi chūzū qìchē choo-dzoo chee-
chur 出租汽车

will you get me a taxi?
qǐng nín bāng wǒ jiào liàng
chūzūchē, hǎo ma? ching
nin bahng wor jyow lyang
choo-dzoo-chur how mah
请您帮我叫辆出租车
好吗？

where can I find a taxi?
zài nǎr kěyǐ zhǎodao chūzū
qìchē? dzai nar kur-yee jow-dow
在哪儿可以找到出租
汽车？

DIALOGUE

**to the airport/to the Xian
Hotel, please** qǐng dài wǒ
dào fēijīcháng/Xiān fàndiàn
dow – fay-jee-chahng

how much will it be?
duōshao qián? dwor-show
chyen

30 yuan sānshí kuài qián
sahn-shur kwai

**that's fine right here,
thanks** jiù zài zhèr, xièxie
jyoh dzai jer hsyeh-hsyeh

taxi driver chūzū sījī choo-dzoo sur-jee 出租司机

taxi rank chūzūchē diǎnr dyenr 出租车点儿

tea (drink) chá chah 茶

tea for one/two, please qǐng lái yí/liǎngge rén de chá ching – run dur 请来一／两个人的茶

teach: could you teach me? nín kěyǐ jiāojiao wǒ ma? kur-yee jyow-jyow wor mah 您可以教教我吗？

teacher lǎoshī low-shur 老师

team duì dway 队

teaspoon cháchí chah-chur 茶匙

tea towel cāwǎnbù tsah-wahn-boo 擦碗布

teenager qīngshàonián ching-show-nyen 青少年

telephone diànhuà dyen-hwah 电话
see **phone**

television diànshì dyen-shur 电视

tell: could you tell him-...? qǐng nín gàosu tà-..., hǎo ma? ching nin gow-soo tah-...-how mah 请您告诉他 … 好吗？

temperature (weather) qìwēn chee-wun 气温

(fever) fāshāo fah-show 发烧

temple (Buddhist) sì sur 寺

(Taoist) guàn gwahn 观

tennis wǎngqiú wahng-chyoh 网球

term (at university, school) xuéqī hsyew-eh-chee 学期

terminus (rail) zhōngdiǎnzhàn joong-dyen-jahn 终点站

terrible zāogāo dzow-gow 糟糕

that's terrible tài zāogāo le lur 太糟糕了

terrific bàngjíle bahng-jee-lur 棒极了

text (message) duǎnxìn dwahn-hsin 短信

(*verb*) fā duǎnxìn fah dwahn-hsin 发短信

Thailand Tàiguó tai-gwor 泰国

than bǐ 比

even more-...-than-... -bǐ-...-gèngduō gung-...-dwor 比 … 更多

smaller than bǐ-...-xiǎo hsyow 比 … 小

thank: thank you xièxie hsyeh-hsyeh 谢谢

thank you very much

fēicháng gǎnxiè fay-chahng gahn-hsyeh 非常感谢

thanks for the lift
xièxie nín ràng wǒ dāle chē rahng wor dah-lur chur
谢谢您让我搭了车

no, thanks xièxie, wǒ bú yào boo yow 谢谢我不要

thanks xièxie

that's OK, don't mention it
bú kèqi kur chee

that nèige nay-gur 那个

that one nèi yíge yee-gur
那一个

I hope that-...-wǒ xīwàng-...
-wor hshee-wahng 我希望 ...

that's nice nà zhèng hǎo nah
jung-how 那正好

is that-...? nà shì-...-ma?
shur-...-mah 那是 ... 吗？

that's it (that's right) duìle dway-
lur 对了

the Chinese has no equivalent for the
English '**the**'

theatre jùyuàn jyew-yew-ahn
剧院

their/theirs tāmende tah-mun-dur
他们的

them tāmen tah-mun 他们

then (at that time) nèi shíhou nay
shur-hoh 那时候

(after that) ránhòu rahn-hoh
然后

there nàr 那儿

over there zài nàr dzai
在那儿

up there zài shàngtou dzai
shahng-toh 在上头

is/are there-...? yǒu-...-ma?
yoh-...-mah 有 ... 吗？

there is/are-... -yǒu-... 有 ...

there you are (giving
something) gěi nǐ gay 给你

Thermos flask rèshuǐpíng rush-
way-ping 热水瓶

these zhèixie jay-hsyeh 这些

they tāmen tahmun 他们

thick hòu hoh 厚

(stupid) bèn bun 笨

thief zéi dzay 贼

thigh dàtuǐ dah-tway 大腿

thin (person) shòu shoh 瘦

(object) xì hshee 细

thing (matter) shìr shur 事儿

(object) dōngxi doong-hshee
东西

my things wǒde dōngxi
我的东西

think xiǎng hsyahng 想

I think so wǒ xiǎng shì zhèiyang wor hsyahng shur jay-yang 我想是这样

I don't think so wǒ bú zhèiyang xiǎng jay-yang 我不这样想

I'll think about it wǒ kǎolǜ yíxia kow-lyew yee-hsyah 我考虑一下

third class sānděng sahn-dung 三等

(hard seat) yìngzuò ying-dzwor 硬座

thirsty: I'm thirsty wǒ kǒukě wor koh-kur 我口渴

this zhèige jay-gur 这个

this one zhèige 这个

this is my wife zhè shì wǒ qīzi jur shur wor chee-dzur 这是我妻子

is this-...? zhèi shìbúshì-...? shur-boo-shur 这是不是 … ?

those nèixie nay-hsyeh 那些

thread *(noun)* xiàn hsyen 线

throat sǎngzi sahng-dzur 嗓子

throat lozenges rùnhóu piàn run-hoh pyen 润喉片

through jīngguò jing-gwor 经过

does it go through-...? *(train, bus)* jīngguò … ma? mah 经过 … 吗 ?

throw/throw away rēng rung 扔

thumb dàmúzhǐ dah-moo-jur 大拇指

thunderstorm léiyǔ lay-yew 雷雨

Thursday xīngqīsì hsing-chee-sur 星期四

Tibet Xīzàng hshee-dzahng 西藏

Tibetan *(adj)* Xīzàngde hshee-dzahng 西藏的

ticket piào pyow 票

DIALOGUE

a return to Xian wǎng Xiān de láihuí piào wahng – dur lai-hway

coming back when? nèitiān yào huílái? shur nay-tyen yow

today/next Tuesday jīntian/xiàge xīngqīèr

that will be 30 yuan sānshí kuài qián chyen

ticket office *(bus, rail)* shòupiàochù shoh-pyow-choo 售票处

tie *(necktie)* lǐngdài 领带

tight *(clothes etc)* xiǎo hsyow 小

it's too tight tài xiǎo le lur 太小了

tights liánkùwà lyen-koo-wah
连裤袜

time shíjiān shur-jyen 时间

what's the time? jǐdiǎn le?
jee-dyen lur 几点了？

this time zhèicì jay-tsur 这次

last time shàngcì shahng-tsur
上次

next time xiàcì hsyah 下次

three times sāncì 三次

Travel tip China occupies
a single time zone, eight
hours ahead of GMT, thirteen
hours ahead of US Eastern
Standard Time, sixteen hours
ahead of US Pacific Time and
two hours behind Australian
Eastern Standard Time. There
is no daylight saving.

timetable (train) lièchē shíkè
biǎo lyeh-chur shur-kur byow
列车时刻表

tin (can) guàntou gwahn-toh
罐头

tinfoil xīzhǐ hshee-jur 锡纸

tin-opener guàntou qǐzi gwahn-
toh chee-dzur 罐头起子

tiny yìdiánrdiǎnr yee-dyenr-dyenr
一点儿点儿

tip (to waiter etc) xiǎo fèi hsyow
fay 小费

tire (US) lúntāi lun-tai 轮胎

tired lèi lay 累

I'm tired wǒ lèi le wor lay lur
我累了

tissues zhǐjīn jur-jin

to: to Shanghai/London
dào Shànghǎi/Lúndūn dow
到上海／伦敦

to China/England
qù Zhōngguó/Yīnggélán chew
大中国／英格兰

to the post office qù yóujú
去邮局

toast (bread) kǎo miànbāo kow
myen-bow 烤面包

today jīntian jin-tyen 今天

toe jiáozhǐtou jyow-jur-toh
脚指头

together yìqǐ yee-chee 一起

we're together (in shop
etc) wǒmen shì yíkuàir de
wor-mun shur yee-kwair dur
我们是一块儿的

toilet cèsuǒ tsur-swor 厕所

where is the toilet? cèsuǒ zài
nǎr? dzai 厕所在哪儿？

I have to go to the toilet
wǒ děi qù fāngbian fāngbian
wor day chew fahng-byen
我得去方便方便

toilet paper wèishēngzhǐ way-
shung-jee 卫生纸

tomato xīhóngshì hshee-hoong-shur 西红柿

tomato juice fānqié zhī fahn-chyeh jur 番茄汁

tomorrow míngtian ming-tyen 明天

tomorrow morning míngtian zǎoshang dzow-shahng 明天早上

the day after tomorrow hòutian hoh-tyen 后天

tongue shétou shur-toh 舌头

tonic (water) kuàngquánshuǐ kwahng-choo-en-shway 矿泉水

tonight jīntian wǎnshang jin-tyen wahn-shahng 今天晚上

too (also) yě yur 也

(excessively) tài 太

too hot tài rè rur 太热

too much tài duō dwor 太多

me too wǒ yě wor 我也

tooth yá yah 牙

toothache yáténg yah-tung 牙疼

toothbrush yáshuā yah-shwah 牙刷

toothpaste yágāo yah-gow 牙膏

top: on top of-...-zài ... shàngtou dzai-...-shahng-toh 在 ... 上头

at the top zài dǐngshang ding-shahng 在顶上

torch shǒudiàntǒng shoh-dyen-toong 手电筒

total (noun) zǒnggòng dzoong-goong 总共

tour (noun) lǚxíng lyew-hsing 旅行

is there a tour of-...? yǒu méiyou wǎng-....-de lǚxíng? yoh may-yoh wahng-....-dur 有没有往 ... 的旅行？

tour guide dǎoyóu dow-yoh 导游

tourist lǚyóu zhě lyew-yoh jur 旅游者

tour operator lǚxíng shè

lyew-hsing shur 旅行社

towards cháozhe chow-jur 朝着

towel máojīn mow-jin 毛巾

town chéngzhèn chung-jun 城镇

  in town (zài) chéngli
(dzai) chung-lee （在）城里

  out of town (zài) chéngwài
chung-wai （在）城外

town centre shì zhōngxīn
shur joong-hsin 市中心

town hall shì zhèngfǔ dàlóu shur-
jung-foo 市政府大楼

toy wánjù wahn-jyew 玩具

track (US) zhàntái jahn-tai 站台

tracksuit yùndòngfú
yewn-doong-foo 运动服

traditional chuántǒng chwahn-
toong 传统

train huǒchē hwor-chur 火车

  by train zuò huǒchē dzwor
hwor-chur 坐火车

**is this the train for
Shanghai?** zhèliè huǒchē
qù Shànghǎi ma? jur-lyeh
hwor-chur chew – mah

sure qù chew

**no, you want that platform
there** búqù, nǐ yào dào
nèige zhàntái qù boo-chew
nee yow dow nay-gur jahn-tai

trainers (shoes) lǚyóuxié lyew-
yoh-hsyeh 旅游鞋

train station huǒchēzhàn hwor-
chur-jahn 火车站

tram yǒuguǐ diànchē yoh-gway
dyen-chur 有轨电车

translate fānyì fahn-yee 翻译

  **could you translate
that?** qǐng nín fānyì yíxia,
hǎo ma? ching nin fahn-
yee yee-hsyah how mah
请您翻译一下好吗？

translator fānyì fahn-yee 翻译

trash lājī lah-jee 垃圾

travel lǚxíng lyew-hsing 旅行

  we're travelling around
wǒmen zài lǚxíng wor-mun dzai
我们在旅行

travel agent's lǚxíngshè lyew-
hsing-shur 旅行社

traveller's cheque lǚxíng
zhīpiào lyew-hsing jur-pyow
旅行支票

tray chápán chah-pahn 茶盘

tree shù shoo 树

trim: just a trim, please (to
hairdresser) qǐng zhǐ xiūxiu
biānr ching jur hsyoh-hsyoh byenr
请只修修边儿

**trip: I'd like to go on a trip
to-...** wǒ xiǎng dào-...-qù wor

hsyahng dow-…-chew 我想到
… 去

trouble (*noun*) máfan mah-fahn
麻烦

I'm having trouble with-…
-wǒde-…-yùdàole diǎnr máfan
wor-duh-… yew-dow-lur dyenr
我的 … 遇到
了点儿麻烦

trousers kùzi koo-dzur 裤子

true zhēnde jun-dur 真的

that's not true bú duì dway
不对

trunk (US: of car) xínglixiāng
hsing-lee-hsyahng 行李箱

trunks (swimming) yóuyǒngkù
yoh-yoong-koo 游泳裤

try (*verb*) shì shur 试

can I try it? kěyi shìyishì
ma? kur-yee shur-yee-shur mah
可以试一试吗？

try on: can I try it on?
kěyi shìyishì ma?
可以试一试吗？

T-shirt T xùshān tee hsoo shahn
T恤衫

Tuesday xīngqīèr hsing-chee-er
星期二

tunnel suìdào sway-dow
隧道

turn: turn left wǎng zuó guǎi

wǎng dzwor gwai 往左拐

turn right wǎng yòu guǎi
往右拐

turn off: where do I turn off?
wǒ děi zài nǎr guǎiwān? wor
day dzai nar gwai-wahn 我
得在哪儿拐弯？

**can you turn the heating
off?** qǐng ba nuǎnqì guānshang
ching bah nwahn-chee-gwahn-
shahng 请把暖器关上？

**turn on: can you turn the
heating on?** qǐng ba nuǎnqì
dǎkāi yíxià dah-kai yee-hsyah
请把暖器打开一下？

turning (in road) zhuǎnwānr
jwahn-wahnr 转弯儿

TV diànshì dyen-shur 电视

twice liǎngcì lyang-tsur 两次

twice as much duō yíbèi dwor
yee-bay 多一倍

twin beds liǎngge dānrénchuáng
lyang-gur dahn-run-chwahng
两个单人床

twin room shuāngrén fángjiān
shwahng-run fahng-jyen
双人房间

twist: I've twisted my ankle
wǒde jiǎobózi niǔle wor-
dur jyow-bor-dzur nyoh-lur
我的脚脖子扭了

type (*noun*) zhǒng joong 种

  another type of-...-lìng
yìzhǒng-....-ling yee-joong
另一种 ...

typical diǎnxíng dyen-hsing
典型

tyre lúntāi 轮胎

U

ugly nánkàn nahn-kahn 难看

UK Yīngguó ying-gwor 英国

umbrella yǔsǎn yew-sahn 雨伞

uncle (father's elder brother) bófù
伯父

  (father's younger brother) shūshu
shoo-shoo 叔叔

  (mother's brother) jiùjiu jyoh-jyoh
舅舅

under-...(in position) zài-...-xià
dzai-...-hsyah 在 ... 下

  (less than) shǎoyú-....-show-yew
... 少于

underdone (meat) bàn shēng bù
shú bahn shung boo shoo 半生
不熟

underground (railway) dìtiě dee-
tyeh 地铁

underpants kùchǎ koo-chah
裤衩

understand: I understand wǒ
dǒng le wor doong lur 我懂了

  I don't understand wǒ bù
dǒng 我不懂

  do you understand? nǐ
dǒngle, ma? 你懂了吗？

unemployed shīyè shur-yur
失业

unfashionable bù shímáo boo
shur-mow 不时髦

United States Měiguó may-gwor
美国

university dàxué dah-hsyew-eh
大学

unlock kāi 开

unpack dǎkāi dah-kai 打开

until-...-zhǐdào-...-wéizhǐ
jur-dow-...-way-jur 只到 ...
为止

unusual bù chángjiàn(de)
chahng-jyen(-dur)
不常见（的）

up shàng shahng 上

  up there zài nàr dzai 在那儿

  he's not up yet tā hái méi
qǐlai tah hai may chee-lai
他还没起来

  what's up? zěnme huí
shìr? dzun-mur hway shur
怎么回事儿？

upmarket gāojí gow-jee 高级

upset stomach wèi bù shūfu way boo shoo-foo 胃不舒服

upside down dàoguolai dow-gwor-lai 倒过来

upstairs lóushàng loh-shahng 楼上

urgent jǐnjí(de) jin-jee(-dur) 紧急（的）

us wǒmen wor-mun 我们

    with us gēn wǒmen yìqǐ gun – yee-chee 跟我们一起

    for us wéi wǒmen wei 为我们

use (*verb*) yòng yoong 用

    may I use-...? wǒ kěyǐ yòng yíxia… ma? wor kur-yee yoong-yee-hsyah-...- mah 我可以用一下…吗？

useful yǒuyòng yoh-yoong 有用

usual (*normal*) píngcháng ping-chahng 平常

    (*habitual*) yuánlái de yew-ahn-lai dur 原来的

V

vacancy: do you have any vacancies? (hotel) zhèr yǒu kòng fángjiān ma? jer yoh koong fahng-jyen mah 这儿有空房间吗？

vacation (holiday) jiàqī jyah-chee 假期

    on vacation xiūjià hsyoh-jyah 休假

vacuum cleaner xīchénqì hshee-chun-chee 吸尘器

valid (ticket etc) yǒuxiào yoh-hsyow 有效

    how long is it valid for? duō cháng shíjiànnei yǒuxiào? dwor chahng shur-jyen nay yoh-hsyow 多长时间内有效？

valley shāngǔ shahn-goo 山谷

valuable (*adj*) bǎoguì(de) bow-gway(-dur) 宝贵（的）

    can I leave my valuables here? wǒ kěyǐ bǎ guìzhòng de dōngxi fàng zài zhèr ma? wor kur-yee bah gway-joong dur doong-hshee fahng dzai jer mah 我可以把贵重的东西放在这儿吗？

van huòchē hwor-chur 货车

vary: it varies jīngcháng biàn jing-chahng byen 经常变

vase huāpíng hwah-ping 花瓶

vegetables shūcài shoo-tsai 蔬菜

vegetarian (*noun*) chīsùde chur-soo-dur 吃素的

very fēicháng fay-chahng 非常

very little hěn xiǎo hun hsyow
很小

I like it very much wǒ hěn
xǐhuan wor hun hshee-hwahn
我很喜欢

via tújīng toojing 途经

Vietnam Yuènán yew-eh-nahn
越南

view jǐng 景

village cūnzi tsun-dzur 村子

vinegar cù tsoo 醋

visa qiānzhèng chyen-jung
签证

visit (*verb*: person) qù kàn chew
kahn 去看

(place) cānguān tsahn-gwahn
参观

I'd like to visit-...-wǒ xiǎng
cānguān-...-wor hsyahng
我想参观 …

voice shēngyīn shung-yin
声音

voltage diànyā dyen-yah 电压

vomit ǒutù oh-too 呕吐

W

waist yāo yow 腰

wait děng dung 等

wait for me děngdeng wǒ wor
等等我

don't wait for me búyòng
déng wǒ boo-yoong 不用等我

**can I wait until my wife
gets here?** wǒ néng děngdào
wǒ qīzi lái ma? nung dung-
dow wor chee-dzur lai mah
我能等到我妻子来吗？

can you do it while I wait?
shìbúshì lìděng kéqǔ? shur-
boo-shur lee-dung kur-chew
是不是立等可取？

**could you wait here for
me?** qǐng zài zhèr děng hǎo
ma? ching dzai jer dung how mah
请在这儿等好吗？

waiter/waitress fúwùyuán foo-
woo-yew-ahn 服务员

waiter!/waitress! fúwùyuán!
服务员

**wake: can you wake me up
at 5.30?** qǐng zài wǔdiǎnbàn
jiàoxing wǒ, hǎo ma?
ching dzai – jyow-hsing wor
请在五点半叫醒我好
吗？

Wales Wēiěrshì way-er-shur
威尔士

walk: is it a long walk? yào
zǒu hén yuǎn ma? yow dzoh hun
yew-ahn mah 要走很远吗？

it's only a short walk zhǐ shì liūdaliūda jur shur lyoh-dah– 只是溜达溜达

I'll walk wǒ zǒuzhe qù wor dzoh-jur chew 我走着去

I'm going for a walk wǒ chūqu sànsan bù choo-chew sahn-sahn 我出去散散步

wall qiáng chyang 墙

the Great Wall of China Chángchéng chahng-chung 长城

wallet qiánbāo chyen-bow 钱包

want: I want a-...-wǒ yào yíge-...-wor yow yee-gur 我要一个

I don't want any-...-wǒ bú yào-... 我不要

I want to go home wǒ yào huíjiā hway-jyah 我要回家

I don't want to wǒ bú yào 我不要

he wants to-... tā xiǎng-... -tah hsyahng 他想 …

what do you want? nǐ yào shénme? shun-mur 你要什么？

ward (in hospital) bìngfáng bing-fahng 病房

warm nuǎnhuo nwahn-hwor 暖和

was: he/she was tā yǐqián shì tah yee-chyen shur 他／她以前是

it was shì 是

wash (verb) xǐ hshee 洗

can you wash these? qǐng xǐxi zhèixie, hǎo ma? ching hshee-hshee jay-hsyeh how mah 请洗这些好吗？

washhand basin liǎnpén lyen-pun 脸盆

washing (dirty clothes) dài xǐ de yīfu yow hshee dur yee-foo 待洗的衣服

(clean clothes) yíxǐ de yīfu yee-hshee-how 已洗的衣服

washing machine xǐyījī hshee-yee-jee 洗衣机

washing powder xǐyīfěn –fun 洗衣粉

wasp huángfēng hwahng-fung 黄蜂

watch (wristwatch) shóubiǎo shoh-byow 手表

water shuǐ shway 水

may I have some water? qǐng lái diánr shuǐ, hǎo ma? ching lai dyenr shway how mah 请来点儿水好吗？

water melon xīguā hshee-gwah
西瓜

waterproof (*adj*) fángshuǐ fahng-
shway 防水

way: it's this way shì zhèitiáo lù
shur jay-tyow 是这条路

　it's that way shì nèitiáo lù
　nay-tyow 是那条路

　is it a long way to-...?
　dào-....-yuǎn ma? dow-...
　-chew yew-ahn mah 到 ...
　远吗？

　no way! bù kěnéng! kur-nung
　不可能

　**could you tell me the way
　to-...?** qǐng nín gàosu
　wǒ, dào-....-zěnme zǒu,
　hǎo ma? ching nin gow-soo
　wor dow-....-dzun-mur dzoh
　how mah

　**go straight on until you
　reach the traffic lights**
　yìzhí zǒu hónglùdēng yee-
　jur dzoh hoong-loo-dung

　turn left wǎng zuǒ guǎi
　wahng dzwor gwai

　take the first on the right
　yào yòubiānr dì yízhuǎn
　yow yoh-byenr dee yee-jwahn

　see **where**

we wǒmen wor-mun 我们

weak (person) ruò rwor 弱

　(drink) dàn dahn 淡

weather tiānqi tyen-chee 天气

website wǎngzhàn wahng-jahn
网站

wedding hūnlǐ hun-lee 婚礼

wedding ring jiéhūn jièzhi jyeh-
hun jyeh-jur 结婚戒指

Wednesday xīngqīsān hsing-
chee-sahn 星期三

week xīngqī hsing-chee 星期

　a week (from) today xiàge
　xīngqī de jīntian hsyah-gur – dur
　jin-tyen 下个星期的今天

　a week (from) tomorrow
　xiàge xīngqī de míngtian ming-
　tyen 下个星期的明天

weekend zhōumò joh-mor
周末

　at the weekend zhōumò
　周末

weight zhòngliàng joong-lyang
重量

welcome: welcome to-...
-huānyíng dào-....-hwahn-ying
dow 欢迎到 ...

　you're welcome (don't mention
　it) búyòng xiè boo-yoong hsyeh
　不用谢

well: I don't feel well wǒ
bù shūfu wor boo shoo-foo
我不舒服

she's not well tā bù shūfu tah
bù shūfu 她不舒服

**you speak English very
well** nǐ Yīngyǔ jiǎngde hěn
hǎo ying-yew jyang-dur hun how
你英语讲得很好

well done! tài hǎole! how-lur
太好了

I would like this one as well
zhèige wǒ yě yào jay-gur wor
yeh yow 这个我也要

well well! āiyā! ai-yah 哎呀

how are you? nín hǎo ma?
how mah

**very well, thanks, and
you?** hén hǎo xièxie, nǐ ne?
hun how hsyeh-hsyeh nee-neh

well-done (meat) lànshú lahn-
shoo 烂熟

Welsh Wēiěrshì way-er-shur
威尔士

I'm Welsh wǒ shì Wēiěrshìrén
wor shur –run 我是威尔士人

were: we were wǒmen yǐqián
shì wor-mun yee-chyen shur
我们以前是

you were nǐmen shì nee-mun
你们是

west xī hshee 西

in the west xībiānr hshee-
byenr 西边儿

West (European etc) Xīfāng hshee-
fahng 西方

in the West Xīfāng
西方

western (adj) xī hshee 西

Western (adj : European etc) xīfāng
de hshee-fahng dur 西方的

Western-style xīshì hshee-shur
西式

Western-style food xīcān
hshee-tsahn 西餐

West Indian (adj) Xī Yìndù
qúndǎo rén hshee yin-doo chun-
dow run 西印度群岛人

wet shī shur 湿

what? shénme? shun-mur
什么？

what's that? nà shì shénme?
nah shur 那是什么？

what should I do? wǒ
yīnggāi zuò shénme? wor ying-
gai dzwor 我应该作什么？

what a view! kàn zhè jǐngr!
kahn jur 看这景儿

what bus do I take?
wǒ gāi zuò nèilù chē?

wor gai dzwor nay-loo chur

我该坐哪路车？

wheel lúnzi lun-dzur 轮子

wheelchair lúnyǐ lun-yee 轮椅

when? shénme shíhou? shun-mur shur-hoh 什么时侯？

　when we get back wǒmen huílai de shíhou wor-mun hway-lai dur 我们回来的时侯

　when's the train/ferry? huǒchē/dùchuán jídiǎn kāi? hwor-chur/doo-chwahn jee-dyen 火车／渡船几点开？

where? nǎr? 哪儿？

　I don't know where it is wǒ bù zhīdao zài nàr

wor boo jur-dow dzai nar 我 不知道在那儿

DIALOGUE

where is the Dragon temple? lóng miào zài nǎr? dzai

it's over there jiù zài nàr jyoh

could you show me where it is on the map? qǐng zài dìtúshang zhǐshì gěi wǒ ba ching – dee-too-shahng jur-shur gay wor bah

it's just here jiù zài zhèr jyoh – jer

see **way**

which: which bus? něilù chē?
nay-loo chur 哪路车？

which one? nǎ yíge? nah
yee-gur

that one nèige nay-gur

this one? zhèige? jay-gur

no, that one búshì, nèige
boo-shur

while: while I'm here wǒ zài
zhèr de shíhou wor
dzai jer dur shur-hoh 我在
这儿的时候

whisky wēishìjì way-shur-jee
威士忌

white bái 白

white wine bái pútaojiǔ poo-tow-
jyoh 白葡萄酒

who? shéi? shay 谁

who is it? shéi? shway 谁

the man who-...-...-de
nèige rén dur nay-gur run ...
的那个人

whole: the whole week
zhěngzheng yíge xīngqī
jung-jung yee-gur hsing-chee
整整一个星期

the whole lot quánbù choo-
en-boo 全部

whose: whose is this? zhèi

shì shéide? jay shur shay-dur
这是谁的？

why? wèishénme? way-shun-mur
为什么？

why not? wèishénme bù?
为什么不？

wide kuān de kwahn dur
宽的

wife qīzi chee-dzur 妻子

Wi-Fi wúxiàn wǎngluò woo-hsyen
wahng-lwor 无线网络

will: will you do it for me?
qǐng gěi wǒ zuò yíxia ching
gay wor dzwor yee-hsyah 请给
我作一下

wind (*noun*) fēng fung 风

window chuānghu chwahng-hoo
窗户

near the window kào
chuānghu kow 靠窗户

in the window (of shop) zài
chúchuāngli dzai choo-chwahng-
lee 在橱窗里

window seat kào chuāng de
zuòwei kow chwahng dur dzwor-
way 靠窗的座位

windy: it's windy yǒufēng yoh-
fung 有风

wine pútaojiǔ poo-tow-jyoh
葡萄酒

can we have some more wine? qǐng zài lái diǎnr pútaojiǔ, hǎo ma? ching dzai lai dyenr – how mah 请再来点儿葡萄酒好吗？

wine list jiǔdān jyoh-dahn 酒单

winter dōngtian doong-tyen 冬天

in the winter dōngtian 冬天

with hé-....yìqǐ hur-....-yee-chee 和 … 一起

I'm staying with-...-wǒ gēn-....zhù zài yìqǐ wor gun-....-joo dzai yee-chee 我跟 … 住在一起

without méiyǒu may-yoh 没有

witness zhèngren jung-run 证人

wok guō gwor 锅

woman fùnǚ foo-nyew 妇女

wonderful hǎojíle how-jee-lur 好极了

won't: it won't start bù dáhuǒ dah-hwor 不打火

wood (material) mùtou moo-toh 木头

(forest) shùlín shoo-lin 树林

wool yángmáo yang-mow 羊毛

word cí tsur 词

work (noun) gōngzuò goong-dzwor 工作

it's not working huàile lur 坏了

world shìjiè shur-jyeh 世界

worry: I'm worried wǒ bù ān wor bwahn 我不安

worse: it's worse huàile hway-lur 坏了

worst zuì huài dzway hwai 最坏

would: would you give this to-...? qǐng nín bǎ zhèige gěi-...., hǎo ma? ching nin bah jay gay-....-how mah 请您把这个给 … 好吗？

wrap: could you wrap it up? qǐng nín bāng wǒ bāo yíxia, hǎo ma? ching nin bahng wor bow yee-hsyah how mah 请您帮我包一下好吗？

wrapping paper bāozhuāngzhǐ bow-jwahng-jur 包装纸

wrist shǒuwànr shoh-wahnr 手腕儿

write xiě hsyeh 写

writing paper xìnzhǐ hsin-jur 信纸

wrong: this is the wrong train wǒmen shàngcuò huǒchēle

wor-mun chung-tswor-lur hwor-chur-lur 我们上错火车了

the bill's wrong zhàngdānr cuòle jahng-dahnr tswor-lur
帐单儿错了

sorry, wrong number
duìbuqǐ, dǎcuòle dway-boo-chee dah– 对不起打错了

sorry, wrong room duìbuqǐ, zhàocuò fángjiān le jow-fahng-jyen 对不起找错房间了

there's something wrong with–...–...-yǒu máobìng yoh mow-bing … 有毛病

what's wrong? zěnmele? dzun-mur-lur 怎么了？

Y

yacht fānchuán fahn-chwahn
帆船

Yangtze Gorge Chángjiāng sānxiá chahng-jyang sahn-syah
长江三峡

Yangtze River Chángjiāng
长江

year nián nyen 年

yellow huángsè hwahng-sur
黄色

Yellow River Huáng Hé hwahng hur 黄河

Yellow Sea Huánghǎi 黄海

yes shìde shur-dur 是的

yesterday zuótiān dzwor-tyen
昨天

yesterday morning
zuótiān zǎoshang dzow-shahng
昨天早上

the day before yesterday
qiántiān chyen-tyen 前天

yet hái 还

DIALOGUE

is it here yet? hái láile
méiyou? lai-lur may-yoh

no, not yet hái méilái may-lai

**you'll have to wait a little
longer yet** nǐ hái yào děng
yídiǎnr yow dung yee-dyenr

yoghurt suānnǎi swahn-nai
酸奶

you (*singular*) nǐ 你
(*singular, polite*) nín 您
(*plural*) nǐmen nee-mun 你们

this is for you zhèi shì gěi
nǐ de jay shur gay nee dur

这是给你的

with you gēn nǐ yìqǐ gun nee
yee-chee 跟你一起

young niánqīng nyen-ching
年轻

your/yours (*singular*) nǐde nee-dur
你的
(*singular, polite*) nínde nin-dur
您的

Z

zero líng 零

zip lāliàn lah-lyen 拉链

**could you put a new
zip on?** qǐng nín bāng wǒ
huànge xīn lāliànr, hǎo
ma? ching nin bahng wor
hwahn-gur hsin – how mah
请您帮我换个新拉链
好吗？

zoo dòngwùyuán doong-woo-yew-
ahn 动物园

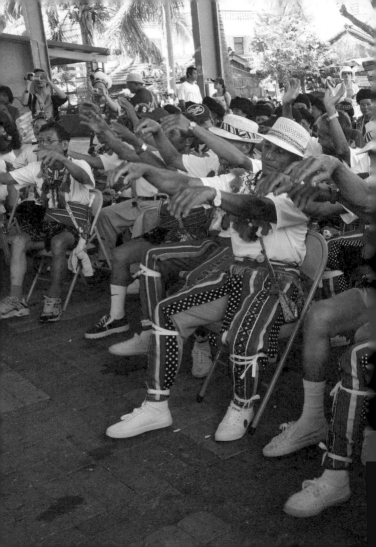

CHINESE
→ ENGLISH

Colloquialisms

You might well hear the following expressions, but on no account should you use any of the stronger ones – they will cause great offence if used by a foreigner.

bèndàn! bun-dahn idiot!

chǔnhuò! chun-hwor idiot!

dàbízi! dah-bee-dzur big nose!

dà tuánjié dah twahn-jyeh ten-yuán note

fèihuà! fay-hwah rubbish!

gàile màorle gai-lur mow-lur absolutely the best

gǔn! goon go away!, get lost!

gǔnchūqù! goon-choo-chyew get out!

húndàn! hoon-dahn bastard!

juéle jweh-lur wonderful, unique

lǎowài! low-wai foreigner!

liǎobude lyow-boo-dur terrific, extraordinary

méizhìle may-jur-lur excellent

nǎli, nǎli nah-lee oh, it was nothing, you're welcome

suànle swahn-lur forget it

suíbiàn sway-byen as you wish

tāmāde! tah-mah-dur hell!, damn!

tài bàngle bahng-lur that's great

tài zāogāole dzow-gow-lur that's terrible

tài zāotòule dzow-toh-lur that's awful

xīpíshì hshee-pee-shur hippy

yángguǐzi! yang-gway-dzur foreign devil!

yāpíshì yah-pee-shur yuppie

yílù píng'ān yee-loo ping-ahn safe journey, bon voyage

yuánmù qiúyú yew-ahn-moo choh-yoo a waste of time (literally: climbing a tree to catch fish)

zāole! dzow-lur damn!, shit!

zhù zuǐ! joo dzway shut up!

zǒu kāi! dzoh go away!

A

ǎi short

Àiěrlán ai-ur-lahn Ireland; Irish

àizībìng ai-dzur-bing AIDS

àn ahn dark; shore

ānjìng ahn-jing quiet

ānquán ahn-choo-en safe

ānzuò ahn-dzwor saddle

Àodàlìyà or-dah-lee-yah Australia; Australian (*adj*)

B

ba bah particle at the end of a sentence to indicate a suggestion, piece of advice etc

bā eight

bǎ measure word used for chairs, knives, teapots, tools or implements with handles, stems and bunches of flowers

bàba bah-bah father

bābǎi eight hundred

bái white

bǎidù ferry

báisè bai-sur white

bái tiān tyen day, daytime

bǎiwàn bai-wahn one million

bàn bahn half

bàndá bahn-dah half a dozen

bàngjíle bahng-jee-lur terrific

bàngōngshì bahn-goong-shur office

bāngzhù bahng-joo help

bànr bahnr partner, boyfriend; girlfriend

bànyè bahn-yur midnight; at midnight

báo bow thin

bàofēngyǔ bow-fung-yew storm

bàozhǐ bow-jur newspaper

bāoguǒ bow-gwor package, parcel

bāokuò bow-kwor include

bǎole bow-lur full

bǎozhèng bow-jung promise; guarantee

báozhǐ bow-jur tissue, Kleenex

bāshí bah-shur eighty

bāyuè bah-yew-eh August

bēi bay cup, glass

běi north

Běi Ài'ěrlán ai-er-lahn Northern Ireland

bēizi bay-dzur cup

bèn bun stupid

běn measure word used for books, magazines etc

bēngdài bung-dai bandage

bǐ bee than

> **bǐ-... gèng** gung even more than-...

> **bǐ nèi duō diǎnr** nay dwor dyenr more than that

biānjiè byen-jyeh border

biānjìng byen-jing border

biānr byenr side

biǎo byow form

biǎodì byow-dee cousin (male, younger than speaker)

biǎogē byow-gur cousin (male, older than speaker)

biáojiě byow-jyeh cousin (female, older than speaker)

biǎomèi byow-may cousin (female, younger than speaker)

biéde dìfang byeh-dur dee-fahng somewhere else

biéde dōngxi byeh-dur doong-hshee something else

bīng ice

bīngdòngde –doong-dur frozen

bìngfáng –fahng ward

bīnguǎn –wahn hotel

bīngxiāng –hsyang fridge

bǐsài game; match; race

bìxū bee-hsyew must

bìyào(de) bee-yow(-dur) necessary

bíyǒu bee-yoh penfriend

bízi bee-dzur nose

bōhào bor-how dial

bōli bor-lee glass (material)

bōli bēi bay glass (for drinking)

bówùguǎn bor-woo-gwahn museum

bózi boh-dzur neck

bù boo no; not; material, fabric

bù duō dwor not much

bù chángjiàn(de) chahng-jyen (-dur) unusual

bú kèqi kur-chee you're welcome, don't mention it

bùfen boo-fun part

bùhǎo boo-how bad

bù jiǔ jyoh soon

bù kěnéng kur-nung impossible

bùliào boo-lyow cloth, fabric

bù lǐmào lee-mow rude

búshì boo-shur no, it is not the case

búshì-... jiùshi-... jyoh-shur either-... or-...

bùtóng boo-toong different; difference

bùxíng boo-sing on foot

búyào! boo-yow don't!

búyàole –lur that's all; nothing else

búyòng xiè hsyeh you're welcome, don't mention it

C

cài tsai dish; meal

cái only

cānchē tsahn-chur buffet car

cánfèi tsahn-fay disabled

cáng tsahng hide

cāngbái –bai pale

cānguān –wahn visit

cāngying fly (noun)

cānjīn tsahn-jin napkin

cāntīng restaurant; dining room

cǎo tsow grass

cǎoyào tsow-yow herbs (medicinal)

céng tsung floor (in hotel etc)

cèsuǒ tsur-swor toilet, rest room

chá chah tea (drink)

chà to (the hour)

chàbuduō chah-boo-dwor almost, nearly

cháchí chah-chur teaspoon

cháhàotái chah-how-tai directory enquiries

chán chahn greedy

cháng chahng long

chànggē –gur sing

chàngpiàn –pyen record (music)

chángtú chēzhàn –too chur-jahn long-distance bus station

chángtú diànhuà dyen-hwah long-distance call

chángtú qìchē chee-chur long-distance bus

chángtú qūhào chew-how dialling code

chāojí shìchǎng chow-jee shur-chahng supermarket

chǎole chow-lur noisy

chāopiào chow-pyow banknote, (US) bill

cháoshī chow-shur damp; humid

cháozhe chow-jur towards

chápán chah-pahn tray

chāzi chah-dzur fork

chē chur city bus

chēfèi chur-fay fare

chēlún chur-lun wheel

chéngbǎo chung-bow castle

chéngjiā –jyah married

chéngkè –kur passenger

chénglǐ –lee in town, in the city

chéngshì –shur city, town

chéngshí honest

chéngzhèn –jun town

chènyī chun-yee shirt

chētāi chur-tai tyre

chēzhàn chur-jahn bus station; bus stop

chī chur eat

chí late

chǐcùn chur-tsun size

chīde chur-dur food

chīsùde chur-soo-dur vegetarian

chóngfù choong-foo repeat

chuán chwahn ship, boat

chuáncāng –tsahng cabin

chuáng chwahng bed

chuángdān –dahn sheet

chuángdiàn –dyen mattress

chuānghu –hoo window

chuānkǒng chwahn-koong puncture

chuánrǎn –rahn infectious

chuántǒng –toong traditional

chuánzhēn –jun fax

chúfáng choo-fahng kitchen

chūkǒu choo-koh exit

chúle-... yǐwài choo-lur-... yee-wai except-..., apart from-...

chǔn silly

chūnjié chun-jyeh Chinese New Year

chūntian chun-tyen spring; in the spring

chúxī choo-hshee New Year's Eve

chǔxù choo-hsyew deposit

chūzū choo-dzoo hire, rent

chūzūchē diǎnr –chur dyenr taxi rank

chūzū qìchē chee-chur taxi

cí tsur word

cídài tsur-dai tape, cassette

cóng tsoong from

cōngcong hurriedly

cónglái bù never (referring to the past or present)

cōngming clever, intelligent

cūnzhuāng tsun-jwahng village

cuò(wù) tswor(-woo) mistake, error; fault

D

dà dah big, large

dǎ hit

dàbó dah-bor brother-in-law (husband's elder brother)

dà bùfen shíjīan dah boo-fun shur-jyen most of the time

dǎcuòle dah-tswor-lur wrong number

dǎ diànhuà dyen-hwah phone, call

dàgài probably

dàhuì dah-hway conference

> Travel tip It's useful to have a business card; Chinese with business aspirations hand them out at every opportunity, and are a little crestfallen if you can't produce one in return. It's polite to take the proffered card with both hands and to have a good look at it before putting it away.

dáhuǒjī dah-hwor-jee cigarette lighter

dài take (something somewhere)

dàilái bring

dàilǐng yóujiàn yoh-jyen poste restante

dàitì instead

dàjíle dah-jee-lur enormous

dàlù main road

dàmǐ uncooked rice

dàn dahn weak; pale

dānchéngpiào dahn-chung-pyow single ticket, one-way ticket

dāndú alone

dāngrán dahn-grahn of course, certainly

dànián sānshí dah-nyen sahn-shur Chinese New Year's Eve

dānrén jiān dahn-run jyen single room

dānshēn dahn-shun single, unmarried

dànshì dahn-shur but

dānyuán dahn-yew-ahn flat, apartment

dǎo dow island

dāo knife

dào to; arrive

dào-... wéizhǐ way-jur until-...

dàodá dow-dah arrive

dàodá shíjiān shur-jyen arrival

dàotián dow-tyen paddy field, rice field

dǎoyóu dow-yoh tour guide

dāozi dow-dzur knife

dàrén dah-run adult

dàshēng de dah-shung dur loud

dàshíguǎn dah-shur-gwahn embassy

dàxióngmāo hsyoong–mow panda

dàxué dah-hsyew-eh university

dàyī dah-yee coat, overcoat

dàyuē dah-yew-eh roughly, approximately

dǎzhàng dah-jahng fight

de dur of (particle inserted between adjective and noun to denote possession)

dé get, obtain

de duō:-... de duō dwor much more-...

Déguó dur-gwor Germany; German (*adj*)

dēng dung light; lamp

děng wait

dēngjì dung-jee check-in

dēngjīkǒu – koh gate (at airport)

dēngjī pái boarding pass

dēngpào dung-pow lightbulb

dì dee floor

  dì èr tiān tyen the day after

dī low

diàn dyen electric; electricity

-diǎn hour; o'clock

diànchí dyen-chur battery

diànchuīfēng dyen-chway-fung hairdryer

diàndòng tìxū dāo dyen-doong tee-hsyew dow shaver

diàngōng dyen-goong electrician

diànhuà dyen-hwah phone

diànhuà hàomǎ bù how-mah phone book

diànhuàtíng phone box

diànnǎo dyen-now computer

diǎnr dyenr a little bit

  ... diǎnr more-...

diànshì dyen-shur television

diàntī lift, elevator

diàntìdāo dyen-tee-dow electric shaver

diànxiàn dyen-hsyen wire; lead

diǎnxíng dyen-hsing typical

diànyā dyen-yah voltage

diànyǐng dyen-ying film, movie

diànyǐng yuàn yew-ahn cinema, movie theater

diànyuán chāzuò dyen-yew-ahn chah-dzwor power point

diànzi dyen-dzur cushion

diàochuáng dyow-chwahng cot

dìbā dee-bah eighth

dìdi younger brother

dì'èr(ge) –gur second

diézi dyeh-dzur dish, bowl; saucer

dìfāng dee-fahng place

dìjiǔ dee-jyoh ninth

dìliǎng dee-lyang second

dìliù dee-lyoh sixth

dìnghūnle –hun-lur engaged (to be married)

dǐngshang: zài dǐngshang dzai ding-shahng at the top

dìngzuò –dzwor reserve

dìqī dee-chee seventh

dìqū dee-chew region

dǐr deer bottom

dìsān dee-sahn third

dìshang dee-shahng on the ground

dìshí dee-shur tenth

dìsì dee-sur fourth

dísīkē –kur disco

dìtǎn dee-tahn carpet

dìtiě dee-tyeh underground, (US) subway

dìtiě zhàn jahn underground station, subway station

dìtú dee-too map

diū dyoh lose

dìwǔ dee-woo fifth

dìyī first

dìzhǐ dee-jur address

dǒng: nǐ dǒngle? doong-lur do you understand?

   wǒ bù dǒng wor I don't understand

dōng doong east

dòng hole; puncture

dōngběi –bay northeast

dōngbiān –byen in the east

dōngnán –nahn southeast

dǒngshì –shur director

dōngtian –tyen winter; in the winter

dòngwù –woo animal

dòngwùyuán –yew-ahn zoo

dōngxi –hshee thing (object)

dōu doh both, all

dǒu steep

dú doo read

duǎn dwahn short

duǎnkù shorts

duànle –lur broken

duǎnwà –wah sock

duì dway right, correct; towards; with regard to; queue; side

duìbuqǐ dway-boo-chee sorry, excuse me

duìfāng fùkuǎn –fahng foo-kwahn collect call

duìhuàn dway-hwahn change (verb: money)

duìhuànlǜ –lyew exchange rate

duìjíle! –jee-lur exactly!

duìle yes, that's it, that's right

duō dwor much; more than

   duōde duō –dur a lot more

duōle:-... duōle –lur far more-...

duōshao? dwor-show how much?, how many? (if answer is likely to be more than ten)

duōxiè –hsyeh thank you very much

duō yíbèi yee-bay twice as much

duō yìdiǎnr yee-dyenr a bit more

duōyòng chātóu –yoong chah-toh adapter

dúpǐn doo-pin drugs, narcotics

dǔzhùle doo-joo-lur blocked

DVD dee-way-dee DVD

E

è ur hungry

Éguó ur-gwor Russia; Russian (*adj*)

èr two

èrbǎi two hundred

èr děng dung second class

ěrduo er-dwor ear

ěrhuán er-hwahn earring

ěr lóng loong deaf

èrlóu er-loh first floor, (US) second floor

èrshí er-shur twenty

értóng er-toong children

èrwàn er-wahn twenty thousand

érxí er-hshee daughter-in-law

èryuè er-yew-eh February

érzi er-dzur son

ěxīn ur-hsin disgusting; nausea

F

fā fah send

fā duǎnxìn fah dwahn-hsin text

Fǎguó fah-gwor France; French (*adj*)

fán fahn bored

fàn meal

fàndiàn fahn-dyen large restaurant; luxury hotel

fǎng fahng imitation

fàng put

fāngbiàn –byen convenient

fángdǐng roof; ceiling

fángfǔjì –foo-jee antiseptic

fángjiān –jyen room

fànguǎnr fahn-gwahnr small restaurant

fāngxiàng –hsyang direction

fángzi –dzur building; house

fángzū –dzoo rent (*noun*)

fànwǎn fahn-wahn rice bowl

fānyì translate; translation; translator

fāshēng fah-shung happen

fāyóujiàn fah-yoh-jyen email

fēi fay fly (*verb*)

fēicháng fay-chahng very, extremely

fēijī fay-jee plane

  zuò fēijī dzwor by air

fēijīchǎng –chahng airport

fèixū fay-hsyew ruins

féizào fay-dzow soap

fēi zhèngshì jung-shur informal

fēn fun minute

fēng fung mad, insane; wind; measure word used for letters

fēngjǐng fung-jing scenery; sights

fēngshàn fung-shahn fan (electrical)

fēngsú fung-soo custom

fěnhóng fun-hoong pink

fēnjī fun-jee extension

fēnkāi separate

fēnzhōng fun-joong minute

Fó for Buddha

Fójiào for-jyow Buddhism; Buddhist

fù(qián) foo(-chyen) pay

fūfù couple (two people)

fùjiāfèi foo-jyah-fay supplement, extra charge

fùjìn foo-jin nearby; near

fùmǔ parents

fùnǚ foo-nyew woman

> **Travel tip** Women travelling in China tend to come across sexual harassment much less than in other Asian countries. Chinese men are, on the whole, deferential and respectful. Being ignored is a more likely complaint, as the Chinese will generally assume that any man accompanying a woman will be doing all the talking.

fùqin foo-chin father

fūren foo-run Mrs

fúshǒu foo-shoh handle

fúwùtái reception

fúwùyuán –yew-ahn receptionist

fùzá foo-zah complicated

G

gàir gair lid

gālí gah-lee curry

gān gahn dry; liver

gǎn catch up

gānbēi! gahn-bay cheers!

gāngbǐ gahng-bee pen

gángkǒu –koh port, harbour

gānjìng gahn-jing clean

gǎnjué gahn-jyew-eh feel

gǎnmào gahn-mow cold (illness)

gǎnrǎn gahn-rahn infection

gāo gow high; tall

gāodiǎndiàn –dyen cake shop

gāomíng gow-ming brilliant

gāoxìng gow-hsing pleased, glad

    hěn gāoxìng jiàndào nǐ hun – jyen dow pleased to meet you

ge gur general all-purpose measure word

gē song

gēbo gur-bor arm

gēbozhǒu –joh elbow

gēchàngjiā gur-chahng-jyah singer

gēge gur-gur elder brother

gěi gay give; for

gējù gur-jyew opera

gēn gun with

gèng:-... gèng gung even more-...

    gèng hǎo how better; even better

Gòngchándǎng goong-chahn-dahng Communist Party

Gòngchándǎngyuán –yew-ahn Communist Party member

gōngchǎng –chahng factory

gòngchánzhǔyì –chahn-joo-yee communism

gōngchǐ –chur metre

gōngdiàn –dyen palace

gōnggòng cèsuǒ tsur-swor public convenience

gōnggong pópo por-por wife's parents-in-law

gōnggòng qìchē chee-chur city bus

gōnggòng qìchē zhàn jahn bus stop

gōnggòng qìchē zǒngzhàn dzoong-jahn bus station

gōngjià –jyah public holiday

> Travel tip Public holidays have little effect on business, with only government departments and certain banks closing. However, on New Year's Day, during the first three days of the Chinese New Year, and on National Day, most businesses, shops and sights will be shut, though some restaurants stay open.

gōngjīn –jin kilogram

gōnglǐ kilometre

gōnglù motorway, (US) highway, (US) freeway

gōngsī –sur company, business, firm

gōngxǐ! gōngxǐ! –hshee congratulations!

gōngyuán –yew-ahn park

gōngzuò –dzwor job; work

gǒu goh dog

gòu(le) –lur enough

guài gwai peculiar

guān gwahn close, shut

guàn jug

guángchǎng gwahng-chahng square

Guǎngdōng –doong Cantonese (adj)

Guǎngdōnghuà –hwah Cantonese (language)

Guǎngdōng rén run Cantonese (person)

guānkǒu gwahn-koh pass (in mountains)

guānle –lur closed

guānménle –mun-lur closed

guānshang le shahng off, switched off

guàntou –toh can, tin

guānyú –yew about, concerning

gúdǒng goo-doong antique

gūgu aunt (father's sister)

guì(le) gway(-lur) expensive

guìzi gway-dzur cupboard

-guo gwor verb suffix indicating a past experience

guóhuà –hwah Chinese painting

guójí –jee nationality

guójì –jee international

guójiā –jyah country, nation; national, state

guòle –lur beyond

guòmǐn allergic

guòqu –chew in the past

guòshí(de) –shur(-dur) old-fashioned

guówài abroad

guòyè –yur overnight

gútou goo-toh bone

gùyì deliberately

gǔzhé gyew-jur fracture

H

hǎi sea

hái still

  hái hǎo ma? how mah are you OK?

hǎibiānr hai-byenr sea; seaside

hǎibīn coast

hǎiguān hai-gwahn Customs

háishi hai-shur or

hǎitān hai-tahn beach

hǎiwān hai-wahn bay

háizi hai-dzur child

hǎn hahn shout

hángbān hahng-bahn flight

hángbān hào how flight number

hángkōng –koong by airmail

hángkōng xìnfēng hsin-fung airmail envelope

Hànyǔ hahn-yew Chinese (spoken language)

hǎo how good; nice; all right, OK

  hǎo, xièxie hsyeh-hsyeh yes, please

hǎochī how-chur delicious

háohuá how-hwah luxurious; posh

hǎojíle how-jee-lur great, wonderful, excellent

hǎokàn how-kahn attractive

hàomǎ how-mah number

hǎo yìdiǎnr yee-dyenr better

hé hur and; river

  hé-… yìqǐ yee-chee together with-…

  … hé-… dōu bù-… doh boo neither-… nor-…

hē drink (*verb*)

hēi hay black

hēi àn ahn dark

hélǐ hur-lee reasonable

hěn hun very

hěnduō hun-dwor a lot, lots; many

hěnkuài di kwai quickly

hézi hur-dzur box

hēzuìle hur-dzway-lur drunk

hóngsède hoong-sur-dur red

hóngshuǐ –shway flood

hòu hoh thick

hòulái later; later on

hóulóng hoh-loong throat

hòumian hoh-myen behind

  zài hòumian dzai at the back

  zài-… hòumian behind-…

hòutiān hoh-tyen the day after tomorrow

hú lake

huā hwah flower

huà picture, painting

huāfèi hwah-fay spend

huài hwai bad

huàile hwai-lur broken

huáiyùn hwai-yewn pregnant

huáji hwah-jee funny

huàjù hwah-jew play (in theatre)

huáng hwahng yellow

huángdì emperor

huángfēng –fung wasp

huángjīn gold

huángsè –sur yellow

huānyíng dào-... hwahn-ying
dow welcome to-...

huāpíng hwah-ping vase

huàr hwar painting, picture

huàxiàng hwah-hsyang portrait

huāyuán hwah-yew-ahn garden

huì hway meeting, conference

huílai come back

huīsède hway-sur-dur grey

huítóujiàn hway-toh-jyen see
you later

huìyì hway-yee meeting,
conference

hūnlǐ hun-lee wedding

huǒ hwor fire

huǒchái hwor-chai matches

huòchē hwor-chur van

huǒchē train

  zuò huǒchē dzwor by train

huǒchēzhàn –jahn railway
station

huǒzāi hwor-dzai fire

huòzhe-... huòzhe-... hwor-jur
either-... or-...

huòzhě or

hùshi hoo-shur nurse

hútòng hoo-toong lane; side street

hùzhào hoo-jow passport

húzi hoo-dzur beard

J

jì jee post, mail (*verb*)

jǐ few

jiā jyah home

  zài jiā dzai at home

jiàgé jyah-gur price

jiǎn jyen cut

jiàn measure word used for
things, affairs etc

Jiānádà jyah-nah-dah Canada;
Canadian (*adj*)

jiānbǎng jyen-bahng shoulder

jiǎndān jyen-dahn simple, easy

jiāng jyang river

jiǎng speak

jiānglái jyang-lai future; in future

jiànkāng jyen-kahng healthy

jiànzhù jyen-joo building

jiǎnzi jyen-dzur scissors

jiǎo jyow foot (of person)

jiào call, greet

jiāochākǒu jyow-chah-koh
junction

jiáodǐ sole (of foot)

jiǎo gēn gun heel (of foot)

jiāojuǎnr jyow-jew-ahnr film
(for camera)

jiāoqū jyow-chew suburb

jiāoqūchē –chur bus (in suburbs)

jiàotáng jyow-tahng church

jiāotōng tú jyow-toong streetmap

jiāoyì huì jyow-yee hway exhibition, trade fair

jiáozhǐtou jyow-jur-toh toe

jiàqī jyah-chee holiday, vacation

jiàqián jyah-chyen cost (*noun*)

jiātíng family

jiǎyá jyah-yah dentures

jiāyóu zhàn jyah-yoh jahn petrol station, gas station

jiàzhí jyah-jur value

jiàzi jyah-dzur shelf

jíbìng illness, disease

jīchǎng bānchē jee-chahng bahn-chur airport bus

jiē(dào) jyeh(-dow) avenue; street

jiè jyeh borrow

jiěfū jyeh-foo brother-in-law (elder sister's husband)

jiéhūn jyeh-hun married

 nǐ jiéhūnle ma? jyeh-hun-lur mah are you married?

jiějie jyeh-jyeh elder sister

jiémùdānr jyeh-moo-dahnr programme

jiérì jyeh-rur festival; holiday

jiēshi jyeh-shur strong

jièzhi jyeh-jur ring (on finger)

jífèi diànhuà jee-fay dyen-hwah payphone

jǐge jee-gur several

 jǐge? how much?, how many? (if answer is likely to be ten or fewor)

jíjiù jee-jyoh first aid

jíjiùxiāng –hsyang first-aid kit

jìn near

jǐngchá jing-chah police; policeman

jīngcháng jing-chahng often, frequent

jīngguò jing-gwor through; via

jīnglǐ manager

jǐngr view

jīngrén de jing-run dur astonishing

jìngzi jing-dzur mirror

jīnhuángsè jin-hwahng-sur blond

jìniànbēi jee-nyen-bay monument

jìniànpǐn jee-nyen-pin souvenir

jǐnjí(de) –dur urgent

jǐnjin just, only

jīnróng wēijī jin-roong way-jee credit crunch

jīnshǔ metal

jīntian jin-tyen today

 jīntian wǎnshang wahn-shahng tonight

jìntóu jin-toh end (of street etc)

jīnwǎn jin-wahn tonight

jīnzi jin-dzur gold

jīqì jee-chee machine

jìshi-… yě jee-shur-… yur even if-…

jìsuànjī jee-swahn-jee computer

jiǔ jyoh nine; alcohol; alcoholic drink

jiù just; then; secondhand

 jiù yìdiǎnr yee-dyenr just a little

jiù yìhuǐr yee-hwayr just a minute

jiúbǎi nine hundred

jiúbājiān jyoh-bah-jyen bar

jiùde jyoh-dur secondhand

jiùhùchē jyoh-hoo-chur ambulance

jiùjiu uncle (mother's brother)

jiùshí jyoh-shur ninety

jiùyuè jyoh-yew-eh September

juǎnqūde jwahn-chew-dur curly

jué búhuì jew-eh boo-hway never (referring to the future)

juéde –dur feel

juédìng decide; decision

juéduì bàng –dway bahng perfect

juéduìde! –dur absolutely!

júhuángsè jyew-hwahng-sur orange (colour)

jùlí joo-lee distance

jùyuàn jyew-yew-ahn theatre

K

kǎchē kah-chur lorry, truck

kāfēi diàn kah-fay dyen café

kāfēiguǎnr –gwahnr café

kāi open (adj)

kāichē kai-chur drive

kāide kai-dur open (adj)

kāile kai-lur open (adj)

kāishǐ kai-shur begin; start; beginning

   yì kāishǐ at the beginning

kāishuǐ kai-shway boiled water

kànbào kahn-bow read (newspaper)

kàngjūnsù kahng-jyewn-soo antibiotics

kànjian kahn-jyen see

kànshū kahn-shoo read (book)

kànyikàn kahn-yee-kahn have a look

kào kow near

kǎoshì kow-shur exam

kǎoxiāng kow-hsyang oven

kè kur lesson; gram(me)

kē measure word used for trees etc

kěài lovely

kěnéng kur-nung maybe, perhaps; possible

kěpà kur-pah horrible

kèqi kur-chee polite

kèrén kur-run guest

kěshì kur-shur but

késou kur-soh cough

kètīng lounge

kěyǐ kur-yee be able

   kěyǐ qǐng ching yes please

   nín kěyǐ-… ma? mah could you-…?

kōng koong empty

kōngjiān –jyen room, space

kōngqì –chee air

kōngtiáo –tyow air-conditioning

kǒukě koh-kur thirsty

kǔ koo bitter

kū cry

kuài kwai quick, fast; sharp; soon; measure word used for lumps or pieces

kuài chē chur express (train)

kuàidì express (mail)

kuài diǎnr! dyenr hurry up!

kuàilè kwai-lur happy

kuàir kwair piece

kuàizi kwai-dzur chopsticks

kuān de kwahn dur wide

kuāng kwahng basket

kuánghuānjié –hwahn-jyeh carnival

kùchǎ koo-chah underpants, men's underwear

kūnchóng kun-choong insect

kùnle kun-lur sleepy

kùnnan kun-nahn difficult; difficulty

kùzi koo-dzur trousers, (US) pants

L

là lah hot, spicy

lā pull

lái come, arrive

láide: nǐ shì cóng nǎr láide? shur tsoong nar lai-dur where do you come from?

láihuí piào lai-hway pyow return/round-trip ticket

lājī lah-jee rubbish, trash

lājīxiāng –hsyang dustbin, trashcan

lán lahn blue

lǎn lazy

lánzi lahn-dzur basket

lǎo low old

lǎolao grandmother (maternal)

lǎoniánren low-nyen-run senior citizen

lǎoshī low-shur teacher

lǎoshǔ low-shoo rat; mouse

Lǎowō low-wor Laos

lǎoye low-yeh grandfather (maternal)

làzhú lah-joo candle

le lur sentence particle indicating something in the past which is still relevant to the present or a change of circumstances in the present or future

-le -lur verb suffix indicat-ing completion of action

lèi lay tired

léiyǔ lay-yew thunderstorm

lěng lung cold

li: zài-… li dzai … lee inside-…

lí lee from; to; pear

-lǐ inside

liǎn lyen face

liǎng lyang two

liàng measure word used for vehicles

liǎngcì –tsur twice

liǎngge dānrénchuáng –gur dahn-run-chwahng twin beds

liǎngge dōu dow both

liǎngge dōu bù doh neither (one) of them

liǎngge xīngqī hsing-chee fortnight

liángkuai –kwai cool

liángxié –hsyeh sandal

liánkùwà lyen-koo-wah tights, pantyhose

liánxi lyen-hshee contact

liányīqún lyen-yee-chewn dress

liányùn lyen-yewn connection

liǎobuqǐ lyow-boo-chee incredible, amazing

lièchē shíkè biǎo lyeh-chur shur-kur byow timetable, (US) schedule

lièzhì lyeh-jur poor

lǐfà lee-fah haircut

lǐfàdiàn –dyen hairdresser's; barber's

lǐfàshī –shur hairdresser's

líhūn lee-hun divorced

límǐ centimetre

límíng dawn

líng zero

lǐng take (someone somewhere)

lǐng tie, necktie

língqián ling-chyen change (*noun*: money)

lìngrén yúkuài ling-run yew-kwai pleasant

lǐngshìguǎn ling-shur-gwahn consulate

lìngwài another, different

lǐng yánglǎojīn de rén –low-jin dur run pensioner

lìng yíge yee-gur another, different; the other one

línyù lin-yew shower

  dài línyù with shower

lìrú for example

liù lyoh six

liùbǎi six hundred

liúgǎn lyoh-gahn flu

liúlì fluent

liùshí lyoh-shur sixty

liúxíng lyoh-hsing popular, fashionable

liúxíngxìng gǎnmào gahn-mow flu

liúxíng yīnyuè yin-yew-eh pop music

liùyuè lyoh-yew-eh June

lǐwù lee-woo present, gift

lìzi lee-dzur example; chestnut

lóng loong dragon

lóu loh floor, storey; building (with more than one storey)

lóushàng loh-shahng upstairs

lóutī loh-tee stairs

lóuxià loh-hsyah downstairs

lǚxíng lyew-hsing travel; tour; journey

lǚxíngshè –shur travel agent's

lǚxíngzhě –jur tourist

> **Travel tip** It used to be government policy to surcharge foreigners on public transport fares and admission tickets for sights. This is no longer the case but the practice lives on anyway, and you might find price discrimination being exercised by unscrupulous shopkeepers.

lǚxíng zhīpiào jur-pyow traveller's cheque

lǚyóuchē lyew-yoh-chur tourist bus, coach

lǚyóuzhě lyew-joh-jur tourist

lǚguǎn lyew-gwahn small hotel

lǜsède lyew-sur-dur green

lù road; way

lúntāi tyre

lúnzi lun-dzur wheel

lùtiān loo-tyen outdoors

lùxiàn loo-hsyen route

lùxiàngdài loo-hsyang-dai video tape

lúzào loo-dzow cooker

M

ma? mah question particle

mā mother

mǎ horse

mà scold

máfan mah-fahn trouble

mǎi buy

mài sell

mǎimài business deal

mǎn mahn full

màn slow; slowly

   hěn màn hun very slowly

   màn diǎnr! dyenr slow down!

mángmang mahng– busy

māo mow cat

máobèixīn mow-bay-hsin pullover

máojīn towel

màopáirhuò mow-pair-hwor fake

máotǎn mow-tahn blanket

máoyī sweater

màozi mow-dzur hat, cap

mǎshàng mah-shahng at once, immediately

mǎtóu mah-toh jetty

Máo zhǔxí mow jyew-hshee Chairman Mao

měi may each, every; beautiful

méi not; does not; no; have not

mèifū may-foo brother-in-law (younger sister's husband)

méi-...-guò -gwor has never; have never

měige may-gur every

měige dìfāng dee-fahng everywhere

měige rén run everyone

méi guānxì gwahn-hshee never mind, it doesn't matter

Měiguó may-gwor America; American (adj)

měijiàn shìqíng may-jyen shur-ching everything

měijiàn shìr shur everything

méi jìnr boring

měilì beautiful

mèimei younger sister

méiqì may-chee gas

měirén may-run everybody

méishìr le may-shur lur safe

měishùguǎn may-shoo-gwahn art gallery

měitiān may-tyen every day

méi wǎnshang wahn-shahng per night

méi wèntí! wun-tee no problem!

méixiǎngdào may-hsyang-dow amazing, surprising

měiyíge may-yee-gur each, every

měiyíge rén run everyone

méiyǒu may-yoh did not; has not, have not; without

méi-...-zhe -zhur was not-...-ing; is not-...-ing

-men suffix indicating the plural

mén mun door

Ménggǔ mung-goo Mongolia; Mongolian (adj)

mǐ metre; uncooked rice

Miǎndiàn myen-dyen Burma; Burmese (adj)

miǎn fèi fay free (no charge)

miánhuā myen-hwah cotton

miǎnshuì myen-shway duty-free goods

miǎo myow second (of time)

mìmǎ mee-mah password

míngbai: wǒ míngba le wor – lur I see, I understand

míngpiàn ming-pyen card

míngtian ming-tyen tomorrow

míngtian zǎoshang dzow-shahng tomorrow morning

míngxìnpiàn ming-hsin-pyen postcard

míngzi ming-dzur name; first name

mòduān mor-dwahn end

mótuōchē mor-twor-chur motorbike

mǒudì moh-dee somewhere

MP sān géshì em-pee sahn gur-shur MP3 format

mùdì cemetery

mùdìdì destination

mùjiān xiūxi moo-jyen hsyoh-hshee interval

mǔqīn moo-chin mother

mùtou moo-toh wood

N

ná nah carry; take

nà that; that one; the

nǎinai grandmother (paternal)

nǎiniú nai-nyoh cow

nǎli? nah-lee where?

nán nahn south; hard, difficult; man

nán cèsuǒ tsur-swor gents' toilet, men's room

nánfāng nahn-fahng in the south

Nánfēi nahn-fay South Africa; South African (adj)

nán fúwùyuán foo-woo-yew-ahn waiter; steward

nánguò nahn-gwor sad

nán háir boy

nánkàn nahn-kahn ugly

nán péngyou pung-yoh boyfriend

nánrén nahn-run man

nǎr? where?

    zài nǎr? dzai where is it?

nǐ qù nǎr? chew where are you going?

nàr there

nà shí nah shur then, at that time

    nà shì-… ma? mah is that-…?

    nà shì shénme? shun-mur what's that?

názhe nah-jur keep

ne nur sentence particle which adds emphasis or conveys the idea 'and what about-…?'

nèi nay that; that one

    nèi? nay which?

nèidì brother-in-law (wife's younger brother)

nèige nay-gur that; that one

nèige shíhou shur-hoh then, at that time

nèixiōng nay-hsyoong brother-in-law (wife's elder brother)

nèi yíge yee-gur that one

néng: nǐ néng-… ma? nung-… mah can you-…?

    wǒ bù néng-… wor I can't-…

nǐ you (singular)

niàn nyen read (aloud)

nián year

niánjì nyen-jee age

    nín duō dà niánjì le? dwor dah nyen-jee lur how old are you?

niánlíng: nín duō dà niánlíng? nyen-ling how old are you?

niánqīng nyen-ching young

niǎo nyow bird

niàobù nyow-buo nappy, diaper

Níbóěr nee-bor-er Nepal; Nepali (*adj*)

nǐde nee-dur your; yours (*singular*)

nǐ hǎo nee how hello; hi; how do you do?

nǐ hǎo ma? mah how are you?

> Travel tip Shaking hands is not a Chinese tradition, though it is now fairly common between men. Businessmen meeting for the first time exchange business cards, with the offered card held in two hands as a gesture of respect – you'll see polite shop assistants doing the same with your change.

nǐmen nee-mun you (*plural*)

nǐmende –dur your; yours (*plural*)

nín you (*singular, polite*)

nínde nin-dur your; yours (*singular, polite*)

niúzǎikù nyoh-dzai-koo jeans

nóng noong strong

nóngchǎng –chahng farm

nóngcūn –tsun countryside

nǚ'ér nyew-er daughter

nǚ cèsuǒ tsur-swor ladies' room, ladies' toilets

nǚ chènshān nyew-chun-shahn blouse

nǚ fúwùyuán foo-woo-yew-ahn waitress; maid; stewardess

nǚ háir hair girl

nǚpéngyou nyew-pung-yoh girlfriend

nǚshì nyew-shur Ms; lady

nǚzhāodài nyew-jow-dai waitress

nuǎnhuo nwahn-hwor warm; mild

nuǎnqì nwahn-chee heating; central heating; radiator

O

Ōuzhōu oh-joh Europe; European (*adj*)

P

pàichūsuǒ pai-choo-swor police station

pán pahn measure word used for round objects

pàng pahng fat

páng pahng side

pángbiān: zài-... pángbiān dzai-... pahng-byen beside the-..., next to-...

pánzi pahn-dzur plate

pǎo pow run

péngchē pung-chur van

pèngtóu dìdiǎn pung-toh dee-dyen meeting place

péngyou pung-yoh friend

pēnquán pun-choo-en fountain

piányi pyen-yee be inexpensive; inexpensive

piào pyow ticket; single ticket, one-way ticket

piàoliang pyow-lyang beautiful; pretty

pífu skin

pígé pee-gur leather

píng'ān ping-ahn safe

píngcháng ping-chahng usual, normal

pīngpāngqiú ping-pahng-chyoh table tennis

píngtǎn ping-tahn flat (*adj*)

píngzi ping-dzur bottle

pǔtōng poo-toong ordinary

Pǔtōnghuà –hwah Mandarin

Q

qī chee seven

qián chyen money

qiánbāo –bow wallet; purse

qiānbǐ pencil

qiánbianr: zài qiánbianr dzai chyen-byenr in front; at the front

qiáng chyang wall

qiángjiān –jyen rape

qiǎngle –lur robbed

qiánmiàn chyen-myen front

qiántiān –tyen the day before yesterday

qiántīng lobby

qiānwàn –wahn ten million

qiánxiōng –hsyoong breast; bust; chest

qián yì tiān tyen the day before

qiānzhèng –jung visa

qiānzì –dzur signature

qiáo chyow bridge

qiǎokèlì –kur-lee chocolate

qiāozhúgàng –joo-gahng rip-off

qībǎi chee-bai seven hundred

qìchē chee-chur car

    zuò qìchē dzwor by car

qìchē chūzū choo-dzoo car rental

qìchē zǒngzhàn dzoong-jahn bus station (for city buses)

qìchē xiūlíchǎng hsyoh- lur-chahng garage (for repairs)

qǐchuáng chee-chwahng get up (in the morning)

qiè chyeh cut

qǐfēi shíjiān chee-fay shee-jyen departure

qíguài(de) chee-gwai(-dur) weird, strange, odd

qí mǎ chee mah horse riding

qīng ching light (not heavy)

qǐng please; ask, request

qīngdàn –dahn mild

qǐng jìn come in

qīngshàonián –show-nyen teenager

qīngxīn –hsin fresh

qióng chyoong poor

qīshí chee-shur seventy

qítā chee-tah other

qìtǐng chee-ting motorboat

qiú chyoh ball

qiúmí sports fan

qiúpāi racket (tennis, squash)

qiūtiān chyoh-tyen autumn, (US) fall; in the autumn/fall

qìxiè chee-hsyeh equipment

qìyóu chee-yoh petrol, (US) gas

qīyuè chee-yew-eh July

qīzi chee-dzur wife

qí zìxíngchē de rén chee dzur-sing-chur dur run cyclist

qù chew go; to

qǔ get, fetch

quánbù choo-en-boo all; all of it, the whole lot

quánguó –gwor national, nationwide

qùnián chew-nyen last year

qúnzi chewn-dzur skirt

R

ránhòu rahn-hoh then, after that

rè rur hot; heat

rèdù rur-doo temperature; fever

rèle rur-lur hot

rén run person

  wǒ shì-... rén wor shur I come from-...

rènao rur-now busy, lively

rēng rung throw

rènhé run-hur any

rènhé rén anybody

rènhé shénme shun-mur anything

rénkǒu run-koh population

rénmín people

rénqún run-chewn crowd

rènshi run-shur know; recognize

rénxíng dào run-hsing dow pavement, sidewalk

rénxíng héngdào hung-dow pedestrian crossing

rèshuǐpíng rur-shway-ping Thermos flask

Rìběn ree-bun Japan

rìjì rur-jee diary

róngyì roong-yee easy

ròu roh meat

ruǎn rwahn soft

ruǎnpán –pahn disk

ruǎnwò –wor soft sleeper, first class sleeper

ruǎnzuò –dzwor soft seat, first class seat

rúguǒ roo-gwor if

Ruìdiǎn rway-dyen Sweden

rùkǒu roo-koh entrance

ruò rwor weak

S

sāi cheek

sāizi sai-dzur plug (in sink)

sān sahn three

sānbǎi three hundred

sānděng sahn-dung third class

sǎngzi sahng-dzur Thursday

sānjiǎokù sahn-jyow-koo pants, panties

sānshí sahn-shur thirty

sānyuè sahn-yew-eh March

sēnlín sun-lin forest

shā shah sand; kill

shāfā shah-fah sofa

shǎguā shah-gwah idiot

shàiyīshéng shai-yee-shung clothes line

shān shahn mountain, hill

shāndòng –doong cave

shàng shahng up; above

  zài-...-shàng dzai above-...

shàngdì God

shāngdiàn –dyen shop

shàngmian: zài-... shàngmian dzai--myen on-...

shàngtou: zài-... shàngtou –toh on top of-...

shāngǔ shahn-goo valley

shǎnguāngdēng shahn-gwahng-dung flash (for camera)

shàngwǔ a.m. (from 9 a.m. to noon)

shāngxīn –hsin sad

shàng xīngqī hsing-chee last week

shàngyī jacket

shàng yícì yee-tsur last time

shǎnpán shahn-pahn memory stick

shànzi shahn-dzur fan (hand-held)

shǎo show less

shāoshāng show-shahng burn (noun)

shǎoshù mínzú show-shoo mind-zoo nationality (for Chinese minorities)

shǎoyú show-yew under, less than

sháozi show-dzur spoon

shēchǐ shur-chur luxury

shéi? shay who?

shéide? shay-dur whose?

shēn shun deep

shēng shung be born; litre

shēng bìngle shung bing-lur ill

shèngdàn jié –dahn jyeh Christmas

shēngqì –chee angry

shēngrén –run stranger

shēngrì –rur birthday

shēngyi business

shēngyīn voice

shéngzi –dzur string; rope

shénjīngbìng shun-jing-bing crazy

shénkān shun-kahn shrine

shénme shun-mur anything; something

  shénme? what?

  shénme shíhòu? shur-hoh when?

  shénme yàng de-...? dur what sort of-...?

  nǐ shuō shénme? shwor sorry?, pardon (me)?

shénme yě méiyǒu yur may-yoh none

shēntǐ shun-tee body

shèshì shur-shur centigrade

shì shur to be; is; are; was; were; will be; it is; it was; yes, it is the case

  shì-... ma? mah is it-...?

shí ten

shī wet

shíbā shur-bah eighteen

shìchǎng shur-chahng market

> **Travel tip** In malls and high street stores, prices are fixed, but there is always leeway for bargaining in small shops and markets. In touristy places, such as fake markets, haggling is essential, as vendors can start at ten or even fifty times what they'll accept.

shìde shur-dur yes, it is the case

shíèr shur-er twelve

shíèr yuè yew-eh December

shìgù shur-goo accident

shíhou: zài-... de shíhou dzai-... dur shur-hoh during-...

shíjiān shur-jyen time

shíjiānbiǎo –byow timetable, (US) schedule

shìjiè shur-jyeh world

shíjiǔ shur-jyoh nineteen

shíliù shur-lyoh sixteen

shímáo shur-mow fashionable

shìnèi shur-nay indoors; indoor

shípǐn diàn shur-pin dyen food store

shíqī shur-chee seventeen; period (of time)

shìqūchē shur-chew-chur city bus

shìr shur thing, matter

shísān shur-sahn thirteen

shísì shur-sur fourteen

shíwàn shur-wahn hundred thousand

shíwù shur-woo food

shíwǔ fifteen

shíwù zhòngdú joong-doo food poisoning

shíyī shur-yee eleven

shíyīyuè shur-yee-yew-eh November

shíyuè shur-yew-eh October

shìzhèngfǔ dàlóu shur-jung-foo dah-loh town hall

shì zhōngxīn shur joong-sin city centre

shízì lùkǒu shur-dzur loo-koh crossroads, intersection

shǒu shoh hand

shòu thin

shòu huānyíng hwahn-ying popular

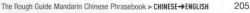

shòuhuòtíng shoh-hwor-ting
kiosk

shǒujī shoh-jee mobile phone,
cell phone

shǒujī chōngdiànqì
shoh-jee choong-dyen-chee
phone charger

shōujù shoh-jyew receipt

shǒujuànr shoh-jwahnr
handkerchief

shòupiàochù shoh-pyow-choo
ticket office; box office

shòushāng shoh-shahng injured

shǒushi shoh-shur jewellery

shǒushù operation

shǒutào shoh-tow glove

shǒutíbāo shoh-tee-bow
handbag, (US) purse

shǒutí diànnǎo shoh-tee dyen-
now laptop

shǒutíxiāng shoh-tee-hsyang
suitcase

shǒutí xíngli shoh-tee hsing-lee
hand luggage

shǒuwànr shoh-wahnr wrist

shǒuxiān shoh-hsyen at first

shǒuyīnjī shoh-yin-jee radio

shǒuzhǐ shoh-jur toilet paper;
finger

shǒuzhuó shoh-jwor bracelet

shū shoo book

shú ripe

shù tree

shuāng shwahng double

shuāngrén chuáng –run
chwahng double bed

shuāngrén fángjiān fahng-jyen
double room

shūdiàn shoo-dyen bookshop,
bookstore

shūfu well; comfortable

shuǐ shway water

shuǐchí –chur sink; swimming
pool

shuǐguǎnr –gwahnr pipe

shuǐguǒ –gwor fruit

shuìjiào –jyow sleep; asleep

shuǐlóng tóu –loong toh tap,
faucet

shuìqún –chewn nightdress

shuìyī pyjamas

shùlín woods, forest

shuō shwor say

shuōhuà –hwah talk

shuōmíngshū leaflet; brochure

shūshu uncle (father's younger
brother)

shùzì shoo-dzur number

sǐ sur die; dead

sì four; Buddhist temple

sìbǎi four hundred

sīchóu sur-choh silk

sì fēn zhī yī fun jur quarter

sījī sur-jee driver

sǐle sur-lur dead

sīrén(de) sur-run(-dur) private

sìshí sur-shur forty

sǐwáng sur-wahng death

sìyuàn sur-yew-ahn Buddhist
monastery

sìyuè sur-yew-eh April

sòng soong deliver; send

sòngfàn fúwù soong-fahn foo-woo room service

sòngxìn delivery (of mail)

suān swahn be sour; sour

suānténg –tung ache

Sūgélán soo-gur-lahn Scotland; Scottish

suíbiàn sway-byen informal

suídào sway-dow tunnel

suīrán sway-rahn although

sùliào soo-lyow plastic

sùliàodài soo-lyow-die plastic bag

sūnnǚr sun-nyewr granddaughter (son's daughter)

sūnzi sun-dzur grandson (son's son)

suǒ swor lock; locked; measure word used for buildings

suǒyǒu de dōngxi swor-yoh dur doong-hshee everything

sùshāir de soo-shair dur plain, not patterned

sùxiàng soo-hsyang statue

T

tā tah he; she; it; him; her

tǎ pagoda

tāde tah-dur his; her; hers; its

tài too (excessively)

tài duō dwor too much

Tàiguó tai-gwor Thailand

tàihǎole tai-how-lur fantastic; well done

tài shòu tai shoh skinny

tàiyáng sun

tàiyángjìng sunglasses

tāmen tah-mun they; them

tāmen quánbù choo-en-boo all of them

tāmende tah-mun-dur their; theirs

tān tahn greedy

tángdì tahng-dee cousin (son of father's brother)

tángjiě –jyeh cousin (daughter of father's brother)

tángkuàir –kwair sweets, candies

tángmèi –may cousin (daughter of father's brother)

tángniàobìng –nyow-bing diabetic

tángxiōng –hsyoong cousin (son of father's brother)

tǎnzi tahn-dzur blanket

táoqì tow-chee pottery

tàoshān tow-shahn jumper

tàozhuāng tow-jwahng suit

tèbié tur-byeh especially

téng tung pain, ache; painful

tiān tyen day; sky

tián sweet (taste)

tiándì field

tiānqì lyen-chee weather

tiáo tyow measure word used for fish and long narrow objects

tiàowǔ tyow-woo dance

tiàozǎo tyow-dzow flea

tiělù tyeh-loo railway

tíng stop

tíngchē –chur park

tíngchēchǎng –chahng car park, parking lot; garage

tíngdiàn –dyen power cut

tíngzi –dzur pavilion

tíqián tee-chyen in advance

tìxūdāo tee-hsyew-dow razor

tǐyùguǎn tee-yoo-gwahn gym

tǒng toong bucket

tóngyì agree

tóu toh head

tōu steal

tóufa toh-fah hair

tóujīn headscarf

tòumíng jiāobù jyow-boo Sellotape, Scotch tape

tóuténg toh-tung headache

tóuyūn toh-yewn dizzy, faint

tú'àn too-ahn pattern

tuán twahn group

tuántǐ twahn-tee party, group

tuì tway cancel

tuǐ leg

tuī push

tuìkuǎn tway-kwahn refund

túpiàn too-pyen picture

tūrán too-rahn suddenly

W

-**wài** outside

wàigōng wai-goong grandfather (maternal)

wàiguó wai-gwor foreign

wàiguó rén run foreigner

wàimian wai-myen outside

wàipó wai-por grandmother (maternal)

wàisūn wai-sun grandson (daughter's son)

wàisūnnǚr –nyewr granddaughter (daughter's daughter)

wài sūnzi sun-dzur grandson (daughter's son)

wàitào wai-tow jacket

wàiyī jacket; coat

wǎn'ān wahn-ahn good night

wǎn wahn late (at night)

wàn ten thousand

wǎncān wahn-tsahn dinner

wǎndiǎn wahn-dyen delay

wǎnfàn wahn-fahn evening meal; supper

wàng wahng forget

wǎng towards; net

wǎngzhàn wahng-jahn website

wǎnhuì wahn-hway party (celebration)

wánjù wahn-jyew toy

wánquándi wahn-choo-en-dee completely

wánr wahnr play (*verb*)

wǎnshang wahn-shahng evening; in the evening

  jīntian wǎnshang jIn-tyen this evening

wánxiào wahn-hsyow joke

Wēi'ěrshì way-er-shur Welsh

wéi way hello

wèi because of; stomach; measure word used politely to refer to ladies, gentlemen, guests etc

wèidao way-dow flavour

Wēiěrshì way-er-shur Wales

wèihūnfū fiancé

wèihūnqī –chee fiancée

wéijīn way-jin scarf

wèir wayr taste; smell

wèishēngjīn way-shung-jin sanitary napkin/towel

wèishēngzhǐ way-shung-jur toilet paper

wèishénme? way-shun-mur why?

  wèishénme bù? why not?

wēixiǎn way-hsyen dangerous

wèn wun ask (a question)

wénhuà dà gémìng wun-hwah dah gur-ming Cultural Revolution

wénjiàn wun-jyen file, document

wèntí wun-tee problem, question

wènxùnchù wun-hsyewn-choo information desk

wénzhàng wun-jahng mosquito net

wénzi wun-dzur mosquito
wǒ wor I; me
wǒde wor-dur my; mine
wǒmen wor-mun we; us
wǒmende –dur our; ours
wòpù wor-poo couchette; sleeper; berth
wòpù chēxiāng chur-hsyang sleeping car
wòshì wor-shur bedroom
wǔ woo five
wù mist; fog
wúbǎi five hundred
wǔfàn woo-fahn lunch
wùhuì woo-hway misunderstanding
wūjiǎor woo-jyowr in the corner of a room
wǔshí woo-shur fifty
wǔshù woo-shoo martial arts
wúxiàn wǎngluò woo-hsyen wahng-lwor Wi-Fi
wǔyuè woo-yew-eh May

X

xǐ hshee wash
xī west
xiā hsyah blind
xià down; below
　xià yícì yee-tsur next time
　xià yíge yee-gur next
　xià xīngqī hsing-chee next week

zài-…-xià dzai under-…
xiàba –bah jaw, chin
xià chē –chur get out
xiàge –gur next
xiàmian: zài-… xiàmian dzai-–myen below-…
xiàn hsyen line; thread
xiān: nǐ xiān qǐng ching after you
xiàndài modern
xiǎng hsyahng want; think
xiāngdāng –dahng quite, fairly
　xiāngdāng duō dwor quite a lot
xiàngdǎo –dow guide
Xiānggǎng –gahng Hong Kong
xiàngjiāo –jyow rubber
xiāngjìn de dur similar
xiàngliàn –lyen necklace
xiàngpí rubber, eraser
xiàngqí –chee chess
xiāngshuǐr –shwayr perfume
xiāngxìn –hsin believe
xiāngyān –yahn cigarette
xiànqián hsyen-chyen cash
xiānsheng hsyen-shung Mr
xiānyàn –yen bright
xiànzài –dzai now
xiào hsyow laugh; smile
xiǎo little, small; tight
xiāofángduì –fahng-dway fire brigade
xiǎofèi –fay service charge; tip
xiǎo húzi hoo-dzur moustache
xiǎojiě –jyeh Miss**

xiǎo lǎoshǔ hsyow low-shoo at sign, @

xiǎolù path

xiǎo qìchē chee-chur car

xiǎo sānjiǎokù sahn-jyow-koo pants, panties

xiǎoshān –shahn hill

xiǎosháor –showr spoon

xiǎoshí –shur hour

> Travel tip China officially has a five-day week, though this only really applies to government offices, which open Monday to Friday approximately 8 a.m. to noon and again from 1 to 5 p.m. Many shops open daily and keep late hours, especially in big cities. Banks usually close on Sundays – or for the whole weekend.

xiǎoshū brother-in-law (husband's younger brother)

xiāoxi –hshee information

xiǎoxī stream

xiǎoxīn! –hsin look out!

xiáozǔ –dzyew group

xiàshuǐdào hsyah-shway-dow drain

xiàtian –tyen summer; in the summer

xiàwǔ afternoon; in the afternoon; p.m.

jīntian xiàwǔ jin-tyen this afternoon

xià yíge yee-gur next

xiàzǎi hsyah-dzai download

Xībānyá hshee-bahn-yah Spain; Spanish (*adj*)

xīběi hshee-bay northwest

xībiānr –byenr in the west

xīcān –tsahn Western-style food

xīcāntīng –tsahn-ting Western-style restaurant

xiě hsyeh blood; write

xié shoe

xiē a little bit

… xiē a bit more-…

xiédǐ –dee sole (of shoe)

xié hòugēn hoh-gun heel (of shoe)

xièxie hsyeh-hsyeh thank you

xièxie, wǒ bú yào wor boo yow no thanks

Xīfāng hshee-fahng West; in the West; Western

Xīfāng de dur Western (*adj*)

xīgài knee

xǐhǎo de yīfu –how dur yee-foo washing (clean)

xǐhuan –hwahn like

xìn hsin letter, message

xīn new

xī'nán hshee-ahn southwest

xìnfēng hsin-fung envelope

xíng hsing all right

xìng surname

xìnggǎn –gahn sexy

xìngkuī –kway fortunately

xíngle –lur that's OK

xǐngle awake

xíngli luggage, baggage
xīngqī –chee week
xīngqī'èr –chee-er Tuesday
xīngqīliù –lyoh Saturday
xīngqīsān –chee-sahn Wednesday
xīngqītiān –tyen Sunday
xīngqīwǔ –woo Friday
xīngqīyī Monday
xìngqu –chew interest
xīngxing star
xìnhào hsin-how signal
xìnshǐ hsin-shur courier
xīnwén hsin-wun news (radio, TV etc)
xīnxiān hsin-hsyen fresh
xìnxiāng hsin-hsyang postbox, mailbox
Xīnxīlán hsin-hshee-lahn New Zealand
xìnyòng kǎ hsin-yoong kah credit card
xīnzàng hsin-dzahng heart
xiōng hsyoong chest
xiōngdì brother
xiōngkǒu –koh chest
xiōngzhào –jow bra
xiōngzhēn –jun brooch
xìshéng hshee-shung string
xīshì hshee-shur Western-style
xiūlǐ hsyoh-lee repair
xiūxiéjiàng –hsyeh-jyang shoe repairer
xiūxiépù shoe repairer
xiūxishi –hshee-shur lounge

xiūxītīng foyer
xiùzhēn fàngyīnjī –jun fahng-yin-jee personal stereo
xiùzi –dzur sleeve
xīwàng hshee-wahng hope
xǐyīdiàn –dyen laundry (place)
xǐyījī washing machine
xīyǐnrén –run attractive
xīyǒu –yoh rare, uncommon
Xīzàng –dzahng Tibet
xǐzǎo –dzow bathe
xǐzǎojiān –jyen bathroom
xuǎn hsyew-ahn choose
xuányá –yah cliff
xǔduō –dwor a lot, lots, plenty of
xuě hsyew-eh snow
xuějiā –jyah cigar
xuéqī –chur term
xuésheng –shung student
xuéxí –hshee learn
xuéxiào –hsyow school
xuéyuàn –yew-ahn college
xuēzi –dzur boot (footwear)
xǔkě zhèng hsyew-kur jung permit (noun)
xūyào hsyew-yow need

Y

yá yah tooth
yágāo yah-gow toothpaste
yājīn yah-jin deposit
yákē dàifu yah-kur dentist
yákē yīshēng yee-shung dentist

yān yen smoke

  nǐ chōu yān ma? choh yen mah do you smoke?

yāndǒu yen-doh pipe

yǎng itch

yángguāng yang-gwahng sunshine

yángmáo yang-mow wool

yángsǎn yang-sahn sunshade

yángtái balcony

yángwáwa yang-wah-wah doll

yànhuì yen-hway banquet

yǎnjing yen-jing eye

yǎnjìng glasses, eyeglasses

yǎnjìngdiàn –dyen optician

yǎnkē yīshēng yen-kur yee-shung optician

yánsè yen-sur colour

yǎo yow bite (by insect)

yāo waist; one

yào want; drug; Chinese medicine

  nǐ yào shénme? shun-mur what do you want?

yàobùrán yow-boor-ahn otherwise

yāodài yow-dai belt

yàodiàn yow-dyen pharmacy

yáodòng yow-doong cave (dwelling)

yàofāng yow-fahng prescription

yàogāo yow-gow ointment

yàomián yow-myen cotton wool, absorbent cotton

yāoqǐng yow-ching invitation; invite

yǎoshāng yow-shahng bite

yàoshi yow-shur key

yáshuā yah-shwah toothbrush

yáténg yah-tung toothache

yě yur also, too

yè night; page

yèli at night; p.m.

yéye yur-yur grandfather **(paternal)**

yèzǒnghuì yur-dzoong-hway nightclub

yī yee one

yìbǎi yee-buy one hundred

yíbàn yee-bahn half

yìbāo yee-bow packet

yìbēi yee-bay cup

yīcéng yee-tsung ground floor, (US) first floor

yícì yee-tsur once

   xià yícì hsyah next time

yìdá yee-dah dozen

yídàkuàir –kwair a big bit

yīděng yee-dung first class

yìdiǎnr yee-dyenr a little bit

   … yìdiǎnr a bit more-…

yìdiánrdiǎnr tiny

yídìng definitely

yīfu dress; clothes

Travel tip Casual clothing is one thing, but looking scruffy will sometimes prompt disrespect, if not contempt. All foreigners are – correctly – assumed to be comparatively rich, so why they would want to dress like peasants is quite beyond the Chinese.

---

yíge yee-gur one

   nǎ yíge? nah yee-gur which one?

yígerén yee-gur-run alone

yígòng yee-goong altogether

yí guànr gwahnr can; jug

yǐhòu yee-hoh after; afterwards

yíhuìr yee-hwayr soon

yǐjīng already

yíkè yee-kur quarter past

yíkuàir yee-kwair piece

yīlǐng collar

yī lóu loh ground floor, (US) first floor

yílù shùnfēng! yee-loo shun-fung have a good journey!

yímā yee-mah aunt **(mother's sister)**

yīmàojiān yee-mow-jyen cloakroom

yímǔ yee-moo aunt **(mother's sister)**

yín(zi) yin(-dzur) silver

Yìndu yin-doo India; Indian **(adj)**

yìng hard

yīngbàng ying-bahng pound sterling

yìngbì coin

yīng'ér ying-er baby

Yīngguó ying-gwor England; Britain; English; British

Yīngguóde –dur English; British

yìngwò ying-wor hard sleeper, second class sleeper

Yīngyǔ ying-yew English **(language)**

yìngzuò ying-dzwor hard seat,

---

third class seat

yínháng yin-hahng bank

yínshuǐ lóngtóu yin-shway loong-toh fountain (for drinking)

yīnwèi yin-way because

yǐnyòngshuǐ yin-yoong-shway drinking water

yīnyuè yin-yew-eh music

yīnyuèhuì –way concert

yìqǐ yee-chee together

yǐqián:-... yǐqián yee-chyen before-...

yìqiān one thousand

yírìyóu yee-rur-yoh day trip

yīsheng yee-shung doctor

yìshù yee-shoo art

yíwàn yee-wahn ten thousand

yǐxià: zài-... yǐxià dzai-... yee-hsyah below, less than

yìxiē yee-hsyeh a few

yí yì yur yee a hundred million

yīyuàn yee-yew-ahn hospital

yīyuè yee-yew-eh January

yìzhí cháoqián yee-jur chow-chyen straight ahead

yǐzi yee-dzur chair

yòng yoong with; by means of; use; in

yōngjǐ –jee crowded

yǒu yoh have; there is; there are

yǒu-... ma? mah is there-...?; are there-...?

yòu right (not left)

yòubiānr yoh-byenr right

yòubìng yoh-bing ill, sick

yǒudúde yoh-doo-dur poisonous

yǒuguǐ diànchē yoh-gway dyen-chur tram

yǒuhǎo yoh-how friendly

yóujì yoh-jee post, mail (verb)

yóujiàn yoh-jyen post, mail

yóujú yoh-jew post office

yóulǎn yoh-lahn tour, visit

yǒu lǐmào yoh lee-mow polite

yǒu máobìng yoh mow-bing faulty

yǒumíng famous

yóunì greasy, oily (food)

yóupiào yoh-pyow stamp

yǒuqián yoh-chyen rich

yǒurén yoh-run somebody, someone; engaged, occupied

yǒushíhòu yoh-shur-hoh sometimes

Yóutàiren de yoh-tai-run dur Jewish

yóuxì yoh-hshee game

yǒuxiào yoh-hsyow valid

yòu yíge yee-gur another, one more

yǒu yìsi yee-sur interesting; funny, amusing

yóuyǒng yoh-yoong swim

yǒuyòng useful

yóuyǒngchí –chur swimming pool

yóuzhèng biānmǎ yoh-jung byen-mah postcode, zip code

yú yew fish

yù jade

yǔ rain

yuǎn yew-ahn far; far away

yuǎnchù: zài yuǎnchù dzai yew-ahn-choo in the distance

yuánlái de dur usual

yuánzhūbǐ –joo-bee ballpoint pen

yúchǔn yew-chun stupid

yùdìng yew-ding reservation; reserve

yuè yew-eh month

yuèfù father-in-law

yuèfù yuèmǔ yew-eh-moo husband's parents-in-law

yuèliang yew-eh-lyang moon

Yuènán yew-eh-nahn Vietnam

yúkuài yew-kwai lovely

yúkuàide yew-kwai-dur enjoyable

yùndòng yewn-doong sport

yùndǒu yewn-doh iron

yùnqi yewn-chee luck

yǔsǎn yew-sahn umbrella

yùshì yew-shur bathroom

yǔyán yew-yahn language

yǔyán kè yew-yahn kur language course

yǔyī yew-yee raincoat

yùyuē yew-yew-eh appointment

Z

záhuòdiàn dzah-hwor-dyen grocer's

zài dzai in; at; on; be in/at a place; again

zài nǎr? where is it?

zài-... de shíhou dur shur-hoh during-...

zài-... hòumian hoh-myen behind-...

zàijiàn dzai-jyen goodbye

zài nàr over there; up there

zài-...-li inside-...

zài-...-pángbiān pahng-byen beside the-..., next to-...

zài-...-shàng shahng above-...

zài-...-shàngmian shahng-myen on-...

zài-...-xià hsyah under-...

zài-...-xiàmian hsyah-myen below-...

zàixiàn dzai-hsyen online

zài-...-yǐxià yee-hsyah below-..., less than-...

zài-...-zhījiān jur-jyen between-...

zài-...-zhōng joong among-...

zájì acrobatics

zāng dzahng dirty, filthy

zànglǐ funeral

zǎo dzow good morning; early

yì zǎo early in the morning

zǎofàn dzow-fahn breakfast

zǎopén dzow-pun bathtub

zǎoshang dzow-shahng morning; in the morning; a.m. (up to 9 a.m.)

jīntian zǎoshang jin-tyen this morning

zàoyīn dzow-yin noise

zázhì dzah-jur magazine

zéi dzay thief

zěnme? dzun-mur how?

    zěnme huí shìr? hway shur what's happening?; what's up?, what's wrong?

    zěnme le? lur what's happening?

zěnmele? what's wrong?, what's the matter?

zhǎi jai narrow

zhāng jahng measure word used for tables, beds, tickets and sheets of paper

zhàngdānr –dahnr bill, (US) check

zhàngfu husband

zhāngláng –lahng cockroach

zhàntái jahn-tai platform, (US) track

zhànxiàn jahn-hsyen engaged

zhànzhù jahn-joo stop

zhǎodào jow-dow find

zhàopiàn jow-pyen photo

zhāotiē jow-tyeh poster

zhàoxiàngjī jow-hsyang-jee camera

zhá tǔdòupiànr jah too-doh-pyenr crisps, (US) potato chips

zhè jur this; the

-zhe verb suffix indicating continuous action or two actions taking place at the same time

zhèi jay this; this one

    zhèi? whose?

zhèicì jay-tsur this time

zhèige jay-gur this; this one

zhēn jun really

zhēnde jun-dur true; genuine, real; sure

zhèngcháng(de) jung-chahng (-dur) normal

zhèngfǔ jung-foo government

zhèngshì jung-shur formal

zhēnguì(de) jung-way(-dur) valuable

zhéngzhěng whole, full

zhēnjiǔ jun-jyoh acupuncture

zhēn láijìn exciting

zhénsuǒ jun-swor clinic

zhèntou jun-toh pillow

zhènyǔ jun-yew shower

zhēnzhèng jun-jung genuine

zhèr jer here

    zài zhèr dzai over here

zhī jur measure word used for hands, birds, suitcases and boats

zhīdao jur-dow know

    wǒ bù zhīdao wor I don't know

zhífēi jur-fay direct flight

zhījiān: zài-... zhījiān dzai-... jur-jyen between-...

zhíjiē jur-jyeh direct

zhǐjīn jur-jin tissue, Kleenex

zhìliàng jur-lyang quality

zhínǚ jin-yew niece

zhǐshi jur-shur only

zhǐténgyào jur-tung-yow painkiller

zhíwù jur-woo plant

zhǐxuě gāobù jur-hsyew-eh gow-boo plaster, Bandaid

zhǐyǒu jur-yoh only

zhìzào jur-dzow make (*verb*)

zhízi jur-dzur nephew

zhì jur cure (*verb*)

zhǐ jur just, only; paper

zhōng joong clock

-zhōng in the middle; between
    zài-...-zhōng dzai among-...

zhòng heavy

zhǒng type; swollen

zhōngdiǎnzhàn –dyen-jahn rail terminus

Zhōngguó joong-gwor China; Chinese (*adj*)

Zhōngguó rén run Chinese (person)

Zhōngguó rénmín run-min the Chinese

Zhōnghuá Rénmín Gònghéguó –hwah run-min goong-hur-gwor People's Republic of China

zhōngjiān: zài zhōngjiān dzai joong-jyen in the middle

zhòngliàng –lyang weight

Zhōngshì –shur Chinese-style

Zhōngwén –wun Chinese (**written** language)

zhōngwǔ noon; at noon

zhōngxīn –hsin central; centre

zhòngyào –yow important

zhōngzhuǎn –jwahn connection

zhōumò joh-mor weekend

zhù joo live (*verb*)

nín zhù nǎr? what's your address?

zhuǎnxìn dìzhǐ –hsin dee-jur forwarding address

zhújiàn de joo-jyen dur gradually

zhǔnbèi hǎo le jun-bay how lur ready

zhù nǐ shùnlì! joo nee shun-lee good luck!

zhuōzi jwor-dzur table

zhǔyào de joo-yow dur main

zhúyì joo-yee idea

zhúzi joo-dzur bamboo

zǐ dzur purple

zìdòng dzur-doong automatic

zìdòng qǔkuǎnjī chew-kwahn-jee cash dispenser, ATM

zìjǐ dzur-jee oneself

zìrán dzur-rahn natural

zìxíngchē dzur-hsing-chur bicycle

zìyóu dzur-yoh free

zìzhù dzur-joo self-service

zǒng dzoong always

zǒng fúwùtái reception desk

zǒnggòng –goong total

zǒngjī operator

zōngjiào –jyow religion

zōngsè –sur brown

zǒngshì –shur always

zǒu dzoh leave, depart, go

zǒuláng dzoh-lahng corridor

zǒuzou go for a walk

zū dzoo hire, rent

zuǐ dzway mouth

zuì drunk

zuì-... ...-est, the most-...

zuǐba -bah mouth

zuì hǎo how best

zuìhòu –hoh eventually; last

zuì huài hwai worst

zuìjìn recently; last, latest

zuò dzwor by; do

zuò fēijī fay-jee by air

zuò huǒchē hwor-chur by rail

zuǒ left

zuǒbiānr –byenr left

zuò fānyì fahn-yee interpret

zuótiān –tyen yesterday

zuótiān wǎnshang wahn-shahng last night

zuótian zǎoshang dzow-shahng yesterday morning

zuòwei –way seat

zuòxià –hsyah sit down

zuǒyòu –yoh about

zúqiúsài football

干锅居

CHINESE
SIGNS

日本料理

YOSHINOYA

Broil BBQ &F

General signs

危险 **wēixiǎn** danger

请勿乱踏草地 **qǐng wù luàntā cǎodì** keep off the grass

军事要地请勿靠近 **jūnshì yàodì, qǐng wù kàojìn** military zone, keep out

禁止入内 **jìnzhǐ rù nèi** no entry

外国人未经许可禁止超越 **wàiguórén wèi jīng xúkě, jìnzhǐ chāoyuè** no foreigners beyond this point without permission

请勿随地乱扔果皮纸屑 **qǐng wù suídì luànrēng guǒpí zhǐxiè** no litter

请勿大声喧哗 **qǐng wù dàshēng xuānhuá** no noise, please

禁止拍照 **jìnzhǐ pāizhào** no photographs

请勿吸烟 **qǐng wù xī yān** no smoking

请勿随地吐痰 **qǐng wù suídì tǔtán** no spitting

人行横道 **rénxíng héngdào** pedestrian crossing

肃静 **sùjìng** quiet

一慢二看三通过 **yī màn, èr kàn, sān tōngguò** slow down, look and then cross

闲人免进 **xiánrén miǎn jìn** staff only

楼下 **lóuxià** downstairs

楼上 **lóushàng** upstairs

Airport, planes

机场 **jīchǎng** airport

机场班车 **jīchǎng bānchē** airport bus

来自 **láizì** arriving from

前往 **qiánwǎng** departing to

起飞时间 **qǐfēi shíjiān** departure time

终点站 **zhōngdiǎnzhàn** destination

预计到达时间 **yùjì dàodá shíjiān** estimated time of arrival

航班号 **hángbānhào** flight number

预计时间 **yùjì shíjiān** scheduled time

延误 **yánwù** delayed

经停站 **jīngtíngzhàn** via

国内航班进站 **guónèi hángbān jìnzhàn** domestic arrivals

国内航班出站 **guónèi hángbān chūzhàn** domestic departures

国际航班进站 **guójì hángbān jìnzhàn**
international arrivals

国际航班出站 **guójì hángbān chūzhàn**
international departures

登记牌 **dēngjìpái** boarding pass

日期 **rìqī** date

行李牌儿 **xínglipáir** baggage check

行李领取处 **xíngli língqǔchù** baggage claim

办理登机手续 **bànlǐ dēngjī shǒuxù** check-in

问讯处 **wènxùnchù** information desk

登机口 **dēngjīkǒu** gate

安全检查 **ānquán jiǎnchá** security control

中转旅客 **zhōngzhuǎn lǚkè** transfer passengers

中转 **zhōngzhuǎn** transfers

过境旅客 **guòjìng lǚkè** transit passengers

侯机室 **hòujīshì** departure lounge

免税商店 **miǎnshuì shāngdiàn** duty-free shop

系好安全带 **jìhǎo ānquándài** fasten seat belts

救生衣 **jiùshēngyī** life jacket

请勿吸烟 **qǐng wù xīyān** no smoking

座位号 **zuòwèihào** seat number

Banks and money

Travel tip China is basically a cash economy, with credit cards only accepted at big tourist hotels, the fanciest restaurants and some tourist-oriented shops; there is usually a four percent handling charge. You can obtain cash advances on a Visa card at many Chinese banks and ATMs.

帐户 **zhànghù** account

帐号 **zhànghào** account no.

银行 **yínháng** bank

中国银行 **Zhōngguó Yínháng** Bank of China

分行 **fēnháng** branch

营业时间 **yíngyè shíjiān** business hours

买价 **mǎijià** buying rate

交款处 **jiāokuǎnchù** cashier

信用卡 **xìnyòng kǎ** credit card

外币兑换 **wàibì duìhuàn** foreign exchange

中国人民银行 **Zhōngguó Rénmín Yínháng** People's Bank of China

卖价 **màijià** selling rate

今日牌价 **jīnrì páijià** today's exchange rate

旅行支票 **lǚxíng zhīpiào** traveller's cheque

元 **yuán** unit of currency

澳元 **Àoyuán** Australian dollar

加拿大元 **Jiānádà yuán** Canadian dollar

人民币 **Rénmínbì** Chinese currency

港币 **Gǎngbì** Hong Kong dollar

英镑 **Yīngbàng** pound sterling

美元 **Měiyuán** US dollar

Bus and taxi travel

长途汽车站 **chángtú qìchē zhàn** long-distance bus station

夜班车 **yèbān chē** all-night bus

公共汽车 **gōnggòng qìchē** bus

快车 **kuàichē** express bus

小公共汽车 **xiǎo gōnggòng qìchē** minibus

区间车 **qūjiānchē** part-route shuttle bus

无轨电车 **wúguǐ diànchē** trolley bus

游览车 **yóulǎnchē** tourist bus

售票处 **shòupiàokǒu** booking office

长途汽车时刻表 **chángtú qìchē shíkèbiǎo** long-distance bus timetable/ schedule

城市交通图 **chéngshì jiāotōngtú** city transport map

始发站 **shǐfāzhàn** departure point

票价 **piàojià** fare

问讯处 **wènxùnchù** information office

月票 **yuèpiào** monthly ticket

一日游 **yí rì yóu** one-day tour

就近下车 **jiùjìn xiàchē** alight on request

先下后上 **xiān xià hòu shàng** allow passengers to alight before boarding

保持车内清洁 **bǎochí chēnèi qīngjié** keep the bus tidy

请勿与司机谈话 **qǐng wù yǔ sījī tánhuà** please do not speak to the driver

老弱病残孕专座 **lǎoruò bìngcānyùn zhuānzuò** seats for the elderly or disabled and for pregnant women

招手上车 **zhāoshǒu chàngchē** stop on request

小卖部 **xiǎomàibù** kiosk

小吃店 **xiǎochīdiàn** snack bar

候车室 **hòuchēshì** waiting room

出租汽车 **chūzū qìchē** taxis

Chinese culture

寺 **sì** Buddhist temple

文化大革命 **Wénhuà Dàgémìng** Cultural Revolution (1966-1976)

天安门 **Tiān'ānmén** Gate of Heavenly Peace

长城 **Chángchéng** the Great Wall

五四运动 **Wǔsì Yùndòng** May 4th Movement (1919)

明 **Míng** Ming Dynasty (1368-1644)

十三陵 **Shísānlíng** Ming Tombs

年画 **niánhuà** New Year prints

塔 **tǎ** pagoda

故宫 **Gùgōng** Forbidden City

八达岭 **Bādálǐng** pass at Great Wall

京剧 **Jīngjù** Peking opera

木偶戏 **mù'ǒuxì** puppet show

清 **Qīng** Qing Dynasty (1644-1911)

宋 **Sòng** Song Dynasty (960-1279)

颐和园 **Yíhéyuán** Summer Palace

唐 **Táng** Tang Dynasty (618-907)

宫 **gōng** Taoist temple

观 **guàn** Taoist temple

庙 **miào** temple

天坛 **Tiāntán** Temple of Heaven

兵马俑 **Bīngmáyǒng** Terracotta Army

辛亥革命 **Xīnhài Gémìng** Xinhai Revolution (1911)

Countries, nationalities

美国 **Měiguó** America; American

澳大利亚 **Àodàlìyà** Australia; Australian

缅甸 **Miǎndiàn** Burma; Burmese

加拿大 **Jiānádà** Canada; Canadian

中国 **Zhōngguó** China; Chinese

英国 **Yīngguó** England; English; UK; British

法国 **Fǎguó** France; French

德国 **Déguó** Germany; German

香港 **Xiānggǎng** Hong Kong

印度尼西亚 **Yìndùníxīyà** Indonesia; Indonesian

爱尔兰 **Ài'ěrlán** Ireland; Irish

日本 **Rìběn** Japan; Japanese

朝鲜 **Cháoxiǎn** Korea; Korean

老挝 **Lǎowō** Laos; Laotian

马来西亚 **Mǎláixīyà** Malaysia; Malaysian

满 **Mǎn** minority people from North-East China

维吾尔 **Wéiwú'ěr** minority people from North-West China

傣 **Dǎi** minority people from South-West China

苗 **Miáo** minority people from South-West China

彝 **Yí** minority people from South-West China

僮 **Zhuàng** minority people from South-West China

蒙 **Měng** Mongol

蒙古 **Ménggǔ** Mongolia

回 **Huí** Muslim minority people

尼泊尔 **Níbó'ěr** Nepal; Nepali

中华人民共和国 **Zhōnghuá Rénmín Gònghéguó** People's Republic of China

菲律宾 **Fēilǜbīn** Philippines; Filipino

俄国 **Éguó** Russia; Russian

苏格兰 **Sūgélán** Scotland; Scottish

新加坡 **Xīnjiāpō** Singapore; Singaporean

西藏 **Xīzàng** Tibet

藏 **Zàng** Tibetan

台湾 **Táiwān** Taiwan; Taiwanese

Travel tip Like most Asian countries, Taiwan has a very family-orientated social structure, and the Taiwanese will be thrilled to hear about your family. Photographs of your loved ones can be particular crowd-pleasers: they often wind up being passed around restaurant tables, train and bus station waiting rooms and hotel lobbies.

泰国 **Tàiguó** Thailand; Thai

威尔士 **Wēi'ěrshì** Wales; Welsh

Customs

中国海关 **Zhōngguó hǎiguān** Chinese Customs

海关 **hǎiguān** Customs

边防检查站 **biānfáng jiǎncházhàn** frontier checkpoint

免疫检查 **miǎnyì jiǎnchá** health inspection

护照检查 **hùzhào jiǎnchá** passport control

报关 **bàoguān** goods to declare

不用报关 **búyòng bàoguān** nothing to declare

绿色通道 **lǜsè tōngdào** green channel, nothing to declare

红色通道 **hóngsè tōngdào** red channel, goods to declare

入境签证 **rùjìng qiānzhèng** entry visa

出境签证 **chūjìng qiānzhèng** exit visa

护照 **hùzhào** passport

过境签证 **guòjìng qiānzhèng** transit visa

旅行证 **lǚxíngzhèng** travel permit

免税物品 **miǎnshuì wùpǐn** duty-free goods

Emergencies

救护车 **jiùhùchē** ambulance

太平门 **tàipíngmén** emergency exit

火警匪警 **huǒjǐng, féijǐng** emergency telephone number: fire, robbery

消防队 **xiāofángduì** fire brigade, fire department

急诊室 **jízhěnshì** first-aid room

派出所 **Pàichūsuǒ** local police station

警察 **jǐngchá** police

公安局 **gōng'ānjú** Public Security Bureau

Entertainment

售票处 **shòupiàochù** box office

入场券 **rùchǎngquàn** cinema ticket

电影院 **diànyǐngyuàn** cinema

迪斯科 **dísīkē** disco

夜场 **yèchǎng** evening performance

全满 **quánmǎn** house full

休息 **xiūxi** interval

京剧 **Jīngjù** Peking Opera

节目单 **jiémùdān**
programme

排 ... **pái** row ...

号 ... **hào** seat number ...

票已售完 **piào yǐ shòu wán** sold out

剧场 **jùchǎng** theatre

剧院 **jùyuàn** theatre

戏院 **xìyuàn** theatre

表演时间 **biǎoyǎn shíjiān** times of performance

Forms

从何处来 **cóng héchù lái** arriving from

出生年月 **chūshēng niányuè** date of birth

籍贯 **jíguàn** father's place of birth

到何处去 **dào héchù qù** heading for

拟住天数 **nǐ zhù tiānshù** length of stay

姓名 **xìngmíng** full name

国籍 **guójí** nationality

性别 **xìngbié (nán/nǚ)** sex (male/female)

护照号码 **hùzhào hàomǎ** passport number

永久地址 **yóngjiǔ dìzhǐ** permanent address

旅客登记表 **líkè dēngjìbiǎo** registration form

签名 **qiānmíng** signature

Geographical terms

自治区 **zìzhìqū** autonomous region

运河 **yùnhé** canal

市 **shì** city

国家 **guójiā** country

县 **xiàn** county

森林 **sēnlín** forest

岛 **dǎo** island

湖 **hú** lake

江 **jiāng** large river

地图 **dìtú** map

山 **shān** mountain, hill

山脉 **shānmài** mountains

海洋 **hǎiyáng** ocean

省 **shěng** province

河 **hé** river

海 **hǎi** sea

镇 **zhèn** town

山谷 **shāngǔ** valley

村 **cūn** village

树林 **shùlín** woods

Health

中医科 **zhōngyīkē** Chinese

medicine department

中药房 **zhōngyàofáng**
Chinese medicine dispensary

牙科 **yákē** dental department

急诊室 **jízhěnshì** emergency

外宾门诊部 **wàibīn
ménzhěnbù** foreign
outpatients

医院 **yīyuàn** hospital

住院处 **zhùyuànchù** hospital
admissions office

内科 **nèikē** medical department

门诊部 **ménzhěnbù**
outpatients

挂号 **guàhào** registration

西药房 **xīyàofáng** Western
medicine dispensary

Hiring, renting

出租自行车 **chūzū
zixíngchē** bikes to rent

租船 **zū chuán** boats to rent

出租 **chūzū** for hire, to rent

Hotels

中国国际旅行社 **Zhōngguó
Guójì Líxíngshè** China
International Travel Service

中国旅行社 **Zhōngguó
Líxíngshè** China Travel
Service

宾馆 **bīnguǎn** hotel

饭店 **fàndiàn** hotel

小卖部 **xiǎomàibù** kiosk

总服务台 **zǒng fúwùtái**
reception

游艺室 **yóuyìshì** recreation
room

电传室 **diànchuánshì** telex
office

Lifts (elevators)

关 **guān** close

下 **xià** down

电梯 **diàntī** lifts, elevators

开 **kāi** open

上 **shàng** up

Medicines

> Travel tip Pharmacies are
> marked by a green cross. Be
> wary of backstreet pharma-
> cies as counterfeit drugs are
> common (check for spelling
> mistakes in the packaging or
> instructions).

抗菌素 **kàngjǔnsù** antibiotics

阿斯匹林 **āsīpǐlín** aspirin

咳鼻清 **kébìqīng** cough
lozenges

棕色合剂 **zōngsè héjì** cough
mixture

止咳糖浆 **zhǐké tángjiāng**

cough syrup

止疼片儿 **zhǐténgpiànr**
painkillers

青霉素 **qīngméisù** penicillin

含碘片 **hándiǎnpiàn** throat
pastilles

剂量 **jìliàng** dosage

失效期 **shīxiàoqī** expiry date

初诊 **chūzhěn** first treatment

外用 **wàiyòng** for external use

一日三次 **yírì sān cì** three
times a day

胃炎 **wèiyán** gastritis

饭前／后温开水送服
**fàn qián/hòu wēnkāishuǐ
sòngfú** to be taken with warm
water before/after food

每四／六小时服一次 **měi
sì/liù xiǎoshí fú yícì** one dose
every four/six hours

一日四次 **yírì sìcì** four times
a day

内服 **nèifú** to be taken orally

每次一个 **měi cì yì gé** one
measure at a time

每次一丸 **měicì yì wán** one
pill at a time

每次一片儿 **měicì yí piànr**
one tablet at a time

必要时服 **bìyào shí fú** when
necessary

Notices on doors

太平门 **tàipíngmén**
emergency exit

入口 **rùkǒu** entrance

出口 **chūkǒu** exit

顾客止步 **gùkè zhǐ bù** no
entry for customers

未经许可禁止入内 **wèi
jīng xúkě, jìnzhǐ rù nèi** no
entry without permission

拉 **lā** pull

推 **tuī** push

闲人免进 **xiánrén miǎn jìn**
staff only

Phones

长途区号 **chángtú qūhào**
area code

用卡电话亭 **yòng kǎ
diànhuà tíng** cardphone

查号台 **cháhàotái** directory
enquiries

分机 **fēnjī** extension

国际长途 **guójì chángtú**
international call

长途电话 **chángtú diànhuà**
long-distance call

电话卡 **diànhuàkǎ**
phonecard

公用电话 **gōngyòng**

diànhuà public telephone

总机 **zǒngjī** switchboard

电话簿 **diànhuàbù** telephone directory

一次一角(毛) **yícì yìjiǎo (máo)** ten fen per call

磁卡电话 **cíkǎ diànhuà** cardphone

Place names

北京 **Běijīng** Beijing

成都 **Chéngdū** Chengdu

敦煌 **Dūnhuáng** Dunhuang

峨嵋山 **Éméishān** Emei Mountains

广州 **Guǎngzhōu** Canton

长城 **Chángchéng** the Great Wall

桂林 **Guìlín** Guilin

杭州 **Hángzhōu** Hangzhou

昆明 **Kūnmíng** Kunming

拉萨 **Lāsà** Lhasa

洛阳 **Luòyáng** Luoyang

南京 **Nánjīng** Nanjing

上海 **Shànghǎi** Shanghai

深圳 **Shēnzhèn** Shenzhen

天津 **Tiānjīn** Tientsin

西湖 **Xīhú** West Lake

西安 **Xī'ān** Xi'an

长江三峡 **Chángjiāng Sānxiá** Yangtze Gorges

Post office

邮局 **yóujú** post office

开箱时间 **kāixiāng shíjiān** collection times

信封 **xìnfēng** envelope

邮筒 **yóutǒng** letterbox, mailbox

信函 **xìnhán** letters

杂志报刊 **zázhì bàokān** magazines and newspapers

包裹单 **bāoguǒdān** parcel form

包裹, 印刷品 **bāoguǒ, yìnshuāpǐn** parcels, printed matter

邮电局 **yóudiànjú** post and telecommunications office

信箱电报 **xìnxiāng** postbox

邮政编码 **yóuzhèng biānmǎ** postcode, zip code

邮票, 挂号 **yóupiào, guàhào** stamps, registered mail

电报纸 **diànbàozhì** telegram form

电报 **diànbào** telegram

电报大楼 **diànbào dàlóu** telegraph building

Public buildings

浴池 **yùchí** baths

学院 xuéyuàn college

领事馆 lǐngshìguǎn
consulate

大使馆 dàshǐguǎn
embassy

工厂 gōngchǎng factory

游泳馆 yóuyǒngguǎn
indoor swimming pool

图书馆 túshūguǎn
library

博物馆 bówùguǎn
museum

中学 zhōngxué
secondary school

体育馆 tǐyùguǎn sports
hall, indoor stadium

体育场 tǐyùchǎng
stadium

大学 dàxué university

Restaurants, cafés, bars

酒吧 jiǔbā bar

咖啡店 kāfēidiàn café,
coffee house

茶楼 chálóu café,
teahouse

茶馆 cháguǎn café,
teahouse

茶室 cháshì café,
teahouse

收款台 shōukuǎntái cashier

冷饮店 lěngyǐndiàn cold
drinks bar

中餐厅 Zhōng cāntīng
Chinese dining room

清真饭店 qīngzhēn fàndiàn
Muslim restaurant

面馆 miànguǎn noodle shop

菜馆 càiguǎn large restaurant

饭店 fàndiàn large restaurant

酒家 jiǔjiā large restaurant

酒楼 jiǔlóu large restaurant

餐厅 cāntīng restaurant; dining
room

快餐 kuàicān snack bar

小吃店 xiǎochīdiàn snack
bar

今日供应 jīnrì gòngyìng
today's menu

素菜馆 sùcàiguǎn vegetarian
restaurant

西餐厅 xī cāntīng Western
dining room

西菜馆 xīcàiguǎn Western
restaurant

Shopping

文物商店 wénwù shāngdiàn
antique shop

工艺美术商店 gōngyì

měishù shāngdiàn arts and crafts shop

自行车 **zìxíngchē** bicycles

付款台 **fùkuǎntái** cash desk

收款台 **shōukuǎntái** cashier

烟酒糖茶 **yān jiǔ táng chá** cigarettes, wine, confectionery, tea

关门 **guānmén** closed

服装店 **fúzhuāngdiàn** clothes shop

男女服装 **nánnǚ fúzhuāng** clothing

化妆用品 **huàzhuāng yòngpǐn** cosmetics

百货商店 **bǎihuò shāngdiàn** department store

家用电器 **jiāyòng diànqì** domestic appliances

换 **huàn** to exchange

食品商店 **shípǐn shāngdiàn** food shop

食品糕点 **shípǐn gāodiǎn** food and confectionery

自由市场 **zìyóu shìchǎng** free market

友谊商店 **yǒuyí shāngdiàn** Friendship store

菜市场 **càishìchǎng** greengrocer

副食品商店 **fùshípǐn**

shāngdiàn grocery store

五金交电 **wǔjīn jiāodiàn** hardware and electrical goods

袜子鞋帽 **wàzi xiémào** hosiery, shoes, hats

日用杂品 **rìyòng zápǐn** household goods

橱房用品 **chúfáng yòngpǐn** kitchenware

妇女用品 **fùnǚ yòngpǐn** ladies' accessories

女装 **nǚzhuāng** ladies' wear

洗衣店 **xǐyīdiàn** laundry

皮革制品 **pígé zhìpǐn** leather goods

> **Travel tip** When bargaining, decide how much you want to pay and then keep obstinately repeating that figure, rather than getting drawn into incremental increases. In fake markets you're likely to see the same thing in the next store along, so having got a price from one place, ask another if they will beat it.

市场 **shìchǎng** market

男装 **nán zhuāng** menswear

乐器行 **yuèqì háng** musical instruments section

新华书店 **xīnhuá shūdiàn** New China bookshop

夜市 **yèshì** night market

开门 **kāimén** open

眼镜店 **yǎnjìngdiàn** optician

复印 **fùyìn** photocopying

照相器材 **zhàoxiàng qìcái**
photographic equipment

钱票当面点清后该不
负责 **qián piào dāngmiàn
diǎnqīng, guòhòu gài bù
fùzé** please check your change
before leaving as mistakes
cannot be rectified

雨伞雨具 **yǔsǎn yǔjù**
rainwear

大减价 **dà jiǎnjià** sale

古旧书店 **gǔjiù shūdiàn**
secondhand bookshop

购物中心 **gòuwù zhōngxīn**
shopping centre

体育用品 **tǐyù yòngpǐn** sports
goods

文具商店 **wénjù shāngdiàn**
stationery

文具用品 **wénjù yòngpǐn**
stationery

牙膏牙刷 **yágāo yáshuā**
toothpaste and toothbrushes

儿童玩具 **értóng wánjù** toys

针织用品 **zhēnzhī yòngpǐn**
underwear

Streets and roads

大街 **dàjiē** avenue

胡同 **hútòng** lane

巷 **xiàng** lane

路 **lù** road

广场 **guǎngchǎng** square

街 **jiē** street

Toilets

Travel tip The Chinese have
almost no concept of pri-
vacy – even public toilets are
built with partitions so low
that you can chat with your
neighbour while squatting.
All leisure activities are done
in large, noisy groups, and a
Western tourist's desire to be
'left alone' is variously inter-
preted as eccentric, arrogant
or even sinister.

有人 **yǒurén** engaged, occupied

男厕所 **náncèsuǒ** gents' toilet,
men's room

男厕 **náncè** gents' toilet, men's
room

女厕所 **nǚcèsuǒ** ladies' toilet,
ladies' room

女厕 **nǚcè** ladies' toilet, ladies'
room

公厕 **gōngcè** public toilets, rest
rooms

盥洗室 **guànxǐshì** toilet, rest
room

无人 **wúrén** vacant, free

Train and underground travel

火车站 **huǒchēzhàn** station

火车 **huǒchē** train

列车到站时刻表 **lièchē dàozhàn shíkèbiǎo** arrival times

列车离站时刻表 **lièchē lízhàn shíkèbiǎo** departure times

开往 … 方向 … **kāiwǎng … fāngxiàng** to …

车次 **chēcì** train number

检票处 **jiǎnpiàochù** barrier

站台 **zhàntái** platform, (US) track

站台票 **zhàntáipiào** platform ticket

问讯处 **wènxùnchù** information desk

火车时刻表 **huǒchē shíkèbiǎo** timetable, (US) schedule

天 **tiān** day

特快 **tèkuài** express

直快 **zhíkuài** through train

快车 **kuàichē** fast train

客车 **kèchē** ordinary passenger train

站名 **zhànmíng** station name

开往 … **kāiwǎng …** to …

旅游车 **lǚyóuchē** tourist train

车次 **chēcì** train number

星期 **xīngqī** week

行李寄存处 **xíngli jìcúnchù** left luggage, baggage checkroom

乘警 **chéngjǐng** railway police

售票处 **shòupiàochù** ticket office

候车室 **hòuchēshì** waiting room

餐车 **cānchē** dining car

硬席 **yìngxí** hard seat

硬席车 **yìngxíchē** hard seat carriage

硬卧 **yìngwò** hard sleeper

硬卧车 **yìngwòchē** hard sleeper carriage

软席 **ruǎnxí** soft seat

软席车 **ruǎnxíchē** soft seat carriage

软卧 **ruǎnwò** soft sleeper

软卧车 **ruǎnwòchē** soft sleeper carriage

紧急制动闸 **jǐnjí zhìdòngzhá** emergency brake

乘务员 **chéngwùyuán** train attendant

地铁 **dìtiě** underground, (US) subway

MENU READER

Food

Essential terms

bowl diézi dyeh-dzur 碟子

chopsticks kuàizi kwai-dzur
筷子

cup bēizi bay-dzur 杯子

dessert tiánpǐn tyen-pin 甜品

fork (for eating) chā chah 叉

fried noodles chǎomiàn
chow-myen 炒面

fried rice chǎofàn chow-fahn
炒饭

glass bōli bēi bor-lee bay 玻璃杯

knife dāozi dow-dzur 刀子

menu càidānr tsai-dahnr 菜单儿

noodles miàntiáo
myen-tyow 面条

plate pánzi pahn-dzur 盘子

rice mǐfàn mee-fahn 米饭

soup tāng tahng 汤

soy sauce jiàngyóu jyahn-gyoh
酱油

spoon sháozi show-dzur 勺子

table zhuōzi jwor-dzur 桌子

excuse me láojià low-jyah 劳驾

could I have the bill, please?
qǐng bāng wǒ jiézhàng, hǎo
ma? ching bahng wor jyeh-jahng
how mah
请帮我结帐好吗？

Basic foods

黄油 **huángyóu** hwahng-yoh butter

奶酪 **nǎilào** nai-low cheese

辣椒油 **làjiāo yóu** lah-jyow yoh chilli oil

辣椒酱 **làjiāo jiàng** jyang chilli paste

椰子油 **yēzi yóu** yur-dzur yoh coconut milk

奶油 **nǎiyóu** nai-yoh cream

豆腐干儿 **dòufu gānr** doh-foo gahnr dried bean curd

大蒜 **dàsuàn** dah-swahn garlic

黄米 **huángmǐ** hwahng-mee glutinous millet

豆瓣辣酱儿 **dòubànr làjiàngr** doh-bahnr lah-jyengr hot soya bean paste

玉米 **yùmǐ** yoo-mee maize

小米 **xiáomǐ** hsyah-mee millet

蚝油 **háoyóu** how-yoh oyster sauce

花生油 **huāshēng yóu** hwah-shung yoh peanut oil

咸菜 **xiáncài** hsyen-tsai pickles

松花蛋 **sōnghuādàn** soong-hwah-dahn preserved eggs

菜籽油 **càizi yóu** tsai-dzur yoh rape oil

大米 **dàmǐ** dah-mee rice

盐 **yán** yahn salt

芝麻油 **zhīma yóu** jur-mah yoh sesame oil

高梁 **gāoliáng** gow-lyang sorghum (similar to corn)

豆油 **dòuyóu** doh-yoh soya bean oil

酱油 **jiàngyóu** jyang-yoh soy sauce

糖 **táng** tahng sugar

番茄酱 **fānqié jiàng** fahn-chyeh jyang tomato paste

素鸡 **sùjī** soo-jee 'vegetarian chicken' (made from soya beans)

小麦 **xiǎomài** hsyow-mai wheat

面粉 **miànfěn** myen-fun wheat flour

Basic preparation and cooking methods

什锦... **shíjǐn...** shur-jin assorted...

...丸 **...wán** wahn ...balls

...圆 **...yuán** yew-ahn ...balls

叉烧... **chāshāo...** chah-show barbecued...

煮... **zhǔ...** joo boiled...

烧... **shāo...** show braised...

... 块儿 ...**kuàir** kwair
...chunks, pieces

香酥 ... **xiāngsū**... hsyang-soo
crispy deep-fried ...

咖喱 ... **gāli**... gah-lee
curried...

炸 ... **zhá**... jah deep-fried...

...丁 ...**dīng** diced...

家常 ... **jiācháng**... jyah-
chahng home-style... (plain)

火锅 ...**huǒguō**... hwor-gwor
... in hot pot, i.e. served with
a pot of boiling water in which
the meat or fish is cooked, also
creating a soup

烤 ... **kǎo**... kow roasted, baked

...片儿 ...**piànr** pyenr ...slices

蒸 ... **zhēng**... jung steamed...

清蒸 ... **qīngzhēng**... ching-
jung steamed...

烩 ... **huì**... hway stewed...

炒 ...**chǎo**... chow stir-fried...

糖醋 ... **tángcù**... tahng-tsoo
sweet and sour...

三鲜 ... **sānxiān**... sahn-
hsyen 'three-fresh'... (with three
ingredients which vary)

Bean curd dishes

麻婆豆腐 **mápó dòufu**

mah-por doh-foo bean curd with
minced beef in spicy sauce

三鲜豆腐 **sānxiān dòufu**
sahn-hsyen 'three-fresh' bean
curd (made with three ingredients)

沙锅豆腐 **shāguō dòufu**
shah-gwor bean curd served
with a pot of boiling water in
which the bean curd is cooked,
also creating a soup

麻辣豆腐 **málà dòufu** mah-lah
bean curd with chilli and wild
pepper

虾仁豆腐 **xiārén dòufu** hsyah-
run bean curd with shrimps

家常豆腐 **jiācháng dòufu**
jyah-chahng home-style bean
curd

Beef dishes

红烧牛肉 **hóngshāo niúròu**
hoong-show nyoh-roh beef
braised in brown sauce

麻酱牛肉 **májiàng niúròu**
mah-jyang beef quick-fried in
sesame paste

酱爆牛肉 **jiàngbào niúròu**
jyang-bow beef quick-fried with
black bean sauce

葱爆牛肉 **cōngbào niúròu**
tsoong-bow beef quick-fried

with spring onions

咖喱牛肉 **gālí niúròu** gah-lee curried beef

时菜牛肉片儿 **shícài niúròupiànr** shur-tsai nyoh-roh-pyenr shredded beef with seasonal vegetables

鱼香 牛肉 **yúxiāng niúròu** yoo-hsyang nyoh-roh stir-fried beef in hot spicy sauce

笋炒牛肉 **sǔnchǎo niúròu** sun-chow stir-fried beef with bamboo shoots

麻辣牛肉 **málà niúròu** mah-lah stir-fried beef with chilli and wild pepper

蚝 油 牛肉 **háoyóu niúròu** how-yoh stir-fried beef with oyster sauce

宫保牛肉 **gōngbǎo niúròu** goong-bow stir-fried beef with peanuts and chilli

茄汁牛肉 **qiézhī niúròu** chyeh-jur stir-fried sliced beef with tomato sauce

Bread, dumplings etc

葱油饼 **cōngyóubǐng** tsoong-yoh-bing spring onion pancake

水饺 **shuǐjiǎo** shway-jyow

Chinese ravioli

饺子 **jiǎozi** jyow-dzur dumplings

锅贴 **guōtiē** gwor-tyeh fried Chinese ravioli

馄饨 **húntun** small Chinese ravioli in soup

馒头 **mántou** mahn-toh steamed bread containing various fillings

蒸饺 **zhēngjiǎo** jung-jyow steamed Chinese ravioli

烧卖 **shāomài** show-mai steamed dumplings open at the top

包子 **bāozi** bow-dzur steamed dumplings with various fillings, usually minced pork

花卷儿 **huājuǎnr** hwah-jwahnr
steamed rolls

三鲜水饺 **sānxiān shuǐjiǎo**
sahn-hsyen shoo-jyow 'three-
fresh' Chinese ravioli (pork,
shrimps and chives)

面包 **miànbāo** myen-bow white
bread

Cold platters

什锦冷盘儿 **shíjǐn lěngpánr**
shur-jin lung-pahnr assorted cold
platter

海杂拌儿 **hǎi zábànr** hai zah-
bahnr seafood cold platter

七彩冷拼盘儿 **qīcǎi lěng
pīnpánr** chee-tsai lung pin-pahnr
'seven colours' cold platter

> **Travel tip** Cold appetizers
> are served first, main courses
> arrive a few minutes later,
> then the meal is finished off
> with soup and perhaps some
> fruit. Rice generally arrives
> about halfway through the
> meal, and is eaten to fill you
> up rather than be mixed with
> your dishes.

Desserts

西瓜盅 **xīgua zhōng** hshee-
gwah joong assorted fruit and
water melon

什锦水果 **shíjǐn shuǐguo**

gēng shur-jin shway-gwor gung
fruit salad

莲子羹 **liánzi gēng** lyen-dzur
lotus-seed in syrup

酸奶 **suānnǎi** swahn-nai
yoghurt

Fish and seafood

鲈鱼 **lúyú** loo-yoo bass

螃蟹 **pángxiè** pahng-hsyeh crab

鱼 **yú** yoo fish

鲳鱼 **chāngyú** pomfret

虾 **xiā** hsyah prawns

加级鱼 **jiājí** jyah-jee red snapper

鱿鱼 **yóuyú** yoh-yoo squid

红烧鲤鱼 **hóngshāo lǐyú**
hoong-show lee-yoo carp braised
in brown sauce

干烧桂鱼 **gānshāo guìyú**
gahn-show gway-yoo Chinese
perch braised with chilli and
black bean sauce

咖喱鱿鱼 **gāli yōuyú** gah-lee
yoh-yoo curried squid

茄汁石斑块儿 **qiézhī
shíbānkuàir** chyeh-jur shur-
bahn-kwair deep-fried grouper
with tomato sauce

火锅鱼虾 **huǒguō yúxiā**
hwor-gwor yoo-hsyah fish and
prawns served with a pot of
boiling water in which they are

cooked, creating a soup

家常鱼块儿 **jiācháng yúkuàir** jyah-chahng yoo-kwair home-style fish

干烧黄鳝 **gānshāo huángshàn** gahn-show hwahng-shahn paddyfield eel braised with chilli and black bean sauce

时菜虾球 **shícài xiāqiú** shoo-tsai hsyah-chew prawn balls with seasonal vegetables

虾仁干贝 **xiārén gānbèi** hsyah-run gahn-bay scallops with shrimps

葱爆海参 **cōngbào hǎishēn** tsoong-bow hai-shun sea cucumber quick-fried with spring onions

蚝油鲍鱼 **háoyóu bāoyú** how-yoh bow-yoo stir-fried abalone with oyster sauce

滑溜鱼片儿 **huáliū yúpiànr** hwah-lyoh yoo-pyenr stir-fried fish slices with thick sauce

鱼香龙虾 **yúxiāng lóngxiā** yoo-hsyang loong-hsyah stir-fried lobster in hot spicy sauce

冬笋炒海参 **dōngsǔn cháo hǎishēn** doong-sun chow hai-shun stir-fried sea cucumber

糖醋鱼块儿 **tángcù yúkuàir** tahng-tsoo yoo-kwair sweet and sour fish

Fruit

苹果 **píngguǒ** ping-gwor apple

杏 **xìng** hsing apricot

香蕉 **xiāngjiāo** hsyang-jyow banana

椰子 **yēzi** yur-dzur coconut

海棠果 **hǎitángguǒ** hai-tahng-gwor crab apple

枣 **zǎo** dzow date

葡萄 **pútao** poo-tow grape

广柑 **guǎnggān** gwahng-gahn Guangdong orange

哈密瓜 **hāmìguā** hah-mee-gwah honeydew melon

龙眼 **lóngyǎn** loong-yahn longan (similar to lychee)

荔枝 **lìzhī** lee-jur lychee

柑子 **gānzi** gahn-dzur orange

桔子 **júzi** joo-dzur orange

桃子 **táozi** tow-dzur peach

梨 **lí** lee pear

柿子 **shìzi** shur-dzur persimmon, sharon fruit

菠萝 **bōluó** bor-lwor pineapple

李子 **lǐzi** lee-dzur plum

石榴 **shíliu** shur-lyoh
pomegranate

沙田柚 **shātiányòu** shah-tyen-
yoh pomelo

橘子 **júzi** joo-dzur tangerine

蜜桔 **mìjú** mee-joo tangerine

西瓜 **xīguā** hshee-gwah water
melon

Lamb and mutton dishes

咖喱羊肉 **gāli yángròu** gah-
lee yahn-roh curried mutton

烤羊肉串儿 **kǎo
yángròuchuànr** kow yahng-
roh-chwahnr lamb kebabs

涮羊肉 **shuàn yángròu**
shwahn yang-roh Mongolian
lamb served with a pot of
boiling water in which the
meat is cooked, also creating
a soup

红烧羊肉 **hóngshāo**
yángròu hoong-show mutton
braised in brown sauce

火锅羊肉 **huǒguō yángròu**
hwor-gwor mutton served
with a pot of boiling water in
which the meat is cooked, also
creating a soup

酱爆羊肉 **jiàngbào yángròu**
jyang-bow mutton quick-fried
with black bean sauce

葱爆羊肉 **cōngbào yángròu**
tsoong-bow mutton quick-fried
with spring onions

时菜羊肉片儿 **shícài
yángròupiànr** shur-tsai yang-
roh-pyenr shredded mutton
with seasonal vegetables

麻辣羊肉 **málà yángròu** mah-
lah stir-fried mutton with chilli
and wild pepper

蚝油羊肉 **háoyóu yángròu**
how-yoh stir-fried mutton with
oyster sauce

Meats

牛肉 **niúròu** nyoh-roh beef

鸡 **jī** jee chicken

鸭 **yā** yah duck

羊肉 **yángròu** yahng-roh lamb;
mutton

肉 **ròu** roh meat (usually pork)

Travel tip In restaurants, the
Chinese don't usually share
the bill. Instead, diners con-
test for the honour of paying
it, with the most respected
winning. You should make
some effort to stake your
claim but, as a visiting guest,
you can pretty much guarantee that you won't get to pay.

猪肉 **zhūròu** joo-roh pork

Noodles

炒面 **chǎomiàn** chow-myen
fried noodles

鸡丝炒面 **jīsī chǎomiàn** jee-sur fried noodles with shredded chicken

肉丝炒面 **ròusī chǎomiàn** roh-sur fried noodles with shredded pork

虾仁炒面 **xiārén chǎomiàn** hsyah-run chow-myen fried noodles with shrimps

炒米粉 **cháomífěn** chow-mee-fun fried rice noodles

面条 **miàntiáo** myen-tyow noodles

Pork dishes

叉烧肉 **chāshāo ròu** chah-show roh barbecued pork

咖喱肉丸 **gālí ròuwán** gah-lee roh-wahn curried meatballs

狮子头 **shīzi tóu** shur-dzur toh a large meatball stewed with cabbage

火锅猪排 **huǒguō zhūpái** hwor-gwor joo-pai pork chop served with a pot of boiling water in which the meat is cooked, also creating a soup

酱爆三样 **jiàngbào sānyàng** jyang-bow sahn-yang pork, pig's liver and kidney quick-fried with black bean sauce

烤乳猪 **káo rǔzhū** kow roo-joo roast sucking pig

米粉蒸肉 **mǐfěn zhēngròu** mee-fun jung-roh steamed pork with rice

宫保肉丁 **gōngbǎo ròudīng** goong-bow roh-ding stir-fried diced pork with peanuts and chilli

鱼香肉丝 **yúxiāng ròusī** yoo-hsyang roh-sur stir-fried shredded pork in hot sauce

冬笋肉丝 **dōngsǔn ròusī** doong-sun stir-fried shredded pork with bamboo shoots

榨菜炒肉丝 **zhàcài chǎo ròusī** jah-tsai chow stir-fried shredded pork with pickled mustard greens

笋炒肉片儿 **sǔnchǎo ròupiànr** sun-chow roh-pyenr stir-fried sliced pork with bamboo shoots

芙蓉肉片儿 **fúróng ròupiànr** foo-roong stir-fried sliced pork

with egg white

青椒炒肉片儿 **qīngjiāo chǎo ròupiànr** ching-jyow chow stir-fried sliced pork with green pepper

时菜炒肉片儿 **shícài chǎo ròupiànr** shur-tsai stir-fried sliced pork with seasonal vegetables

滑溜肉片儿 **huáliū ròupiànr** hwah-lyoh stir-fried sliced pork with thick sauce

回锅肉 **huíguō ròu** hway-gwor roh boiled then stir-fried pork

Poultry and poultry dishes

时菜扒鸭 **shícài páyā** shur-tsai pah-yah braised duck with seasonal vegetables

佛跳墙 **fó tiào qiáng** for tyow chyang chicken with duck, pig's trotters and seafood stewed in rice wine (literally: Buddha leaps the wall)

茄汁鸡脯 **qiézhī jīpú** chyeh-jur jee-poo chicken breast with tomato sauce

咖喱鸡块儿 **gālí jīkuàir** gah-lee jee-kwair curried chicken pieces

酱爆鸡丁 **jiàngbào jīdīng** jyang-bow jee-ding diced chicken quick-fried with black bean sauce

冬笋鸡片儿 **dōngsǔn jīpiànr** doong-sun jee-pyenr chicken slices with bamboo shoots

冬菇鸡片儿 **dōnggū jīpiànr** doong-goo chicken slices with mushrooms

香酥鸡 **xiāngsū jī** hsyang-soo jee crispy deep-fried whole chicken

香酥鸭 **xiāngsū yā** yah crispy deep-fried whole duck

辣子鸡丁 **làzi jīdīng** lah-dzur jee-ding diced chicken with chilli

麻辣鸡丁 **málà jīdīng** mah-lah diced chicken with chilli and wild pepper

香菇鸭掌 **xiānggū yāzhǎng** hsyang-goo yah-jahng duck's foot

Travel tip To avoid stomach complaints, eat at places that look busy and clean, and stick to fresh, thoroughly cooked food. Beware of food that has been pre-cooked and kept warm for hours. Fruit you've peeled yourself is safe; other uncooked foods may have been washed in unclean water.

with mushroom

茄汁煎软鸭 **qiézhī jiān ruǎnyā** chyeh-jur jyen rwahn-yah fried duck with tomato sauce

家常焖鸡 **jiācháng mènjī** jyah-chahng mun-jee home-style braised chicken

北京烤鸭 **Běijīng kǎoyā** bay-jing kow-yah Peking duck

酱爆鸭片儿菜心 **jiàngbào yāpiànr càixīn** jyang-bow yah-pyenr tsai-hsin sliced duck and green vegetables quick-fried with black bean sauce

葱爆烧鸭片儿 **cōngbào shāoyāpiànr** tsoong-bow show-yah-pyenr sliced duck quick-fried with spring onions

宫保鸡丁 **gōngbǎo jīdīng** goong-bow jee-ding stir-fried diced chicken with peanuts and chilli

怪味儿鸡 **guàiwèirjī** gwai-wayr-jee whole chicken with peanuts and pepper (literally: strange-tasting chicken)

汽锅蒸鸡 **qìguō zhēngjī** chee-gwor jung-jee whole chicken steamed in a pot

红烧全鸭 **hóngshāo quányā** hoong-show choo-en-yah whole duck braised in brown sauce

红烧全鸡 **hóngshāo quánjī** choo-en-jee whole chicken braised in brown sauce

Rice

炒饭 **chǎofàn** chow-fahn fried rice

蛋炒饭 **dàn chǎofàn** dahn fried rice with eggs

鸡丝炒饭 **jīsī chǎofàn** jee-sur fried rice with shredded chicken

肉丝炒饭 **ròusī chǎofàn** roh-sur fried rice with shredded pork

虾仁炒饭 **xiārén chǎofàn** hsyah-run fried rice with shrimps

米饭 **mǐfàn** mee-fahn rice

稀饭 **xīfàn** hshee-fahn rice porridge

叉烧包 **chāshāobāo** chah-show-bow steamed dumplings with pork filling

Seasonings, spices

桂皮 **guìpí** gway-pee Chinese cinnamon

丁香 **dīngxiāng** ding-hsyang cloves

茴香 **huíxiāng** hway-hsyang fennel seed

五香面儿 **wǔxiāng miànr** woo-hsyang myenr 'five spice' powder

生姜 **shēngjiāng** shung-jyang ginger

辣椒 **làjiāo** lah-jyow chilli, chilli peppers

辣椒粉 **làjiāo fěn** fun chilli powder

胡椒 **hújiāo** hoo-jyow pepper

盐 **yán** yahn salt

醋 **cù** tsoo vinegar

Snacks

豆沙酥饼 **dòushā sūbǐng** doh-shah soo-bing baked flaky cake with sweet bean paste filling

火烧 **huǒshāo** hwor-show baked wheaten bun

糖火烧 **táng huǒshāo** tahng baked wheaten bun with sugar

油饼 **yóubǐng** yoh-bing deep-fried savoury pancake

油炸糕 **yóuzhágāo** yoh-jah-gow deep-fried sweet pancake

馅儿饼 **xiànrbǐng** hsyenr-bing savoury fritter

烧饼 **shāobǐng** show-bing sesame pancake

春卷儿 **chūnjuǎnr** chun-jwahnr spring rolls

豆沙包 **dòushābāo** doh-shah-bow steamed dumpling with sweet bean paste filling

油条 **yóutiáo** yoh-tyow unsweetened doughnut sticks

Soups

开水白菜 **kāishuǐ báicài**
kai-shway bai-tsai Chinese
cabbage in clear soup

酸辣汤 **suān là tāng** swahn lah
tahng hot and sour soup

汤 **tāng** soup

竹笋鲜蘑汤 **zhúsǔn xiānmó
tāng** joo-sun hsyen-mor
soup with bamboo shoots and
mushrooms

西红柿鸡蛋汤
xīhóngshì jīdàn tāng
hshee-hoong-shur jee-dahn soup
with eggs and tomato

榨菜肉丝汤 **zhàcài ròusī
tāng** jah-tsai roh-sur soup with

shredded pork and pickled
mustard greens

时菜肉片儿汤 **shícài
ròupiànr tāng** shur-tsai roh-
pyenr soup with sliced pork and
seasonal vegetables

菠菜粉丝汤 **bōcài fěnsī
tāng** bor-tsai fun-sur soup with
spinach and vermicelli

三鲜汤 **sānxiān tāng** sahn-
hsyen 'three-fresh' soup (prawns,
meat and a vegetable)

圆汤素烩 **yuántāng sùhuì**
ywahn-tahng soo-hway vegetable
chowder

Typical combinations

红烧 ... **hóngshāo...** hoong-
show ...braised in soy sauce

干烧 ... **gānshāo...** gahn-show
...braised with chilli and black
bean sauce

麻酱 ... **jiàngbào...** jyang-bow
...quick-fried with black bean
sauce

葱爆 ... **cōngbào...** tsoong-
bow ...quick-fried with spring
onions

鱼香 ... **yúxiāng...** yoo-hsyang
stir-fried... in hot spicy sauce

(literally: fish fragrance; not always with fish)

笋炒 ... **sǔnchǎo...** sun-chow
stir-fried... with bamboo shoots

宫保 ... **gōngbǎo...** goong-bow
stir-fried... with peanuts and chilli

滑溜 ... **huáliū...** hwah-lyoh
stir-fried... with sauce

冬笋 ... **dōngsǔn...** doong-sun
...with bamboo shoots

辣子 ... **làzi...** lah-dzur ...with chilli

麻辣 ... **málà...** mah-lah
... with chilli and wild pepper

蟹肉 ... **xièròu...** hsyeh-roh
...with crab

火腿 ... **huótuǐ...** hwor-tway
...with ham

冬菇 ... **dōnggū...** doong-goo
...with mushrooms

香菇 ... **xiānggū...** hsyang-goo
...with mushrooms

蚝油 ... **háoyóu...** how-yoh
...with oyster sauce

榨菜 ... **zhàcài...** jah-tsai
...with pickled mustard greens

时菜 ... **shícài...** shur-tsai
...with seasonal vegetables

虾仁 ... **xiārén...** hsyah-run
...with shrimps

茄汁 ... **qiézhī...** chyeh-jur
...with tomato sauce

番茄 ... **fānqié...** fahn-chyeh
...with tomato sauce

Vegetables

茄子 **qiézi** chyeh-dzur
aubergine, eggplant

竹笋 **zhúsǔn** joo-sun
bamboo shoots

豆芽 **dòuyá** doh-yah
bean sprouts

> **Travel tip** As for table
> manners, it's impolite to show
> your teeth, so if you use a
> toothpick, cover your mouth
> with the other hand. Slurping
> soup is normal, even rather
> polite. You don't have to eat
> with chopsticks; all restau-
> rants have knives (*daozi*) and
> forks (*chazi*). Tofu dishes are
> eaten with a spoon.

卷心菜 **juǎnxīncài** jwahn-hsin-
tsai cabbage

胡萝卜 **húluóbo** hoo-lwor-bor
carrots

白菜 **báicài** bai-tsai Chinese
cabbage

青豆 **qīngdòu** ching-doh green
beans

蘑菇 **mógu** mor-goo mushrooms

菠菜 **bōcài** bor-tsai spinach

红薯 **hóngshǔ** hoong-shoo sweet
potato

西红柿 **xīhóngshì** hshee-hoong-
shur tomato

蔬菜 **shūcài** shoo-tsai vegetables

Vegetable dishes

烧茄子 **shāo qiézi** show chyeh-
dzur stewed aubergine/
eggplant

烧胡萝卜 **shāo húluóbo** hoo-
lwor-bor stewed carrot

烧三鲜 **shāo sānxiān** sahn-
hsyen stewed 'three-fresh'
vegetables

炒玉兰片儿 **chǎo
yùlánpiànr** chow yoo-lahn-pyenr
stir-fried bamboo shoots

炒豆芽 **chǎo dòuyá** doh-yah
stir-fried bean sprouts

炒白菜 **chǎo báicài** bai-tsai
stir-fried Chinese cabbage

海米白菜 **hǎimǐ báicài** hai-
mee stir-fried Chinese cabbage
with dried shrimps

韭菜炒 鸡蛋 **jiǔcài chǎo
jīdàn** jyoh-tsai-chow jee-dyen
stir-fried chives with eggs

黄瓜炒鸡蛋 **huángguā
chǎo jīdàn** hwahng-gwah chow
jee-dahn stir-fried cucumber
with eggs

鱼香茄子 **yúxiāng qiézi**
yoo-hsyang chyeh-dzur stir-fried
aubergine in hot spicy sauce

冬笋扁豆 **dōngsǔn biǎndòu**
doong-sun byen-doh stir-fried
French beans with bamboo
shoots

烧二冬 **shāo èr dōng** show
er doong stir-fried mushrooms
and bamboo shoots with
vegetables

鲜蘑豌豆 **xiānmó wāndòu**
hsyen-mor wahn-doh stir-fried
peas with mushrooms

炒土豆丝 **chǎo tǔdòusī** chow
too-doh-sur stir-fried shredded
potato

炒萝卜丝 **chǎo luóbosī**
lwor-bor-sur stir-fried shredded
turnip

菠菜炒鸡蛋 **bōcài chǎo
jīdàn** bor-tsai — jee-dahn stir-
fried spinach with eggs

西红柿炒鸡蛋 **xīhóngshì
chǎo jīdàn** hshee-hoong-shur
stir-fried tomato with eggs

Drink

Essential terms

beer píjiǔ pee-jyoh 啤酒

bottle píngzi ping-dzur 瓶子

coffee kāfēi kah-fay 咖啡

cup bēizi bay-dzee 杯子

glass bōlibēi bor-lee-bay 玻璃杯

milk niúnǎi nyoh-nai 牛奶

mineral water kuàngquánshuǐr
kwahng-choo-en-shwayr
矿泉水儿

orange juice xiānjúzhī hsyen-
jyew-jur 鲜橘汁

rice wine mǐjiǔ mee-jyoh 米酒

soft drink qìshuǐr chee-shwayr
汽水儿

sugar táng tahng 糖

tea chá chah 茶

water shuǐ shway 水

whisky wēishìjì way-shur-jee
威士忌

jiǔshuǐ zài wài drinks not
included 酒水在外

**a cup of tea/ a cup of tea/
coffee, please** yì bēi chá/
kāfēi bay 一杯茶／咖啡

another beer, please
qǐng zài lái yì bēi píjiǔ
ching dzai lai yee bay pee-jyoh
请再来一杯啤酒

a glass of Maotai (lái) yì bēi
Máotáijiǔ yee bay mow-tai-
jyoh（来）一杯茅台酒

Beer

啤酒 **píjiǔ** pee-jyoh beer

冰镇啤酒 **bīngzhèn píjiǔ** bing-jun iced beer

青岛啤酒 **Qīngdǎo píjiǔ** ching-dow most famous type of Chinese beer

Coffee, tea etc

红茶 **hóngchá** hoong-chah black tea

菊花茶 **júhuāchá** joo-hwah-chah chrysanthemum tea

咖啡 **kāfēi** kah-fay coffee

绿茶 **lǜchá** lyew-chah green tea

茉莉花茶 **mòli huāchá** mor-lee hwah-chah jasmine tea

乌龙茶 **wūlóngchá** woo-loong-chah oolong tea, famous semi-fermented tea, half green, half black

花茶 **huāchá** hwah-chah scented tea

牛奶咖啡 **niúnǎi kāfēi** nyoh-nai kah-fay white coffee, coffee with milk

Soft drinks

可口可乐 **kěkou kělè** kur-koh kur-lur Coke

果子汁 **guǒzizhī** gwor-dzur-jur fruit juice

冰水 **bīngshuǐ** bing-shway iced water

崂山可乐 **Láoshān kělè** low-shahn kur-lur Chinese variety of cola made from Laoshan water

柠檬汽水儿 **níngméng qìshuǐr** ning-mung chee-shwayr lemonade

牛奶 **niúnǎi** nyoh-nai milk

矿泉水儿 **kuàngquánshuǐr** kwahng-chwahn-shwayr mineral water

橘子汽水儿 **júzi qìshuǐr** joo-dzur chee-shwayr orangeade

橘子汁 **júzizhī** joo-dzur-jee orange juice

菠萝汁 **bōluozhī** bor-lwor-jur pineapple juice

酸梅汤 **suānméitāng** swahn-may-tahng sweet-sour plum juice

Wine, spirits etc

白兰地 **báilándì** bai-lahn-dee brandy

香槟酒 **xiāngbīnjiǔ** hsyang-bin-jyoh champagne

白干儿 **báigānr** bai-gahnr clear spirit, distilled from sorghum grain

白酒 **báijiǔ** bai-jyoh clear spirit, distilled from sorghum grain

法国白兰地 **fǎguó báilándì** fah-gwor bai-lahn-dee cognac

干红葡萄酒 **gān hóng pútaojiǔ** gahn hoong poo-tow-jyow dry red wine

干白葡萄酒 **gān bái pútaojiǔ** dry white wine

金酒 **jīnjiǔ** jin-jyoh gin

果子酒 **guǒzijiǔ** gwor-dzur-jyoh liqueur

茅台酒 **Máotáijiǔ** mow-tai-jyoh Maotai spirit

红葡萄酒 **hóng pútaojiǔ** hoong poo-tow-jyoh red wine

黄酒 **huángjiǔ** hwahng-jyoh rice wine

老酒 **láojiǔ** low-jyoh rice wine

朗姆酒 **lángmǔjiǔ** lahng-moo-jyoh rum

苏格兰威士忌 **Sūgélán wēishìjì** soo-gur-lahn Scotch whisky

炒土水儿 **qìshuǐr** chee-shwayr soda water

汽酒 **qìjiǔ** chee-jyoh sparkling wine

味美思 **wèiměisī** way-may-sur vermouth

俄得克酒 **édékèjiǔ** ur-dur-kur-jyoh vodka

威士忌 **wēishìjì** way-shur-jur whisky

白葡萄酒 **bái pútaojiǔ** poo-tow-jyoh white wine

葡萄酒 poo-tow-jyoh **pútaojiǔ** wine

Picture credits

All photography by Tim Draper, © Rough Guides, except front cover © Justin Guariglia/Corbis